DELICIOUS
ENCOUNTERS

Revised Edition with a section on Exotic Curries

Innovative Recipes for Festive Occasions,
Formal Entertainment, Impromptu Dinners
Parsi, Indian, Western Flavours

DELICIOUS ENCOUNTERS
Revised Edition with a section on Exotic Curries

Innovative Recipes for Festive Occasions,
Formal Entertainment, Impromptu Dinners
Parsi, Indian, Western Flavours

KATY DALAL

VAKILS, FEFFER AND SIMONS PVT. LTD.
Hague Building, 9, Sprott Road,
Ballard Estate, Mumbai-400 001

Copyright © 1999 Vakils, Feffer and Simons Pvt. Ltd.
All rights reserved.

First printing 2000
Revised Edition 2003

Price in India Rs. 230/-

Published by Bimal A. Mehta for
Vakils, Feffer and Simons Pvt. Ltd.
Hague Building, 9, Sprott Road,
Ballard Estate, Mumbai-400 001.

Printed by Arun K. Mehta at
Vakil & Sons Pvt. Ltd., Industry Manor,
Appasaheb Marathe Marg, Worli,
Mumbai 400 025.

ISBN 81-87111-62-3

Contents

Introduction	1

SECTION 1

The Fabulous Curries of India	9
Malwani Crab Curry	10
Saraswat Prawn Curry	11
Prawn Kofta Curry	12
Parsi Pomfret and Prawn Patia Curry	13
Goanese Ambot Tik Curry with Shark or Sting-ray or Cat-fish	14
Chettinad or Hot Madrasi Curry	15
Bengali Chingri Malai or Prawn Curry	16
White Creamy Hyderabadi Chicken Curry	17
Kerala Duck Curry	18
Parsi Mutton Curry	19
Moghlai Shehenshahi Mutton Curry	20
Slow Cooked Parsi Kheema Curry	21
North Indian Kofta Curry	22
The Parsi Pora or Omlette Curry	23
Khat-Khate – Goanese Vegetable Curry	24
Hyderabadi Green Nergisi Kofta Curry	26
Lobster Curry	27

SECTION 2

A Sunday Parsi Dhansakh Lunch	28
Fried Bhing Roes	29
Fried Lobsters	29
Tarela Bhinda Ma Chatpati Marghi	30
(Sweet and Hot Chicken served with Baby Lady Fingers)	
Wagharela Chawal *(Fried Rice for Dhansakh)*	31
Gosht Na Kavab *(Mutton Kababs)*	31
Gosht Nu Dhansakh *(Mutton Dhansakh)*	32
Keri-No-Ambakaliyo	33
(Sweet and Sour Mangoes in Sugar Gravy)	
Badam Nu Custard *(Almond Custard)*	34
Malai-Badam Ni Kulfi	34
(Cream and Almond Kulfi)	

SECTION 3

For The Love of Tandoor	35
Tandoori or Barbecue Party	37
Stuffed Tandoori Murghi	38
Tandoori Murghi	39
Murgh Tikkas	39
Malai Tandoori Murghi	40
Tandoori Mutton Leg	41
Badami Tandoori Murghi	41
Tandoori Mutton "Seek Soti"	42
Tandoori Shammi-Kababs on Seeks	42
Barbecued Pork Chunks with Prunes	43
Tandoori Pomfret	44
Tandoori Ghol Fish Fillets	44
Tandoori Lobsters	45
Tandoori Tiger Prawns	45
Tandoori Stuffed Brinjals	46
Garlic-Tomato Sauce	46
Tandoori Stuffed Coloured Peppers	47
Yoghurt Sauce	47
Large Stuffed Tandoori Potatoes	48
Tandoori Cauliflower	49
Barbecued whole Bananas or Figs served with Sweet Whipped Cream	49

SECTION 4

Mirror Food	50
Russian Salad	50
Lobster Thermidor on a Mirror	51
The Geisha's Fan	52
Cold Ramas on Glass	53
Devilled Eggs on Mirrors	54
Crab or Lobster Stuffed Grapefruit Cocktail	55
Chicken Hawaiian Salad	57
Mirror Chicken	59
Roast Chicken on Mirror	60

SECTION 5

Cold Cuts	61
Today's Party Food	62

Mayonnaise	63

Fillings for Sandwiches:

Prawn Mayonnaise	63
Cheese and Mushroom Mayonnaise	63
Herb Mayonnaise	63
Mayonnaise with Green Peppercorns and Dill	64
Gherkin and Boiled Egg Mayonnaise	64
Mayonnaise with Walnuts, Apples, Celery and Olives	64
Pineapple Mayonnaise	64
Ham Mayonnaise	64
Orange and Chikoo Mayonnaise	64
Cherry and Apple Mayonnaise	64

Sandwich Fillers – Savoury Butter for Sandwiches:

Butter with Chicken	65
Fish Butter	65
Ham Butter	65
Crab Butter	65
Cheese-Gherkin-Dill Butter	65
Cheese and Walnut or Almond Butter	65
Prawn and Chilli Butter	65
Green Grapes and Onion Butter	66
Mushroom Butter	66
Uses for Mayonnaise Mixtures and Savoury Butter	66
Pie Cases	67

SECTION 6

An English Tea in Your Rose Garden	68
Fresh Raspberry and Strawberry Cream Cake	71
Strawberry Shortcake	72
Pavlova	73
Black Forest Cherry Cake	74
My Apple Brulée	75
Lemon Meringue Pie	76
Baba Au Rum or Savarin	77
Dundee Cake	78
A Royal Fruit Cake – Dundee Cake	79
Chocolate Fudge Cake	80
French Apple Tart	81
Banana Bread	82
Walnut Brownies	82
Almond and Butter Biscuits	83
Strawberry Fresh Paneer Tart	84
A Pure Cream Tart	85
Tarte Tatin	86
Almond Brittle	87
Bread and Butter Pudding	87
A Spotlight on Nowzer Iranpour	88
Mixed Fruit Cheesecake	89
Amaretto Mousse	90
Mixed Fruit Crême Brulée	90

SECTION 7

A Whiff of French Food	91
Flemish Style Asparagus	93
Sole Au Beurre De Citron Vert – Dover Sole *(Pomfrets Stuffed with Lime Butter)*	93
Navarin of Lamb	94
Poisson Flambé Sea Bass *(1 Large Ramas Barbecued)*	95
Poulet À La Bourguignon *(A Variation of Boeuf Bourguignon)*	96
Poached Provençal Chicken	97
Ravioli	98
Sausages and Spaghetti	99
A Daube from Avignon	100
Crepes Aux Fraises *(Strawberry Pancakes)*	101
Oeufs À La Neige Aux Roses *(Snow Eggs with Rose Petals)*	102
Mousse Au Chocolat Et Au Menthe *(Minted Chocolate Mousse)*	103
Fig Jam Provençal Style	103
Caramelised Apple Cake	104
Chocolate Cake	105
Almond Biscuits	105
Fruit Cake	106
Orange Cake	106
Apple Tart	107

SECTION 8

A Meal without Chillies for Edmee Guyon and Ronald Macdougall	108
Fish Cakes with Mushroom Sauce	109

Boiled Asparagus with Hollandaise Sauce	110
Vegetables Au Gratin	111
Savoury Chicken with Chips	112
Saffron and Egg Pulao	113
Crême Caramelle	114
A Spring Breakfast in Lonavala	115
Fresh Bombay Ducks Fried	116
A Magical Mouthful	117
For The Vegetarian "Magical Mouthful"	118
Sautéed Prawns	118
Mamma's Banana Fritters	119
Kanda-Papeta-Per-Eda	119
(Eggs on Savoury Potatoes and Onions)	

SECTION 9

Al Fresco Lunches with Old Friends	120
Ripe Mango Salad	120
Pomfrets Stuffed with Cheese and Prawns	121
Prawn Masala Toasts	122
Sweet, Sour and Hot Pork	122
Apple Mousse with Brandy	123
Baked Peaches and Strawberries	123

SECTION 10

New Year's Dinner at Twilight	124
Potage A La Marquise	124
Heavenly Chicken-breasts with Apples and Cream Accompanied by Fluffy Potatoes	126
Spanish Rice or Paella	127
Peach Melba	128

SECTION 11

Summer Shades and Splashes	129
Peach, Broccoli and Almond Salad	129
Fish Fillets Chilled with Prawn Mayonnaise	130
Spaghetti Bolognaise	131
Chicken Stuffed Tomatoes	132
Rum and Macaroon Trifle Pudding	133
Katy Dalal's Moussaka	134
Brinjals Baked with Cheese and Prawns	136
Shahjahani Murghi	137

Hyderabadi Pasande Gosht	138
Cauliflower-No-Pulao	139
Cherries Jubilee	139
Pineapple Meringue Pie	140
Bengal Toast	141
Cheese Fish Fillets with Hot Tomato Sauce	142
Bombay Hot Pot	143
Pure Nectar	144

SECTION 12

Some Popular Chinese Items I Cook	145
Large Pomfret Steamed and Lightly Fried in Black Bean Sauce Hunan Style	146
Black Bean Sauce Hunan Style	147
Manchurian Chicken	147
Chinese Hot & Sour Soup	148
Chilli Hot Prawns	148
Sautéed Vegetables	149
Pineapple Chicken	149
Prawns with Honey and Peaches	150
Chinese Style Braised Chicken Wings	150
Honey and Ginger Chicken	151
American Chop Suey	152
Vegetable Hakka Noodles	153
Chinese Prawn Fried Rice	154
Pineapple Sauce	155
Drums of Heaven	156
Broccoli with Lemon and Butter Bake	156
Bird's Nests with Chicken Mince or Stir-fried Vegetables	157

SECTION 13

Christmas Specialities	158
Stuffed Roast Chicken	158
Christmas Pudding with Brandy Sauce	159
Coq Au Vin	160
Crepes Suzette	161

SECTION 14

Some Very Unusual and Simple Recipes	162
Golden Pumpkin Surprise	162

A Passion for Peppers	164
Dry Fruit Stuffed Peppers	164
Mince Stuffed Red Peppers	165
Golden Pepper Pulao	166
Red Pepper Mushroom Pulao	167
Khichri with Vegetable Stuffed Green Peppers	168
Red Peppers Stuffed with Cottage Cheese and Peaches Served on Tomato Rice	169

SECTION 15

A Riceless Lunch for My Friends	170
Chicken with Strawberry Jelly	170
Fish Florentine	171
Creamed Mutton Kashmiri Style	172
Papeta Ma Gosht *(Mutton and Potato Stew)*	173
Mango Shrikhand	174
Mango Freezer Ice-Cream	174

SECTION 16

An Extra-Ordinary Lunch	175
Cheese Souffle	175
Himalayan Murghi	176
Curled Fish Fillets in an Almond Sauce	177
Saffron Rice with Meatballs and Cottage Cheese	178
Topli Nu Paneer	179
Caramel Topped Vanilla Ice-Cream	179

SECTION 17

Some Favourite Party Dishes	180
Tandoori Bade Jhinge	180
Mango and Sliced Chicken Salad	181
Pahari Murghi	182
Pear Flan	183
Cointreau Ice-Cream	183
A Luxurious Diwali Meal with Twinkling Lamps, Flowers and Sparklers	184
Ramas Fish Baked with Sliced Potatoes	184

Moghlai Gosht Raswala	185
Mushroom and Tomato Stuffed Omelettes	186
Beetroot Pickle	186
Mutton Khurma	187
Shah-i-Tukhra	188
Shah-i-Tukhra (Method 2)	188

SECTION 18

A Lunch for Friends	189
Prawn Stuffed Avocados	189
Daraius's Chicken Delight	190
Chicken Patties with Hot Mushroom Sauce	191
Liver with Oranges	192
Apple Surprise	193
Chocolate Ice-cream	193

SECTION 19

A Lunch with My Favourite Cousins	194
Tiger Prawns and Ripe Mango Salad	194
Roast Mutton Chops	195
Bouillabaisse – Our Family Style	196
Apricot Ice-cream	197
Rice and Almond Kheer	197

SECTION 20

A Special Lunch for Easter	198
Mushroom and Chicken Soup	198
Cold Ramas Mousse	199
Chicken with Vegetables, Chips and Fruit	201
Herb, Prawn and Fish Pulao	202
An Indian Cheesecake	203

SECTION 21

A Shikar Bird Reared for Local Consumption	204
Bater Shahzada or Baked Stuffed Quails	205
Bater Zafrani – Quails in Saffron Sauce	206

INTRODUCTION

When I wrote my first cook book "Jamva Chaloji", I knew precisely what I was going to write about and which recipes I would include in it. The book seemed to have formed by itself. Its reception was so very gratifying that I was emboldened to compile recipes that I had already collected for the second book. Books number three and four were to be companion volumes – rather – straight forward books which would appeal to many women all over India. However, I wanted the second book to be different. It had to be light and colourful and include not only Indian recipes but also some world-famous recipes that we had been cooking for our clients down the years.

Cookery books with foreign recipes are available but range in price from Rs. 500/- to about Rs. 1800/- and over. Not everyone has this sort of money to spend, so I felt impelled to write a book which would include recipes from different countries which could be adapted to Indian taste buds. For instance, there is a very famous French recipe called "Boeuf Bourguignon", that is "Beef from a place called Burgundy". Now, I don't eat beef, nor do millions of Indians; but I liked everything about the contents of the recipe and so I changed it to "boneless chicken" and called it "Poulet à La Bourguignon". It turned out to be a hit with my clients in Bombay, most of whom were high fliers and had been to Europe and seen the world and experienced different cuisines. Another example, a Spanish recipe called "Paella", which I call "Spanish Rice", has become so popular that not only are we regularly called upon to cater it for small parties and functions, but we have also cooked it for navjotes and weddings where the guests were over a thousand people.

I want this book to bring pleasure into the life of the person who reads it and sees the pictures. I have included various breakfast, brunch, lunch, tea-time and dinner menus which the owner of the book can mix and match, in order to entertain friends, relations or clients.

The world has come so close to our finger tips that one cannot divorce oneself from it and remain segregated. Over the years, one's awareness increases that there is much to know outside our own warm and comfortable circle.

During the last eight years living in Lonavala, close to nature, I have felt the empty space in my consciousness filling out by a greater awareness to growing things like flowers, plants, fruits and vegetables.

The best month of all in Lonavala is February. The flower trees burst forth in fragrance and many shades of green adorn the tiny garden. The plants and trees are rejuvenated with spring's sap. The cold is still in the air, the mornings are misty. By five a.m. the birds start twittering till there is a crescendo of song bursting from the mulberry trees. I slowly wake, grope for my shawl and go to the verandah outside my bedroom and sit on the swing. It's still dark although a silvery glimmer exists and you can discern the garden, the road, the hills and a few stars, which still shine. Suddenly, it's six o'clock and wisps of light are seen in the East. "Ushas", the

Rigvedic dawn, slowly emerges, turning the sky violet, maroon, pink, orange and red. And suddenly the Sun bursts forth.

The flowers, mainly roses, all seem to blossom collectively and fill the air with their fragrance. We have numerous flowerpots on the little lawn in front of the house and a large number in the vegetable garden at the back, which gets more sunlight. This must be affecting the roses, as the ones at the back, appear larger with stems bowed down by the weight of the heavy flowers which are a riot of colours. There are pink, paler pink, bright orange, red, crimson, white with streaks of red, peach coloured with red lines, yellow and lemon coloured ones and a pinkish white. I never pluck a single rose unless it's imperative to do so.

Throughout the year, the vegetable garden yields seasonal vegetables — potatoes, spring onions, carrots, red and white radish, three types of papri, ridge gourds, soft smooth-skinned gourds, red and white pumpkins, drumsticks, chillies, coriander, cabbages, lemongrass, mint, peppermint, spinach, some frenchbeans, beetroots, sour limes and large black brinjals. One year, there were so many brinjals, I made pickle with them. Herbs are always there. By April they die out with the heat. Anise, Basil, Thyme, Sage, Celery, Parsley are all planted regularly in October and November. By March, only the Parsley and Celery remain. These herbs can surprise you with their delicate aromas, fresh or dry. Nowadays you get dried herbs packaged in India but, I suggest you buy the original French dried ones.

Parsley and Celery are all-time favourites in salads and soups, vegetables and bakes. The aniseed can be used sparingly in soups and main dishes but sage is especially used in combination with onions for stuffing chickens and turkeys. I use it lavishly in all chicken items.

In India we use a lot of vanaspati ghee and mustard oil which can be heavy on the heart. Cooking in butter and olive oil for a change, can drastically reduce fat intake in the body.

So come, open the garden gate and experience some of the delightful surprises we have in store for you.

COUNTRY HOLIDAY LIFESTYLE

When we are in our little home at Lonavala our lifestyle changes. The children, who see plenty of samosas, kachoris, khaman patties, khandvi, dhoklas, cutlets and gungroos in Mumbai, insist on some bland, continental type of vegetarian and non-vegetarian snacks, brunches and suppers. For them I always have a few tempting items in store which I would like to share with you.

During the winter and rainy seasons, they like to have heavy-bodied soup and a snack item with toast. I had devised some lovely soups with French names when I used to cater for the Freemason's Hall in Mumbai and a few have been included in this book.

Frankly speaking, one gets tired of tomato soups, plain chicken soups, gazpacho and sweet corn and chicken soup after a time, so I hope you will like our home preparations better.

Lonavala is really fun time. We take the dining table outdoors and eat alfresco. After the monsoons, the garden is lush and green and to eat surrounded by greenery and floral blossoms of various colours and scents gives one a feeling of contentment, and bliss permeates the mind. The birds and butterflies are almost fearless of humans. If we are very fortunate we may see a humming bird or a hoopoe or kingfisher.

Sometimes the children want to have an elegant meal. Out come all the lovely crockery and table cloths. It's a tradition to serve fish and salad only on the plates which look like fishes. They were a present from my brother Sohraab and his wife Khorshed. The large serving dish is decorated with slices and chunks of fruit and vegetables to make a delightful centrepiece and the fish mayonnaise or fish fillet and chips or fried whole pomfret is served on individual plates. The noise and laughter around the table as the children rag and tease each other, makes all the trouble in the kitchen worthwhile.

When it rains heavily in the monsoon, and the days are sombre, I sit on the verandah with my pet African Grey Parrot, Kasu, and think dreamily of what I should cook for lunch — a poached chicken in the Provençal French manner — when Daraius shouts out that he would like banana karkarias (fritters). I was thinking of baking a banana loaf for tea, so I end up making both the items for tea. In the night I would like to cook boneless chicken in butter with lovely golden orange carrots, green peas, broad beans and julienned frenchbeans.

Freny, my daughter, is a great one for splashing sauces and grating fresh pepper on her food. Beetroot pickle is a ritual to be had at Lonavala and so is watermelon pickle. My friend Betty had made some when I visited her in Texas thirty years ago. I'm including the recipe here. It's so simple to make and the good thing is that you eat the juicy red flesh and make the pickle from the white RIND of the watermelon.

I also make green karvanda pickle in Lonavala as there are virtually wild bushes full of the fruit all over the hills.

Another must is a dessert, after meals. We manage some fast items so that we spend the minimum time fussing in the kitchen. The simpler the item, the better. Freny's chocolate mousse turns out very well and I normally end up with my caramel custard and different types of trifles with and without ice creams. Jellies with sauces are other simple items.

My husband Feroze has a sweet tooth. He just has to have something sweet with his tea so I end up making Parsi sweet items like bhakhras, sweet round biscuit type pastries, chapats or pancakes stuffed with chopped nuts and fresh coconut, karkarias or fritters with banana and raisins, sev and rava — all-time Parsi festival favourites which can be had at breakfast, tea and along with lunch and dinner.

THE STORE CUPBOARD

One very important item that most people overlook in their holiday homes is the condition of their store cupboards. Do not be lazy about stocking it well. It will save you innumerable headaches and unnecessary trips to the bazaar. Sometimes we reach home at ungodly hours and it's a relief to know that there will always be something to eat even if we reach Lonavala after midnight.

I buy the bulk of my vegetables, meat, fish and chicken in Mumbai. The items are cut, washed and packed as and how I will need them. The fish will be sliced as well as filleted. The mutton will be cubed and minced. The chicken will be deboned as well as cut with the bones. I freeze everything for two days in Mumbai and then pack them in coolers and re-freeze immediately on arrival in Lonavala.

I top up all the ground masalas such as turmeric, chilli, sambhar and Parsi dhansakh masalas. I also see to it that my spice bottles are filled with black peppercorns, cloves, cinnamon, cumin, coriander, mace, nutmeg, cardamoms, fenugreek, fennel seeds, mustard seeds, bay leaves and dried Kashmiri chillies.

Masalas such as ginger-garlic paste, jeera-garlic and coconut curry are taken in bottles. Cooked onion, fried onion, potato-shoestrings and wafers are also included, in airtight packages as they keep in good condition for over a month.

Generally, I keep a very large collection of teas. You could call me tea-mad. I have tea from Coorg and Assam, at least ten varieties of fruit teas, eight packet teas and numerous types of tea bags. We keep coffee beans brought for me from Coorg by Freny's friend Silloo, as well as two instant coffee brands. We also keep powdered as well as condensed milk. Cocoa powder is always there for making desserts and sauces.

Essences such as rose, vanilla, saffron, cardamom and milk masala are kept at all times. The milk here in Lonavala is so good that the whole family welcomes chilled milk with a few drops of essence.

Dried fruits such as dates, raisins, currants, apricots, peels and cherries, as well as salted cashew nuts, charoli and almonds are kept for sweet-making and cake-baking.

Refined oil is kept in 5 kg. plastic cans. My friends Indu and Aruna, who run a dairy with German cows, keep me supplied with the best pure ghee that there is.

An assortment of dals such as pink masoor dal (lentils), black masoor (lentils), mung dal, chana dal, tuvar dal, val dal, chora (black eyed peas) are kept in small quantities so they don't get spoiled.

I don't keep too much canned food. It is likely to spoil. Baked beans and ham tins will definitely be found along with packets of spaghetti, macaroni, and sweet and salted biscuits. Cheese tins are always there for snacks and bakes.

I'm not very fond of meats so I like to keep some dried Bombay ducks, baby shrimps and fish fillets of dahra and surmai.

Tomatoes, potatoes and onions of the best quality come from Byculla, so I bring them to Lonavala along with ginger, garlic and fresh coriander.

We normally eat some vegetables that grow in the garden. Fruit, eggs, milk, butter and bread are bought locally as the need arises.

The knack is to know what items in your store cupboard will last longest and what items will perish quickly so that you can plan your menus suitably. At our house we have guests turning up at the oddest hours and I have to always have items to fall back upon. No one goes away without being fed, no matter what the time. In such instances, cheese, pastas, chutneys and pickles can come very handy. I make yellow Parsi dhan-dal and white basmati rice and serve it with my brinjal pickle which is very much like a patia; then I quickly soak some dried Bombay ducks, clean and flake them, apply some chilli powder and turmeric, and deep-fry them. Served with sweet mango chutney or a hot "methia" pickle it's a complete meal, served within 25 – 30 minutes. For a sweet, I make a simple rava with semolina, milk and sugar.

If the guests don't want to eat rice, I boil some noodles and serve them with a cheese sauce containing some vegetables. If no vegetables are around, I add some green or dried herbs, some crushed walnuts or almonds and some raisins or mushrooms. For a sweet, I quickly bake an apple pudding or prepare a rice kheer.

So, one's first priority in stocking the store cupboard is our basic rice, dal, sugar, salt, flour and different types of oils and ghee. And the imperishable pastas in various shapes. Potatoes, onions, tomatoes and fresh and dried chillies should never be absent from the kitchen.

Fruits can be a very helpful item. Apples are long lasting and can be very quickly stewed in sugar syrup and served with blancmange or custard powder.

If you have bananas, you can make fritters with them or even bhajias. Bhajias go a long way to help as you can serve them at breakfast, lunch, tea or dinner and best of all, they can be made with innumerable vegetables such as potatoes, onions, spinach, raw tomatoes, brinjals, cabbage, cauliflower, chillies, capsicum, red pumpkin, sweet potatoes, prawns, fish, and boiled eggs. But for all this you have to remember to keep rava, maida, ata and gram flour.

Rice can be used in various ways. If you have yoghurt, make a yoghurt curry and yellow rice khichri to which you can add fried onions, potatoes and whole spices. If you can't just think straight, make a dried fruit pulao with kesar or saffron. Serve this with a pink lentil masala dal or serve black lentils with rotis or bread and serve the pulao with sweet pickles.

All recipes mentioned above are to be found in my book "JAMVA CHALOJI".

Some important dried and long-lasting items are honey, sun-dried tomatoes, olives, garlic, and dried and canned mushrooms. You can make a fast "Dhingri Pulao" if you have mushrooms. Keep some Tomato Sauces and Ketchups, Tabasco or Capsico bottles handy. The green jeera Capsico comes in very handy, sprinkled over food and snacks. Chicken and vegetable stock cubes also come in very useful to flavour rice or potatoes.

So you see, your store cupboard will never let you down as long as you look after it.

THE MOST IMPORTANT COOKING UTENSILS IN YOUR KITCHEN

1. Pots, Pans and Dekchis of various sizes, Non-stick frying pans and saucepans, Pressure Cookers and a Rice Cooker.
2. Wooden Board for chopping and a separate one for making Rotis.
3. Gas, Kerosene, Coal or Electric Stove and a Gas or Electric Oven.
4. Knives for cutting bread, meat, chicken, to fillet fish and to cut fruits.
5. Iron Tava, Frying Pans and Skillets.
6. A Double Boiler.
7. Roasting Tins and Trays, Casseroles, Flan Rings, Soufflé Dishes, Loaf Tin, Swiss Roll Tin, Tart Moulds and Cake Tins with removable bases.
8. Food mill or a "Moulin Légume".
9. A Mixer-Grinder-Juicer
10. Mortar and Pestle.
11. Whisks of various sizes.
12. Measuring Jar, Measuring Cups and Spoons.
13. Kadhais, a Wok, and a Two-handled Frying Pan.

14. Piping-Bag and Nozzles.
15. Kitchen Scales.
16. Storage Bottles in varying sizes.
17. Containers with Lids to keep food fresh in the refrigerator.

THE BEGINNING OR HOW IT ALL BEGAN: A FAMILY BACKGROUND

I grew up in the shadow of my paternal grandmother, Cooverbai Frenchman, with whom we lived in Bandra, a suburb of Mumbai. We lived on the first floor of a large bungalow surrounded by a huge garden with various birds, dogs, chickens and cats. Cooverbai was a very good cook and so were her daughters, Khorshed Balsara and Hilla Shroff. She turned her daughter-in-law, Piroja, into a good cook too.

Cooverbai was married at the age of nineteen to a handsome young man called Meherji Hormusji Frenchman, who lived a whole sub-continent away in Rawalpindi and who worked as a Guard in the British Railways.

As a new bride Cooverbai was taken under the wing of her sister-in-law, Meherbai Boga, who was quite literally the uncrowned Queen of Rawalpindi. She was married to Bomanji and was the Chatelaine of his brother Nusserwanji's vast estates, hotels and businesses.

Her house was always bustling with guests. 'Fooiji', had given orders to all the 'Victoria-wallahs' (horse carriages) of Rawalpindi Railway Station that, 'Any Parsi alighting at the station was to be brought home straightaway at her expense'. To run her enormous household took energy and acumen. At all times there were three chief cooks, numerous underlings, Indian maids for the womenfolk, carriage coachmen, syces, gardeners and a secretary. It took several men to keep the garden in shape.

The young bride Cooverbai who had gone with such high hopes to Rawalpindi was faced with tragedy upon tragedy within a decade of her marriage. Her husband was pierced with poisoned "khanjhar" in the stomach by Pathan robbers who tried to make off with the "khazana" the train was carrying for the British Government. The honest, and handsome young man put up a stubborn and unexpectedly courageous fight. He was finally overpowered and thrown out of the running train. He crawled the long miles to the nearest station, which was Kahan. He had a wound on his forehead, his palms were slashed into ribbons by the Pathans and his intestines were hanging out of his stomach all covered with mud as he had crawled on his hands and knees. He lived for 13 days and finally succumbed to the poison, which had been applied on the curved daggers. The young doctor who treated him met me accidentally fifty years after this event and described the happenings to me first-hand. Homi, the eldest son was 11 years old, Khorshed 9, papa- Nariman was 5 and little Hilla was 2 years old. The whole world had come crashing down upon the young widow who was 32 years old. Stunned and bereft, Meherbai guided her in all matters. The British Government gave compensation to the widow and the three eldest were put into boarding schools. Meherbai looked after Hilla who was her pet.

Bad times came upon the family. The patriarch, Hormusji "Halwan" Frenchman, Meherbai and Meherji's father, was murdered. His food sent in a tiffin box to the railway office where he worked was found poisoned.

Cooverbai moved back to Mumbai with her furniture and her memories. She first lived in Mahim in Pitle-ni-Wadi, then shifted closer to the school where her sons were kept — Bapaimai Batha's Boarding School. Later on, she shifted to Cusrow Baug, but felt sad at seeing "yellow walls", so in 1941 she shifted to Bandra.

Beautiful, young, strong and vigorous Cooverbai's hand was sought in marriage by several people amongst whom was a dear friend of Meherji's. But she refused all offers saying "who would look after my children if I had others from a new marriage?" So she lived her life, mostly on "brun-pao and chai" and saved each pice she could, for her daughters' marriages.

Cooverbai died at the age of 73. She had educated herself. She wrote and spoke English and read Wordsworth, Scott, Dickens and Shakespeare. A woman of indomitable courage and fortitude, she left behind her a legacy of loyalty, forthrightness, courage and the message that there was no shame in honest labour of any sort. She died when I was 14, with her hand in mine. That was the day I grew up.

Cooverbai had learnt her lessons well in Rawalpindi. She was a good cook and trained her daughters well. She ran her household with an iron hand till the day she died. I learnt almost all the western dishes incorporated in this book, from her. She made four different types of mutton chops, she loved to bake cakes and savouries and enjoyed visits every Saturday with me, to her daughter Hilla's house. My aunt had a cook but on Saturdays she cooked fancy items from magazines and cookbooks. So Saturday became the highlight of my young life. I developed a desire to learn cooking for myself and little dreamt that one day I would be feeding a couple of thousand people per day.

This book is dedicated to the two people who mean the world to me:

- *My mother, Piroja Frenchman who upon being orphaned at the age of seven, spent the next 18 years in the Avabai Petit Orphanage, initially as a student and subsequently as a helper, acquiring skills of sewing, painting, embroidery and above all cooking which she lovingly passed on to me.*

- *My husband, Feroze Dalal who introduced me to the diverse culinary delights that the world has to offer when I accompanied him on his trips abroad.*

This book would not have seen the light of day without the painstaking and diligent efforts of Jeroo Khansaheb and Rhea Mitra who helped me with the typing of the book and those of Jamshed Billimoria who came all the way from Bangalore to take the excellent photographs therein.

SECTION 1

THE FABULOUS CURRIES OF INDIA

The curry dish has become very famous all over the world. Nowhere is it so popular as in the London Restaurants where many people associated with India in the past or present, congregate to eat its delicious curries, mutton curries, kofta curries, egg curries and vegetable curries. All these curries are differently spiced and are eaten with great relish with accompaniments such as white rice, green peas pulaos, kachumbers, raitas and papads.

Some scholars feel that it was Madrasi influence that led to the popularization of curry. Others feel that it is the Goanese whose influences popularized the dish. Whatever the explanation, I feel that Westerners are wrong to dump all Indian dishes into a "curry" vacuum. I don't feel that we can lump yoghurt and dal gravies into the curry slot. Nor can we call vegetables cooked in masalas as curries.

A true curry is one which first and foremost contains fresh coconut, red dried chillies, broiled coriander seeds, tamarind and fresh curry leaves. Hence, I have selected those recipes which include these items.

I hope you will enjoy cooking them and eating them with your families.

MALWANI CRAB CURRY

Preparation Time: 25 mins. • Cooking Time: 22 mins. • Serves: 6-8

3 huge crabs, cleaned and cut into pieces. Be careful to remove all the dead man's fingers
15 large, red hot Resampatti chillies ⎫
8 large garlic cloves ⎪
2 large grated onions ⎬ Grind fine with a little water
2 tbsps. coriander seeds, broiled ⎪
1 tbsp. poppy seeds ⎪
2 tsps. black pepper corns ⎪
1 tsp. aniseeds ⎭
Coconut milk from 1½ coconuts
4 large tomatoes, skinned and roughly chopped
4 split green chillies
2 star anise
6 berries Triphala
1 cup thin tamarind water
3 sprigs curry leaves
Rock Salt
Sesame Oil

- Cut up the crabs carefully. Detach the claws and tap each one with force, once only. Cut the center of the crab into four pieces and remove the grey dead man's fingers from it. Wash thoroughly 3 times. Salt and set aside.
- Grind the masala till fine.
- Remove the first strong coconut milk and then remove the thinner milk second time around.
- Place 2 large spoons of sesame oil in a strong bottomed vessel. Add the curry leaves and place on high heat. When the leaves crackle, add the ground masala, lessen the heat and stir well for 2 minutes. Then add the thinner coconut milk and stir well. When it comes to a boil, add the crab pieces, the split green chillies, the Star Anise and the Triphala berries. Allow to boil for 10 to 12 minutes. Taste for salt. Then add the tamarind water.
- Add the thick coconut milk and allow to simmer on a low fire for a further 7 to 10 minutes.
- Eat with white, freshly boiled rice, cucumber and peanut kachumber, onion salad and papads.

SARASWAT PRAWN CURRY

Preparation Time: 15-20 mins. • Cooking Time: 30-35 mins. • Serves: 4-6

600 gms. shelled, deveined prawns
½ fresh coconut, grated
6 Reshampatti chillies, deseeded
4 green chillies
1 tbsp. coriander seeds
1 tsp. cumin seeds
1 tsp. poppy seeds
1 tsp. fennel seeds
6 garlic cloves
1 tsp. grated, fresh ginger
7 black pepper corns
3 mace flowers

} Grind till soft and buttery with ½ cup of water

1 small onion, finely chopped
2 tomatoes, finely chopped
¼ cup fresh coriander, finely chopped
2 sprigs curry leaves
Salt
Coconut oil or any other refined oil

- Wash the prawns twice, salt them and set aside.
- Place 3 tablespoons of oil in a dekchi along with the curry leaves on a medium flame. Allow the leaves to crackle and add the tomatoes and coriander. When the tomatoes become soft, add the prawns and cook for 5 minutes, stirring all the time.
- Then add the finely ground masala and mix it vigorously into the tomato gravy. Crush the onion by hand and add to the masala.
- Then add 2½ cups of water and allow to boil vigorously for a further 5 minutes. Lower the flame and simmer for 10 more minutes before taking the curry off the fire. Taste for salt.
- Serve with fried mullets or mandlis or mackerels along with white rice.

PRAWN KOFTA CURRY

Preparation Time: 25 mins. • Cooking Time: 40-45 mins. • Serves: 4-6

My family loves to eat prawns – in any form. One of their prawn favourites is my prawn ball curry. The prawn mixture has to be carefully prepared, otherwise the koftas will disintegrate.

For the Koftas:

500 gms. shelled, deveined prawns, (small size will do)
4 green chillies
2 tbsps. green coriander leaves, chopped
1 tsp. ginger-garlic paste
½ tsp. turmeric powder
½ tsp. chilli powder
½ tsp. cumin powder

} Mash or grind together

1 egg, whisked
Salt

For the Curry:

½ coconut, grated, and milk removed
½ coconut, ground fine
10-12 Kashmiri chillies
1½ tbsps. coriander seeds
1 tsp. cumin seeds
1 tsp. turmetic powder
1 tsp. anar dana powder
1 tsp. black pepper corns
2 onions

} Grind fine in a little water

2 raw mangoes (whilst in season), skinned and cut into 4 pieces each
6 bundles of drumsticks, make 4 pieces of each, boiled in salted water
3 tomatoes, finely chopped
3 sprigs curry leaves
Salt
Peanut oil

- First make the curry. Take a large vessel and put in half a cup of oil and the curry leaves.
- Place the vessel on a medium flame and allow the leaves to crackle. Then put in the ground masala and fry it well till red. Add 3 cups of water and salt to taste and leave the vessel on a medium flame.
- Whilst the curry is being made, and is being brought to boil, wipe the prawns in a soft cloth to dry them. Then mash them on a curry stone along with the green chillies, coriander, ginger and garlic paste and the turmeric, chilli and cumin powders. Mash well. Whisk an egg and add it to the prawn mixture. Keep in a cool place till you make the curry and boil it. Taste for salt.
- When the curry is boiling, wet both your hands and make small balls, the size of a sour lime, and drop them one by one into the hot liquid. Allow to remain on the boil for 10 minutes.
- Pour the coconut milk into the boiling curry. Taste for salt. Then place on a low flame and allow to simmer for 10 more minutes.
- This curry must be eaten with white rice dotted with green peas, fried vegetable bhajias, an onion, cucumber and spring onion kachumber and fried or roasted papads.

PARSI POMFRET AND PRAWN PATIA CURRY

Preparation Time: 25 mins. • Cooking Time: 30 mins. • Serves: 8-10

3 large pomfrets, each sliced into 5 pieces after discarding the heads
500 gms. large prawns, shelled and deveined
3 large onions, finely chopped ⎫
1 coconut, grated ⎪
15 Red Kashmiri chillies ⎬ *Finely ground in ½ cup vinegar*
10 large garlic cloves ⎪
1½ tbsps. broiled cumin seeds ⎪
1 tsp. mustard seeds ⎭
2 tbsps. Parsi Dhansakh masala
4 large tomatoes, skinned and chopped
8 baby black brinjals
8 baby tomatoes
4 drumsticks, cleaned, each cut into 4 pieces and tied up into bundles of 3
2 green capsicums, finely sliced
½ cup finely chopped fresh coriander leaves
2 split whole green chillies
½ cup crushed jaggery
3 sprigs curry leaves
Salt
Sesame oil or any other refined oil

- Wash the pomfret slices and the prawns twice. Salt them and keep them in separate containers till needed.
- Take a large flat-bottomed pan. Place it on a medium flame with ½ cup of oil. Add the curry leaves, stir and then add the finely ground masala and the dhansakh masala. Fry it till red and a nice aroma emits from it. Add any left over vinegar and the chopped tomatoes and lower the flame and add the prawns. Stir, cover and allow to simmer for 10 minutes.
- Once the prawns have softened, gently add the pomfret slices and shake the vessel from side to side until the fish is covered with the masala.
- Try to avoid using water, but if it is necessary, sprinkle a little at a time.
- When the pomfret slices are cooked, taste for salt.
- Cut the baby brinjals in 4, but keep the pieces attached to the stem. Deep fry in hot oil and add to the cooked patia. Add the baby tomatoes as well as the bundled drumsticks. Simmer for 5 minutes more. Cover with the finely chopped coriander.
- This unusual gravy is eaten on all auspicious Parsi occasions with yellow toover dal and boiled white rice, or with vegetable khichdi or vegetable pulao. If served with yellow dal and rice, sweet mango pickle is a must. If eaten with khichdi, papads are served without fail. If served with a vegetarian pulao, kachumber is served with the dish.

GOANESE AMBOT TIK CURRY WITH SHARK OR STING-RAY OR CAT-FISH

Preparation Time: 15 mins. • Cooking Time: 40 mins. • Serves: 6

500 gms. shark, sting-ray or catfish pieces
3 large tomatoes, chopped
2 onions, chopped
12 Kashmiri chillies ⎫
1 tbsp. coriander seeds ⎪
1 tsp. cumin seeds ⎪
1 tsp. turmeric powder ⎬ Grind in ½ cup sugarcane vinegar
8 large cloves of garlic ⎪
1" fresh ginger ⎪
10 black peppercorns ⎪
2 cloves ⎪
1" cinnamon ⎪
3½ tsps. sugar ⎭
3 kokum fruits
3 sprigs curry leaves
Salt
Refined peanut oil

- Cut the fish into 2" to 3" pieces. Wash thrice and salt and set aside.
- Place the chopped onions and curry leaves in 3 tbsps. of oil in a large saucepan or tapeli. Cook over a medium flame till soft and pink. Add the tomatoes and when soft, add the ground masala and stir for 5 minutes. Then add 2 cups of water and bring to a fast boil. Add the kokum.
- Put the fish pieces in the boiling gravy for 7 minutes. Then keep on simmer for 6 minutes more. Add the sugar and taste for salt.
- Serve with boiled rice and a raw green salad.

CHETTINAD OR HOT MADRASI CURRY

Preparation Time: 22 mins. • Cooking Time: 45-50 mins. • Serves: 6-8

1 kg. 250 gms. chicken pieces of medium size
1 large coconut, grated
16-18 Reshampatti chillies ⎫
10 cloves garlic
2" piece ginger root
1" piece fresh or dry turmeric
1" piece amba halad   ⎬ Grind very fine in a little water
2 tbsps. coriander seeds, broiled
1 tbsp. poppy seeds, broiled
1 tbsp. fennel seeds, broiled
½ tsp. cumin seeds
½ tsp. seeds of green cardamoms
1 tsp. black peppercorns   ⎭
3 bay leaves
2 star anise
3 baby onions, sliced
4 large tomatoes, skinned and coarsely chopped
1 cup thin tamarind water
2 fresh lime leaves
½ cup finely chopped coriander leaves
3 sprigs curry leaves
Salt
Sesame Oil

- Wash the chicken pieces twice, salt them and set aside.
- Place a large vessel on medium heat. Add 3 tablespoons of sesame oil to the pan. When hot, add the 2 fresh lime leaves and 3 sprigs of curry leaves to the pan and roast lightly for 1 minute. Lower the flame, cover the pan and cook for a further 1 minute.
- Slice the 3 baby onions and add them to the pan and stir fry till golden brown in colour. Then add the bay leaves, star anise, and the large cinnamon piece and stir for 1 minute before adding the chicken pieces. Stir, cover the vessel and allow the chicken to simmer in its own juice over a very low flame at least 7 minutes.
- When the chicken has roasted well, add the finely ground masala. Keep the flame low. Stir the masala and the chicken vigorously. Taste for salt. Add 3 cups of water and the tamarind water and the tomatoes. Simmer for 20 minutes till the chicken is tender and the gravy has thickened. Remove from the fire.
- Serve covered with the chopped coriander leaves along with boiled rice, pickle and papads.

BENGALI CHINGRI MALAI OR PRAWN CURRY

Preparation Time: 20 mins. • Cooking Time: 25-30 mins. • Serves: 6

This is a delicious preparation but I have made some minor changes in the recipe. I felt that the original recipe had too much turmeric paste and too much garam masala. My own version of this delicious curry is given below.

20 large Tiger prawns, shelled and deveined and washed
1 coconut for milk
2 Kashmiri chillies, ground to a paste
2" piece turmeric, ground to a paste
2 onions, ground to a paste
1" crushed ginger root, ground to a paste
1 tsp. crushed garlic, ground to a paste
4 green cardamoms, lightly crushed
2 cloves
1 large (2") piece of circular Singapore cinnamon
2 tsps. sugar
2 sprigs curry leaves
Salt
Pure Ghee

- Place 3 tablespoons of ghee in a large dekchi. When hot, add the curry leaves, the cardamoms, cloves and cinnamon and stir for 1 minute. Then add the pulped onion, stir well and add the ground chilli paste, turmeric paste, ginger and garlic pastes. Stir fry over a low fire for 3 to 5 minutes. Then add the prawns and salt. Keep the flame on low and cover the vessel for 7 minutes.
- Add the coconut milk and sugar. Taste for salt.
- Allow the curry to boil for 12 minutes before removing it from the fire.
- Serve sprinkled with freshly chopped green coriander along with white rice or Radha Ballavis.

WHITE CREAMY HYDERABADI CHICKEN CURRY

Preparation Time: 20 mins. • Cooking Time: 30-35 mins. • Serves: 6

1 kg. chicken cut into 8 pieces
2 large onions, finely chopped
Milk from 1 whole large coconut
1 gm. saffron
150 gms. boiled, skinned almonds, ground
    to a paste in one cup warm water
8 green chillies, deseeded ⎫
1 tbsp. cumin seeds, broiled ⎪
1 tbsp. fennel seeds, broiled ⎬ Ground fine in a little water
6 cloves garlic ⎪
1" piece fresh ginger ⎭
1 cup cream
3 bay leaves
1-2" piece cinnamon
3 cloves
10 black peppercorns
4 lightly crushed green cardamoms
½" shahjeera
Salt
Ghee

- Wash the chicken pieces and salt them and cover them with the ground green chilli paste and keep in a cool place for 2 hours.
- Place the onions and 2 tablespoons of ghee in a large vessel. Put over a medium flame and cook the onions till soft and pink.
- Add the bay leaves, cinnamon piece, cloves, peppercorns, and green cardamom and shahjeera, and fry along with the onions for 2 minutes.
- Add the marinated pieces of chicken to the onions and stir gently. Lower the flame, cover and allow the chicken pieces to cook in their own juice. Carefully strain the coconut milk and add it to the pan and allow to simmer for 20 minutes, stirring the contents of the pan every 5 minutes.
- Strain the liquidized almonds into the chicken gravy which should not be removed from the fire. Taste for salt.
- Heat the saffron, mix it in ½ cup of hot water and add it to the simmering chicken.
- Gently stir the cream with a pinch of fine salt and stir it into the cooked chicken in a circular motion. Remove the vessel from the fire after 2 minutes.
- This curry can be eaten with hot parathas or kulchas or a light potato-cauliflower pulao.

KERALA DUCK CURRY

Preparation Time: 10-15 mins. • Cooking Time: 35-45 mins. • Serves: 6

1 large duck, cut into 8 pieces
3 potatoes, skinned and chopped into thick chips
2 onions, chopped fine
4 green chillies, chopped fine
½ cup fresh coriander, chopped fine
2 tomatoes, finely chopped
Milk of 1 large coconut
8 Reshampatti chillies ⎫
1 tbsp. coriander seeds ⎪
8 large cloves garlic ⎬ *Grind fine in water*
1 large round tamarind, as big as a sour lime ⎪
10 curry leaves ⎭
1½ tbsps. garam masala
1 tsp. chilli powder
1 tsp. turmeric powder
1 tsp. black pepper powder
½ tsp. mustard seeds
Salt
Oil

- Fry the potato chips and set aside. Wash the duck twice and salt it.
- Apply garam masala, chilli, turmeric and black pepper powders to the pieces. Then place ½ cup of oil in which the potatoes had been fried, in a frying pan. Place on medium heat and fry the duck until the pieces are golden brown. You will have to fry the duck in two batches, so use more oil if you have to.
- Place the chopped tomatoes in a vessel. Add the coconut milk and the masala and place on medium heat. Stir and bring to a boil.
- Crush the onions, chillies and coriander with a pinch of fine salt and add them to the curry. After allowing it to boil for 5 minutes, add the duck pieces and more water if you want to and cook till the pieces are tender. Taste for salt. Then fry the mustard seeds in 2 teaspoons of oil, allow to crackle and add to the curry.
- Once you have removed the duck curry into a dish, cover with the fried chips.
- Serve with white rice, green chilli and cucumber salad and sour lime pickle.

PARSI MUTTON CURRY

Preparation Time: 15 mins. • Cooking Time: 50 mins. • Serves: 6-8

1 kg. mutton chunks with bone
5 medium sized potatoes, skinned and cut into 4 pieces each
4 large tomatoes, skinned and pulped
4 drumsticks, cleaned and each cut into 4 pieces

1 fresh coconut
18 large Kashmiri chillies, deseeded
10 large cloves garlic
1½ tbsps. coriander seeds, broiled
1 tbsp. sesame seeds, broiled
1 tbsp. poppy seeds, broiled
½ cup chana (grams)
½ cup peanuts
} Grind fine in ½ cup of water

3 sprigs curry leaves
½ cup tamarind water
Salt
Sesame oil

- Wash the meat. Prepare the potatoes and wash them. Then cook the meat and potatoes in 4 to 5 cups of water with salt in a pressure cooker till tender.

- Take 3 tablespoons of sesame oil and place it in a large vessel on medium heat. When the oil is hot add the curry sprigs and allow to crackle and then add the ground soft coconut masala. Stir the masala for 5 minutes on a low fire till a good aroma arises out of it.

- Then add the mutton soup from the pressure cooker and allow to boil briskly on a medium flame. Once the curry has boiled for 7 minutes, add the pulped tomatoes and the cooked mutton and potatoes. Lower the heat and allow the curry to thicken. Simmer for 10-15 minutes. Remove from the fire.

- Serve with white rice cooked with bay leaves, sour lime wedges, onion slices and papads.

MOGHLAI SHEHENSHAHI MUTTON CURRY

Preparation time: 25 mins. • Cooking time: 1 hour • Serves: 8-10

For the Mutton:
1 kg. boneless mutton chunks with 6 to 8 nali pieces
2 tsps. ground ginger-garlic paste
Salt
2 tbsps. pure ghee

For the Ground Masala:
1 large coconut, grated
16 red deseeded Kashmiri chillies
2 tbsps. broiled coriander seeds
1 tbsp. broiled sesame seeds
6 large cloves garlic

} Grind very fine in ½ cup of water

For the Nut Masala:
100 gms. boiled, skinned almonds
100 gms. cashewnuts
4 mace flowers
½ tsp. cardamom seeds

} Grind fine in ¼ cup of water

For the Curry:
2 finely chopped onions
1 tsp. turmeric powder
½ cup tamarind water
Rock Salt
Pure Ghee

- Wash the mutton chunks and nali pieces and apply the ginger-garlic paste and salt. Keep aside for ½ hour in a cool place.
- Take a pressure cooker. Place the ghee in it and put it on a medium flame. When the ghee becomes hot, add the mutton and nali pieces and keep stirring for 3 minutes. Add 4 to 5 cups of water and cook till the mutton is soft and tender.
- Place 2 tablespoons of ghee in a large tapeli and place it on medium heat. Add the chopped onions and turmeric and cook till soft and pink. Then add the ground coconut masala and cook till red. Add the mutton soup and bring to a strong boil. Add salt to taste. Be careful because the soup will be salty. Add the mutton and nali pieces and stir gently for 5 minutes. Then add the nut paste thinned a little with the curry and lower the flame and allow to simmer for 10 minutes so the curry becomes smooth and thick. Add the tamarind water and allow to simmer for a further 5 minutes. Remove from the fire.
- Serve hot with kachumber, papads and a green peas pulao.

SLOW COOKED PARSI KHEEMA CURRY

Preparation time: 15 mins. • Cooking time: 45 mins • Serves: 6-8

850 gms. good shoulder kheema or minced mutton
4 onions, finely chopped
5 tomatoes, skinned and finely chopped
6 green chillies, deseeded and finely chopped
½ cup finely chopped fresh coriander leaves
2 tsps. Kashmiri chilli powder
1 tsp. turmeric powder
2 tsps. Parsi Dhansakh Masala

Seeds of 3 green cardamoms
1 1" piece cinnamon
1 star anise
3 cloves } Dry grind very fine
10 black peppercorns
3 mace flowers
1 tsp. shahjeera

½ cup raisins, soaked in sugar water
½ cup vinegar
½ cup sugar } Mixed well
Milk of 1 large coconut
500 gms. potatoes, skinned and cubed into ½" pieces and soaked in salted water
3 sprigs curry leaves
Salt
Pure Ghee

- Put the chopped onions and the curry sprigs into a large vessel along with ½ cup of pure ghee.
- Place on a medium flame and allow to cook till soft and pink.
- Place the kheema in a thali and mix salt and the ginger-garlic paste into it.
- Add the chopped green chillies, coriander leaves, red chilli powder, turmeric powder and the dhansakh masala and stir for 2 minutes. Then mix in the marinated kheema. Reduce the heat to low and allow to simmer for 7 minutes. Mix well, add 3 cups of water and cook the mince till the water has evaporated. Do not raise the heat. This will take some time.
- After the water has dried up, strain the coconut milk into the kheema and allow to come gently to a boil. Sprinkle the fine dry ground masala on top of the kheema. Mix and cook for 10 minutes more. By this time the kheema must be very soft and tender.
- To the kheema add the raisins and the vinegar-sugar mixture and cook the kheema until you have as much curry as you desire.
- Deep fry the potatoes in hot oil and scatter over the kheema.
- This is served always with plain or vegetable khichdi or vegetable pulao along with mango methia pickle and papads.

NORTH INDIAN KOFTA CURRY

Preparation time: 20 mins. • Cooking time: 35-45 mins. • Serves: 6-8

For the Koftas:

700 gms. fine minced meat
2 tsps. ginger-garlic paste
1 tbsp. freshly ground red chilli powder
1" cinnamon ⎫
3 cloves ⎪
9 black peppercorns ⎬ Dry ground very fine
1 star anise ⎪
½ tsp. caraway seeds ⎪
2 mace flowers ⎭
3 eggs
½ cup finely chopped fresh coriander leaves
Salt

For the Curry:

1 large coconut, grated ⎫
14-16 Kashmiri chillies ⎪
2" fresh ginger root ⎪
2 finely chopped onions ⎬ Finely ground with ½ cup of water
Seeds of 3 cardamoms ⎪
1 tbsp. coriander seeds ⎪
1 tbsp. poppy seeds ⎪
1 tsp. cumin seeds ⎭
1 tsp. shahjeera
4 to 5 cups mutton bone soup
Juice of 3 sour limes
3 sprigs of curry leaves
Salt
Ghee

- Take a large thali and place it on the kitchen table. Place the mince on it along with ginger-garlic paste and salt to taste and mix well. Also sprinkle the freshly ground red chilli powder, the hot spice masala and the finely chopped green coriander leaves on the mince. Mix everything well. Then make a hollow in the mince. Whisk the eggs and put them in the hollow and mix well and evenly. Make into a large round ball and cover and keep in a cool place till needed.

- Place 3 tablespoons of ghee and the curry sprigs in a large vessel over a medium flame. When hot, put in the ground masala and stir it well for 3 minutes until it is red hot. Then add the mutton soup and bring the curry to a strong boil.

- Wet your hands with water and make small, tightly packed balls, the size of a sour lime from the minced meat and drop them into the boiling curry. Do not stop until all the meatballs have been plunged into the hot curry. Then allow to cook on a boil for 10 minutes. Do not use a spoon to mix the curry. Hold the vessel with both your hands covered with thick tea towels or napkins, and shake the vessel from side to side. After the boiling period is over, simmer for 5 minutes. Remove from the fire and add the lime juice.

- Serve with hot pulao rice, pineapple salad and onion slices.

THE PARSI PORA OR OMELETTE CURRY

Preparation time: 12 mins. • Cooking time: 35-40 mins. • Serves: 6-8

The eleventh month of the Parsi calender is sacred to the angel Behman. Through the 30 days, Parsis do not eat mutton or chicken. They eat plenty of eggs and fish. It is during this period that this particular curry is cooked. It is very delicious.

For the Omelette:
7 large eggs
3 small spring onions, finely chopped
1 large raw tender mango, finely chopped (when in season)
6 green chillies, deseeded, and finely chopped
¼ cup fresh coriander leaves, finely chopped
1 cut tsp. red chilli powder
1 tsp. ginger-garlic paste
½ tsp. turmeric powder
½ tsp. garam masala
Salt

For the Curry Masala:
1 coconut, grated
12 red chillies
½ cup broken cashews
1 tbsp. coriander seeds
1 tsp. cumin seeds
1 tsp. fennel seeds
1 tsp. poppy seeds
1 tsp. sesame seeds
1 tsp. amchoor powder
1" piece of turmeric, fresh or dry
1" piece root ginger

} Grind fine in a little water

Juice of 2 sour limes
4 small onions, cut horizontally and sliced
4 large tomatoes, each cut into 8 pieces
2 sprigs curry leaves
Salt
Refined Oil

- Place the sliced onions in a large langri or any other flat bottomed vessel. Add half a cup of oil and the curry leaves and place on medium heat. When the onions become golden in colour, add the tomatoes and cook till soft.
- Add the finely ground masala to the onions and stir for 5 minutes. Add 3 cups of water and bring the curry to a boil. Simmer on a low heat and add salt. Remove from the fire after 10 minutes.
- Take a frying pan, preferably a non-stick one. Cover the bottom with a thin layer of oil.
- Crack the eggs in a large bowl. Mix in the onions, mango pieces, green chillies, coriander, red chilli powder, turmeric powder, ginger-garlic paste, the garam masala and salt.
- Try to make 10 to 12 omelettes from this mixture.
- Place the frying pan on medium heat. When hot, put a ladle full of the omelette mixture into the frying pan and swirl it around to form a neat circle. Allow to cook for 2 minutes and flip over the other side. When golden-red remove from the frying pan, place on a wooden board and roll over the omelette. When cold, cut it into thick strips.
- When all the omelettes have been cooked and it is time to eat, bring the curry to a boil, add the omelette pieces. Remove from the fire and sprinkle the lime juice over the curry.
- Serve with white rice and fried dry Bombay Ducks.

KHAT-KHATE – GOANESE VEGETABLE CURRY

Preparation time: 35 mins. • Cooking time: 40-45 mins. • Serves: 6-8

The true Goanese and other Konkan people use a spice which is very unusual in the cooking of this curry. It is popularly known as triphala or tirphal and consists of berries which are picked in the month of October in Maharashtra and Karnataka. This spice is barely known outside these regions. The seeds of these berries are discarded, when the fruit which is kept in the hot sun to dry, split open. This spice has a strong aromatic smell and should therefore be sparingly used. These seeds are used for people who are sick with dysentery as it has an anti-flatulent effect.

These berries are especially used to flavour items such as dals, peas and beans, which are not easy to digest.

A number of vegetables can be used to make this curry. Select any four, five or six from my list and cut them into ½" squares, except for the Frenchbeans, which look nice if kept in 1½" pieces. You may use any of these vegetables: potato, sweet potato, carrots, papaya (semi-ripe), yam plain, purple yam, red pumpkin, raw bananas, white gourd and drumstick pieces. Take 1 cup each of the 5 different vegetables.

10-12 red chillies, Goan, Kashmiri or Begdi
¾ large coconut, grated
1" piece turmeric
1" piece fresh ginger
12 black peppercorns
1 tbsp. broiled coriander seeds
Seeds of 3 cardamoms
} Grind fine in ½ cup water

150 gms. toover dal, soaked for 1 hour
150 gms. dried white peas, soaked overnight
1 cup tamarind water
½ cup crushed jaggery
9 berries of triphala
Salt
3 tbsps. ghee
½ tsp. cumin
3 sprigs curry leaves
1 tsp. sugar

- Clean the drumsticks, cut each into 3 to 4 pieces, boil in slightly salted water and keep aside.

- Top and tail the frenchbeans, if using them, and boil them in salted water to which you have added a pinch of soda-bi-carb and 1 teaspoon of sugar. When tender, drain from the water and set aside

- Cut all the other vegetables into ½" cubes and wash them and place them in a large vessel. Boil them till tender in 4 cups of salted water. Retain the vegetables in water.

- Cook the toover dal and the dried peas in salted water in 2 pressure cookers till tender. Add a pinch of turmeric powder.

- Take 3 tablespoons of ghee. Place it in a large thick bottomed langri. Put in the ghee and place the vessel over a medium heat. When the ghee heats

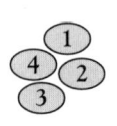

Stuffed Tandoori Murghi (pg. 38)
Tandoori Murghi (pg. 39)
Tandoori Cauliflower (pg. 49)
Tandoori Pomfret (pg. 44)

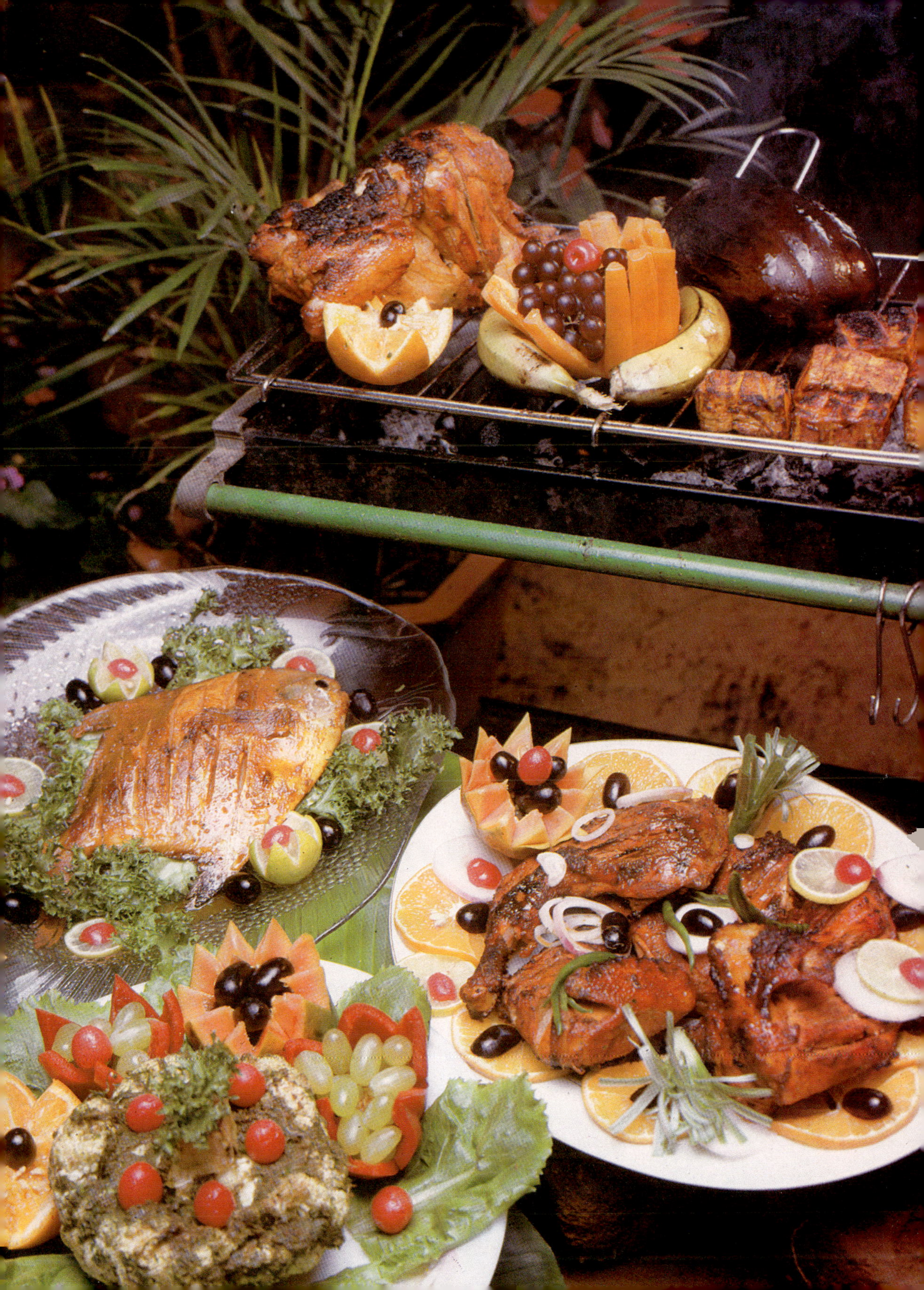

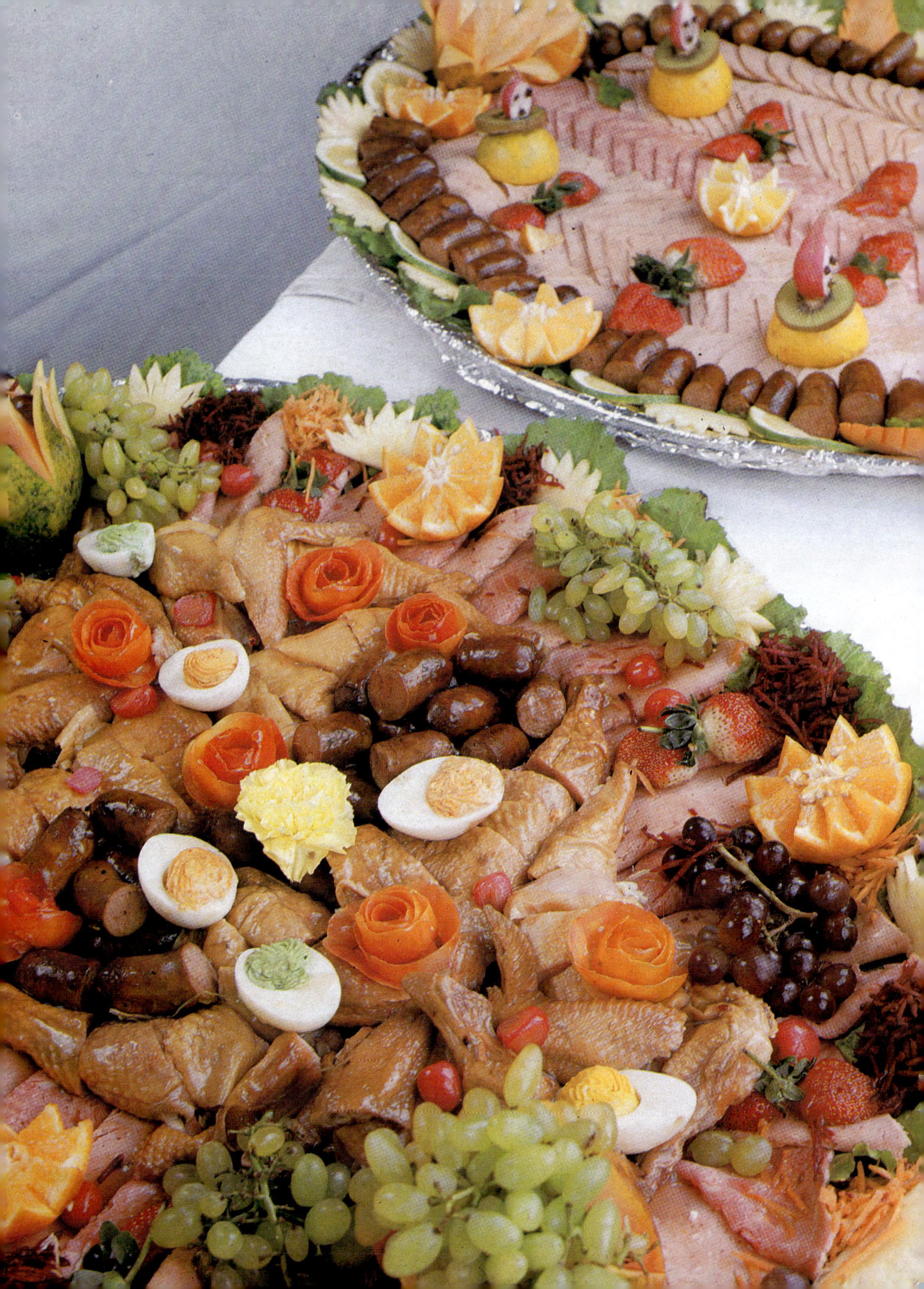

up, add the cumin and the curry leaves and allow them to crackle. Add the finely ground coconut masala and stir vigorously for 3 minutes. Then add the cooked toover dal with its soup, the drained peas and the vegetables. Do not shake or mix with a spoon. Hold the vessel with 2 tea napkins and shake the vessel so that everything mixes well and the vegetables are coated with the curry masala.

- Add the tamarind juice, crushed jaggery and very lightly crushed triphale berries and allow the vegetables to simmer over a low fire for 10 minutes.
- If using frenchbeans, add them last to the mixture. The vegetable curry will look nice with its dark green colour.
- Serve with masala fried rohu, mackerels or surmai slices, fried rice or khichdi, papads and hot mango pickle in oil.

Cold Cuts – Chicken, Devilled Eggs (pg. 54)

HYDERABADI GREEN NERGISI KOFTA CURRY

Preparation time: 20 mins. • Cooking time: 40-50 mins. • Serves: 6-8

For the Koftas:

700 gms. minced mutton – very fine
8 boiled eggs
1 tbsp. ginger and garlic juice
8 green chillies deseeded ⎫ Grind to
2 tbsp. fresh coriander leaves ⎭ a paste
10 black peppercorns
1 star anise
1" cinnamon stick ⎫ Dry grind
2 cloves ⎬ to a fine
3 flowers mace ⎭ powder
Seeds of 2 green cardamoms
2-3 eggs
Salt

For the Curry:

Milk of 1 coconut
½ fresh coconut grated
1 cup fresh coriander leaves
    tightly packed
12-16 green chillies deseeded
1" piece turmeric ⎫ Grind
10 large garlic cloves ⎬ exceedingly
2 tbsp. broiled coriander seeds ⎨ fine in
1 tbsp. broiled fennel seeds ⎬ water.
1 tsp. broiled cumin seeds ⎭
1 cup broken cashew nuts
½ cup grams (chana)
2 finely chopped onions
3 curry sprigs
Juice of 3 sour limes
Salt
Pure ghee or peanut oil

- Shell the boiled eggs and cut each into 2 elongated pieces.
- Place the mince in a thali. Add salt and the ginger-garlic juice and then mix in the chilli and coriander paste and the dried spice powder. Taste for salt.
- Make a hollow in the centre of the mince. Whisk the raw eggs and place them in the hollow and then mix it all up. Make a ball and place it in the refrigerator.
- Make the curry by putting half a cup of ghee or oil in a flat bottomed pan. Place the vessel on a medium flame, and when the ghee gets hot put in the curry leaves. Stir for 1 minute and add the green masala and mix well. Lower the flame and allow the masala to cook well. Add 2 cups of water and bring the mixture to a boil on a slow heat. Then when it is boiling add the coconut milk. The heat should be lowered.
- Take some mince, make it into a ball and place it on your left palm and flatten it out. Then place a piece of egg on it and shape the mince around it in an oval-egg shape. Press tightly. You will get 16 nergisi koftas.
- Raise the heat under the curry and drop 8 koftas gently into the boiling curry. Cook the koftas for 10 minutes until they are firm.
- Once the koftas are cooked remove them into a tray with a large perforated spoon, and place the remaining 8 koftas in the curry and cook them for 10 more minutes until they are firm. Place all the koftas together in the vessel and remove from the heat.
- Sprinkle the lime juice over the curry.
- Serve immediately with white basmati rice, bhindi bhaji, papads and a tomato-beetroot salad.

LOBSTER CURRY

Preparation time: 20 mins. • Cooking time: 30-35 mins. • Serves: 4-6

This curry is very easy to make and has very few ingredients in it so that the eater's concentration is not broken away from the sweetness of the lobster flesh. It is a very hot favourite in our house. Its hot and tangy taste is difficult to duplicate.

6 medium sized lobsters
2 small onions finely chopped
Milk of ½ a fresh coconut
½ fresh coconut grated ⎫
10 Red Kashmiri chillies deseeded
6 Red Reshampatti chillies deseeded
10 large garlic cloves
2 tbsp. broiled coriander seeds ⎬ Grind exceedingly fine with water.
1 tsp. broiled cumin seeds
1 tsp. broiled sesame seeds
1 tsp. broiled poppy seeds
1" ginger root
1 ball of cleaned tamarind slightly bigger than a sour lime ⎭
4 split green chillies deseeded
1 raw mango skinned and cut into chips
3 sprigs curry leaves
Salt
Sesame, coconut or peanut oil

- Clean the lobster well. Remove the central vein. Leave the shells, they add colour and taste to the curry. Salt and set aside.
- Place 2 table spoons of oil in a vessel, add the curry leaves and place on a medium fire. Allow to crackle for 1 minute and then add the finely ground masala and mix well for 3 minutes. Lower the flame and allow the masala to cook for a further 3 minutes. Take care it does not scorch. Then add 3 cups of water and increase the heat and bring the curry to a boil. Add the lobster pieces in the boiling curry.
- When the lobster flesh is soft, add the mango chips and the chopped onions both first crushed in your palm. Then taste for salt.
- When the mango chips have softened, add the coconut milk and the split green chillies. Bring to one boil and remove from the fire. Keep covered for 3 minutes.
- Serve at once with white basmati rice, with green peas, chopped raw onion and cucumber kachumber and papads.

SECTION 2

A SUNDAY PARSI DHANSAKH LUNCH

Sundays are sacrosanct to a Parsi. He eats his "dhansakh" in the afternoon and has a long siesta afterwards. In the countryside of Gujarat the men slept in the open, on huge verandahs covered with grass matting to take advantage of the wind. In the cities they sleep under fans or in AC rooms. This "dhansakh" is the one thing you cannot separate a Parsi from, be he in India, U.K., U.S.A., Canada, Europe, Singapore, Australia, Africa or New Zealand.

"Dhansakh" consists of an almond coloured simple fried rice, meat or chicken chunks cooked in red lentils and vegetables, mutton kababs and a kachumber - salad of raw onions, cucumbers, fresh ginger, coriander, mint and pieces of sour lime. Alongside, we have sweet mango pickle, ambakaliyo – a semi-ripe mango preparation, dried Bombay ducks and raw mangoes in brine. This whole list conjures up the "dhansakh". Ask any non-Parsi friend what he would like to eat and the immediate response is "dhansakh". It is cooked in thousands of Parsi homes but in each and every home the taste will be different. No two "dhansakhs" will taste the same. This is because of the masala that is used to spice the dal and heighten its flavour. Old people used to keep their dhana-jeera recipe, the real name of the dhansakh masala, a secret. I have found that Cooverbai's recipe cooks the best possible dhansakh and so I have given it at the end of my book 'JAMVA CHALOJI'. The ground masala must be locked in an airtight bottle.

To go with the dhansakh I selected some unusual items, – fried Bhing roes, fried Lobsters, a chicken cooked in Kashmiri chillies, hot spices, cashew nuts, almonds, saffron, curds, shahjeera and mace. This chicken gravy is topped with very tender lightly fried lady's-fingers. To take the heat off, we can serve chilled sweet curd along with the meal, or better still, large topli paneers, a longtime Parsi favourite dying out now. To end the meal, "badam-malai" kulfi should be served. I have given quantities sufficient for a meal for 10 – 12 persons.

FRIED BHING ROES

Preparation Time: 2 hrs. • Cooking Time: 20-25 mins. • Serves: 10-12

8 bhing roes divided into two parts
3 tbsps. red chilli powder
2 tbsps. turmeric powder
1 tbsp. black pepper powder
juice of 4-6 sour limes
coarse salt to taste

- Very carefully wash the roes and place on a large tray. Separate each roe from the centre into two parts. Apply the chilli, turmeric, black pepper powder and salt. Sprinkle the lime juice, turn over and marinade for 2 hours. According to my friend, Munchi Cama, at this stage the roes should be steamed covered in mulmul cloth and then fry in hot til or sesame oil.
- Place the roes in hot oil and cover the frying pan with a lid. Lower the heat and cook for 5-7 minutes. Now turn them over and fry without covering. Cut each roe into 4 or 6 pieces depending on the size of the roe.
- Serve the fried roes immediately with slices of sour lime as they are best enjoyed whilst hot. You may increase the chilli powder if you wish.

FRIED LOBSTERS

Preparation Time: 2 hrs. • Cooking Time: 45 mins. • Serves: 10-12

12 large lobsters deveined and cleaned: keep the tail and head shell
14 red Kashmiri chillies
2 tbsps. jeera
2 large cloves garlic
1 tbsp. black peppercorns
½ tbsp. mustard seeds
1 tbsp. lightly roasted sesame seeds
} *Grind all these ingredients to a pulp*
juice of 3 sour limes
sesame oil for frying
salt to taste

- Grind the masala to a pulp with the lime juice.
- Wash the lobsters, devein, shorten the long whiskers and marinate in the masala for 2 hours.
- Heat an iron skillet with sesame oil and place 4 of the lobsters in the pan, stomach side down. Cover and cook over a low fire for 7 to 10 minutes. Uncover, turn over and fry for a further 3 to 4 minutes. Remove and place in a flat dish and keep warm till all the lobsters are tender and cooked well. Serve at once.

TARELA BHINDA MA CHATPATI MARGHI
(Sweet and Hot Chicken served with Baby Lady Fingers)

Preparation Time: 25 mins. • Cooking Time: 1 hr. • Serves: 10-12

3 chickens, (1 kg. each) cut legs and breasts into 8 pieces each. Discard neck and wings.
750 gms. tender baby lady fingers
500 gms. onions, finely chopped
400 gms. tomatoes, skinned, deseeded and finely chopped

1½ tsps. fresh turmeric ⎫
1½ tbsps. fresh garlic ⎪
1½ tbsps. fresh ginger ⎪
16 Kashmiri chillies ⎪
8 green chillies ⎬ *finely ground*
2 star anise or badiyan ⎪
1 tbsp. black peppercorns ⎪
½ tbsp. shahjeera ⎪
½ tbsp. mace or javantri ⎪
½ tbsp. cinnamon ⎪
½ cup almonds ⎪
½ cup cashewnuts ⎭

1 cup thick curd
2 gms. saffron, heated and soaked in ½ cup hot water
1 tsp. sugar
pure ghee or oil
salt to taste

- Wash the chicken pieces well, apply salt and set aside.
- Grind all the spices till soft with half a cup of water.
- Apply the masala to the chicken pieces and marinate for 2 hours.
- Place a large heavy-bottomed pan on the fire. Add a cup of ghee and then add the finely chopped onions. Cook till the onions are soft but not brown. Add the chicken pieces and mix well. Lower heat, cover and allow it to cook in its own juices for 10 to 15 minutes. Uncover and add the tomatoes and 2 cups of water and cook till the tomatoes have softened. Pinch the chicken and check its tenderness. When you feel that the chicken is done rub the saffron strands in the water till you get a dark orange colour. Add to the chicken. Beat the curd with 1 teaspoon of sugar until well whisked and add it to the chicken. Simmer for 10 minutes.
- Wash and dry the lady fingers. Lightly salt them after you have topped and tailed them.
- Heat half a kadhai or fry pan with oil. When hot, add the lady fingers in small batches. Fry till tender but still green. Serve separately or sprinkled over the chicken.

WAGHARELA CHAWAL
(Fried Rice for Dhansakh)

Preparation Time: 5 mins. • Cooking Time: 35-45 mins. • Serves: 10-12

1 kg. best quality basmati rice
3 large onions, sliced, deep fried
2 pieces cinnamon, 1" long
10 black peppercorns
6 cloves
4 black large cardamoms
3 star anise
3 mace flowers
5 bay leaves
salt to taste

- Wash the rice well. Place in a rice cooker along with the fried onions, spices and salt to taste. Add sufficient water. If you like, add ½ cup of ghee or oil in which the onions had been fried. Cook till tender and every grain is separate.

GOSHT NA KAVAB
(Mutton Kababs)

Preparation Time: 15 mins. • Cooking Time: 40-50 mins. • Serves: 12-16

500 gms. mashed potatoes
750 gms. minced meat
1½ tbsps. fresh ginger ⎱ grind
1½ tbsps. garlic ⎰ to a
1½ tbsps. fresh turmeric ⎱ paste
8 green chillies deseeded finely chopped
250 gms. finely chopped onions
150 gms. finely chopped fresh coriander
75 gms. finely chopped fresh mint
1 tbsp. turmeric powder if fresh turmeric is not available
1½ tbsps. chilli powder
1½ tbsps. dhansakh masala
1 tbsp. garam masala
8 eggs well whisked
salt to taste
oil for frying

- My great grandmother Soonamai used to get her kabab mutton ground in an oval stone quern by her maid Diwali in the Kashmiri Wazwan style. I distinctly remember the use of fresh turmeric.

- Mix the mutton with the ginger, garlic, turmeric, green chillies and salt. Add all the chopped onion, coriander and mint and mix up with the mutton in a tray. Add the mashed potatoes.

- Add all the powdered spices and mix well. Add the whisked eggs, mix well into the spiced mutton and set aside for half an hour.

- Wet your hands and make round balls according to the size you need. Deep fry in a kadhai of hot oil till golden brown.

- Makes 40 to 60 kababs.

GOSHT NU DHANSAKH
(Mutton Dhansakh)

Preparation Time: 25 mins. • Cooking Time: 1¼ hrs. • Serves: 12

1 kg. mutton leg chunks including nali
450 gms. pink masoor dal
200 gms. toover dal
500 gms. skinned, finely chopped tomatoes
1 large bunch spring onions finely cut
400 gms. red pumpkin chopped into 1" squares
250 gms. brinjal chopped into 1" squares
2 bunches tiny methi bhaji washed and cut
4 leaves of white radish, chopped
1 teacup chopped coriander
8 green chillies finely chopped
4 green mangoes
6 drumsticks peeled and each cut into 4 pieces and boiled in salted water
3 sprigs curry leaves
1½ tbsps. ginger-garlic paste for the dal
1½ tbsps. ginger-garlic paste for the mutton
400 gms. potatoes, skinned and halved (optional)
1½ tbsps. turmeric powder
2½ tbsps. Kashmiri chilli powder
4 tbsps. dhansakh masala
2 tbsps. keri sambhar masala
2 tbsps. garam masala
pure ghee
salt to taste

- Wash the mutton, apply salt, ginger-garlic paste and cook in a pressure cooker with 5 cups of water, until tender.
- Wash and chop all the vegetables such as the pumpkin, brinjal, spring onions, methi bhaji, radish leaves, coriander and green chillies. Place them in a pressure cooker. Wash the dals 2 to 3 times and add to the chopped vegetables. If using the potatoes, add them now. Pour 8 cups of water. Add salt to taste. Add the ginger-garlic paste, turmeric powder and chilli powder. Allow to cook till soft.
- Place 1 cup of ghee or oil in a large dekchi and place on medium heat. Drop in the washed curry leaves. When they begin to sizzle, add tomatoes, dhansakh masala, keri sambhar masala, garam masala and stir non-stop till the tomato is reduced to a pulp and the spices completely cooked. Remove the vessel from the flame. Peel the raw mangoes, chop each into 4 pieces, and add to the tomato mixture in the dekchi.
- Once the dals are cooked, remove the potato pieces and set aside. The mutton should also be thoroughly cooked and the soup strained and set aside.
- Pass the dal through a large sieve or grind it in a moulin legume. Use the soup to help pass it through the moulin.
- Pour the dal and soup mixture into the dekchi with the cooked tomatoes and masalas and place over a low heat and keep stirring for 10 minutes. Add the boiled mutton pieces and some more soup only if the dal is still very thick. When the dal starts boiling add the cooked potatoes and the boiled drumstick bundles and taste for salt.

- Serve along with the rice and kababs and add a dollop of pure ghee and finely chopped coriander on top of the serving dish.
- Accompany with roasted dried bombay ducks, onion kachumber or gor amli ni kachumber, both given in "JAMVA CHALOJI' and therefore not repeated here. Use the dhansakh masala given at the end of "JAMVA CHALOJI' as well as raw mango pickled in brine if you have made any.

Most important, serve with Keri-no-ambakaliyo.

KERI-NO-AMBAKALIYO
(Sweet and Sour Mangoes in Sugar Gravy)

Preparation Time: 30 mins. • Cooking Time: 45 mins. • Serves: 20

2 kgs. sugar
1½ kgs. mangoes. If raw and small in size peel and keep whole. If semi-ripe Rajapuri mangoes, cut into 1" chunks
300 gms. tiny pearl onions, skinned
10 smashed green cardamoms
5 cloves
3 pieces cinnamon each 1" long
3 bay leaves
½ kg. jaggery
pinch of salt

- Skin the mangoes and keep whole if small or cut into pieces if large.
- Place the sugar, jaggery and 1 cup water in a heavy bottomed pan on a low fire. Add the whole spices and stir till the sugar and jaggery have melted. Add a pinch of coarse salt.
- When the sugar mixture starts to bubble add the whole, skinned baby onions and mangoes. Lower the heat and cook till soft.
- Cool and fill in glass containers. Refrigerate.

BADAM NU CUSTARD
(Almond Custard)

Preparation Time: 30 mins. • Cooking Time: 40-50 mins. • Serves: 15

1 cup almonds boiled, skinned and ground in ¼ cup rose water
½ cup boiled, sliced almonds
3 litres milk
3 cups sugar
¾ tin condensed milk
12 eggs
1½ tsps. vanilla essence
1 tsp. nutmeg and green cardamom powder
butter for greasing the baking dish or tin

- Place the milk in a large, heavy, flat-bottomed vessel and bring to a quick boil. Add the sugar and cook over a medium flame, stirring the milk non-stop, till almost a quarter has evaporated. Remove from fire, add condensed milk. Stir and cool.
- Whisk the eggs well and add them to the milk along with the vanilla and nutmeg-cardamom powder. Stir and add the ground almonds. Preheat the oven for 10 minutes. Pour the milk in a large rectangular pyrex dish or aluminium tray. Bake at 350°F for 40 minutes. Once the custard is steady, sprinkle sliced almonds on top, lower the flame and bake for 10 minutes till the top is golden brown. Cool. Chill and serve.

MALAI-BADAM NI KULFI
(Cream and Almond Kulfi)

Preparation Time: 40 mins. • Cooking Time: 30 mins. • Serves: 20

3 litres milk
½ litre thick cream
3 cups of sugar
1½ cups almonds boiled, skinned, ground in ½ cup rose water
Remove the seeds from 5 green cardamoms and tie them in a muslin cloth with a long string

- Place the milk in a large, heavy bottomed pan and bring to a quick boil. Add sugar, lower the flame and stir the milk non-stop till almost half of it has evaporated. Add the muslin with cardamom seeds and hold the long string. Add the ground almonds, cream and lower the flame and keep stirring. The almonds should not stick to the bottom of the vessel. Remove from the fire after 10 minutes and cool. Remove the muslin packet.
- Empty the almond milk into long aluminium cylinders covered at both ends or triangular moulds with covers. Freeze overnight before serving.

SECTION 3

FOR THE LOVE OF TANDOOR

I learned how to grind a wonderful masala for Tandoori Murghi about twenty years ago from one of my cooks. The masala is ground, and whipped yoghurt is added to it. The chicken is washed, cuts are made into the flesh and it is then salted and soaked in fresh lime juice for an hour or two, after which it is mixed into the yoghurt masala and allowed to marinate in a freezer for 24 hours.

The tandoori method of grilling in a tandoor or U shaped oven is millennia old. In fact, millions of years ago some prehistoric man dropped a chunk of raw meat by mistake into a fire and realized that it tasted better than the raw meat he had been eating, and thus evolved – the BARBECUE.

In India the Tandoor goes back a long way. I was at a Harappan site called Kalibangan, on the Ghaggar, excavating and exploring the site for a month. The dates went back to 3200 B.C. and more. Amongst some wonderful finds like a western W.C., possible agnikulas (vedic fire-altar), a tandoor shaped vessel was also found.

But what about those of us who do not have a modern Tandoor? I overcame the absence by using round and rectangular coal choolas. You get thin long iron skewers called "Seeks". You take three to four chicken quarters and pass each piece twice through the "Seek". Now you thread 2, 3 or 4 pieces on each "Seek" according to the breath of your "choola". Heat some coals till red hot and place them on the "jali" of the "choola" and place the "seeks" against the top of the "choola" and gently rotate them till the chicken pieces are cooked. Dip a soft piece of muslin into ghee and pat it against the chicken. It will give a sheen to the barbecued chicken. Remove from the "seeks" onto a serving platter and serve with lime wedges and green chillies.

You can barbecue pomfrets, ghol fish fillets, baby ramas and large prawns in the same masala. Personally, I like to make slight changes so all the items don't taste the same. I also stuff whole small chickens, stitch them up with thread and marinate them whole for 24 hours and then slowly cook them over hot coals. I also make tandoori cauliflower, stuffed tandoori large potatoes and brinjals. For the vegetables I have a different masala.

Sometimes, instead of red Kashmiri chillies I grind green deseeded, large, long chillies which are not as hot as the small ones, and use garam masalas.

Today our Tandoori Murghi has become very popular in Mumbai and is served at lunches and wedding parties for hundreds of people.

The secret of a good tandoori or barbecue lies in the masalas and spices you use to marinade the chicken, mutton, fish, wild game or birds.

Many spices and herbs had medicinal values. They were used to make the digestive juices flow, to titillate the palate and most important of all, to tenderize the meat. Because of the power of the tenderizer we can cook the tandoori or barbecue till soft and tender and within the space of 20-30 minutes, or if using the U shaped tandoor, in much lesser time.

This tandoor can be partially buried in the ground or can be placed above ground, or be incorporated into a platform and the sides of the platform around the mouth of the tandoor are used for sitting, placing platters, condiments, etc. The tandoor is fed with hot coals at its bottom from a small opening. The place between the tandoor and bricked platform is covered with sand which is a good conductor of heat.

There are small terracotta tandoors for family use and large commercial ones which are made with the help of metal rings over which clay is used or thick slabs and rings of dried terracotta, the upper part being shaped like a water jar. It is cured by using spinach leaves when used for the first time. You can use a combination of salt and oil to cover the insides or even jaggery. It should be used at short intervals for several days before being used in earnest. You can burn wood or charcoal or aromatic wooden chips to cook food in the tandoor. Of course, I use the metal sigris which make things easier for me but I cannot really cook a nan without excessive trouble. If using an original tandoor you just slap your raw flour nan onto the insides of the hot tandoor, pierce it with a seek, overturn it and the nan is golden brown and cooked in minutes. This nan baking is now a fine art in Pakistan and India and a major triumph of Punjabi culture. The nans are small and triangular when served in city restaurants but where it is the primeval meal in remote areas, they are even larger than our dinner plates.

The Secrets of The Marinades

You will be surprised at the various spices used as tenderizers from ancient times in India. The same are used today in fancy restaurants, sophisticated kitchens and everyday homes. The most powerful tenderizer is the raw papaya pulp, the raw pulp of the pineapple and raw fig pulp. Dried pomegranate seed powder and the dried powder of the raw mango is copiously used. So is fresh lemon juice, tamarind pulp and fresh sour yoghurt or curds. You will notice that out of this list of tenderizers, my first and most important recipe for Tandoori Murghi includes FOUR of them. Lemon juice, tamarind pulp, fresh yoghurt and amchoor or dried mango powder. Lastly, the spices are ground in sugarcane vinegar which is also a world famous tenderizer.

Sometimes meat is beaten with a metal or wooden mallet to tenderize it. Indian mutton is very, very tough and I advocate this beating before marinading it. I have never, ever used raw fig pulp. The ready made tenderizers which are available to us in the market can never come upto scratch in comparison with the real articles.

You can devise your own masalas once you have gained sufficient confidence in yourself. The choices are infinite. You must select what masalas, spices and nuts will go best with what you want to tandoor and everything will set itself into place. Keep a brave heart and have plenty of adventurous spirit. You can use traditional vegetable pulps of garlic, ginger, onion, fresh green and red dried chillies, coriander, fresh or dry mint, fried onions, cloves, cinnamon, black peppercorns, mace, saffron, raisins, plums, apricots, pistachios, almonds, cashew nuts, walnuts, peanuts and freshly grated coconut ground to a pulp. I use onions and coriander finely ground and cooked lightly in oil and mixed with lime juice and sugar to marinade cauliflowers to be barbecued. For stuffing whole chickens for barbecuing I use vegetable stew, sweet and sour vegetables, kheema and boiled eggs and then I stitch up the chicken with a needle and thick thread, marinade it with the basic barbecue masala for twenty four hours and cook it slowly over a hot coal fire, dabbing the chicken with a soft muslin piece dipped in pure ghee. The tender flesh sizzles as it cooks golden, red, brown and dark and is a great pleasure to eat, hot, tender and soft on the inside and crisp and chewy on the outside.

YOU CAN PLAN A WHOLE MEAL AROUND YOUR TANDOORI OR BARBECUE PARTY

1. Serve the tandoori with lashings of green cos lettuce, iceberg lettuce or endive lettuce dotted with sprigs of parsley, pine nuts, red pepper pieces and a French Dressing.
2. You can serve bowls of fluffy mashed potatoes heavily buttered and covered with coarse flakes of black pepper.
3. You can serve a vegetarian rice pulao studded with cashew nuts and raisins.
4. You can serve slices of boiled beetroots, slices of cucumber, slices of spring onions and slices of tomatoes topped with grated fresh ginger and grated red carrots sprinkled with a sugar and lime dressing.
5. You can serve it with boiled potatoes and boiled eggs in a mayonnaise dressing.
6. You can serve thick stalks of celery, chopped apples and orange segments whisked with cream.
7. You can serve fresh figs split into halves topped with carrot halwa as a sweet ending.
8. You can serve toasted, garlicky French bread.
9. You can serve thick finger chips alongside with a tomato and garlic sauce.
10. You can serve buns stuffed with a mixture of butter, chives and minced walnuts.
11. You can serve sweet chopped bananas in a yoghurt mixture of sugar, cardamom, saffron and seedless grapes.
12. You can serve sliced brown onions in a vinegar, sugar and green chilli dressing along with plain boiled rice.
13. You can serve a salad with segments of sweet lime mixed with shredded basil and finely chopped lettuce, spring onions and red radishes, all mixed in a dressing of almond oil and lime juice.
14. You can serve it with mushrooms cooked in baby onions in a light white sauce coated with chopped parsley.
15. You can serve the barbecue with a bowl of boiled, buttered, fresh corn sprinkled over with fresh coriander.
16. The barbecue can be served with a bowl of boiled rajma beans tossed in a salad with chopped coloured peppers, potatoes and raw onions in a chaat gravy like sweet chutney made with dates, tamarind and red chillies.
17. You could serve a large bowl of tender boiled and buttered garden peas, topped with finely cut fresh mint.
18. The vegetarian barbecue could be served with a sweet, hot ragra.

19. The brinjal barbecue could be served with sev-batata-purees covered with a green chutney, a sweet chutney and garlic chutney.

20. The stuffed large potatoes barbecued in the hot ashes and coals should be served with baked beans and soft buttered rolls.

21. Iced cucumber, apple and tomato soups can also be served with buttered toasts as accompaniments.

22. Baked eggs, baked mushrooms, baked spinach, baked vegetables, baked celery, baby onions and red carrots could also be a hot and healthy accompaniment.

23. Pickled onions, raw mangoes, date chutnies, mango chutnies, mango murabbas can be served with vegetable khichdi.

STUFFED TANDOORI MURGHI

Preparation Time: 30 mins. • Marinated Overnight • Cooking Time: 40 mins.
• Serves: 8-10.

3 chickens, 1 kg. each
1 unit tandoori masala (as given in the recipe for TANDOORI MURGHI)
500 gms. mutton mince
500 gms. onions
300 gms. breadcrumbs
2 tbsps. ginger-garlic paste
1 tsp. turmeric powder
1 tsp. Kashmiri chilli powder
1 tsp. garam masala powder
1 cup vinegar
½ cup sugar
½ cup fresh coriander, finely chopped.
¼ cup mint, finely chopped
oil
salt

- Wash the three chickens inside-out. Clean out the pelvic cavity. Marinate in sour lime juice and salt for 2 hours in a cool place. Make small slits on the thighs and drumsticks.

- Chop the onions fine and fry in 1 cup oil on a medium flame till soft and pink. Mix the mince with salt and the ginger-garlic paste and add it to the frying onions. Cook the mince till tender, adding water one cup at a time. Add the spices and cook till the mince is soft. Add the sugar and vinegar and mix well.

- Lay the mince in a thali and add the chopped mint and coriander leaves and the breadcrumbs. Stuff the chickens and stitch them up from both sides and tie the legs together with a cord. Apply the tandoori masala all over the chickens. Freeze.

- Thaw the chickens and roast over white-hot coals half an hour before serving.

- Serve with parathas, onion rings, cucumber slices and finely chopped coriander.

TANDOORI MURGHI

Preparation Time: 20 mins. • Marinated Overnight • Cooking Time: 30-40 mins
• Serves: 6-8

6 legs of chicken
6 breasts of chicken
10 gms. aji-no-moto ⎫
juice of 3 sour limes ⎬ For the first marinade
salt ⎭

100 gms. Kashmiri chillies ⎫
50 gms. tamarind ⎪
25 gms. skinned garlic cloves ⎬ Grind together in 1 cup sugar-cane vinegar for the second marinade
10 gms. cinnamon ⎪
10 gms. cloves ⎭

500 gms. fresh yoghurt
25 gms. mango powder (amchoor)
2 tsps. jalebi colour
3 tbsps. ghee
salt
4 iron skewers

- Wash the chicken well and make three diagonal slits on the breast pieces. Make two small slits on the drumsticks and three on the thigh portions. Do not cut through and through.
- Salt the chicken and mix in the lime juice and the aji-no-moto and allow to stand for an hour.
- In a vessel whisk the yoghurt, jalebi colour and the mango powder. Then mix in the ground masala very thoroughly and add the chicken pieces and coat them well with the yoghurt mixture. Prepare one day in advance and keep cool in the freezer or refrigerator. Taste for salt.
- The next day, half an hour before you need the chicken, light a coal fire and allow the coals to turn white. Fix three pieces of chicken on each skewer and place them across the hot coals on the sigri. The chicken should not touch the coals. Turn the skewers so that both sides are evenly roasted. Dampen a small piece of cloth with ghee and baste the chicken to give it a shiny appearance and to improve its taste.
- Serve with green chillies, sliced onions and sour lime wedges.

MURGH TIKKAS

12 pieces of filleted breasts, each cut into three pieces
4 very thin iron skewers

- The same masala and procedure as for TANDOORI MURGHI, but double skewer the pieces whilst roasting them. Serve with chillies and onion slices over a bed of lettuce.

MALAI TANDOORI MURGHI

Preparation Time: 15 mins. • Marinated Overnight • Cooking Time: 30 mins. • Serves: 6

8 chicken breasts
250 gms. malai or cream
200 gms. thick yoghurt
1 tbsp. white pepper powder
1 large green chilli, deseeded and crushed
1 tsp. ajino-moto
salt
pure ghee

- Wash the chicken breasts and make three diagonal slashes on each of them without cutting through the meat. Apply salt and the aji-no-moto and set aside.
- Whisk the cream along with the yoghurt. Mix in the white pepper and the green chilli.
- Add the chicken to the yoghurt and marinate overnight in the refrigerator.
- To serve, place the chicken breasts on an iron grid or skewer and allow it to dip towards the flame. Rest the skewer on the edges of the coal chullah or sigdi. Turn the skewers to roast the chicken evenly on all sides. Do not burn the flesh. Dab the chicken with a piece of cloth dipped in pure ghee. Cook till tender and serve hot with onion rings.

TANDOORI MUTTON LEG

Preparation Time: 25 mins. • Cooking Time: 2½-3½ hrs. • Serves: 10

1 large 3 kg. leg of mutton
2 units of tandoori masala as given for TANDOORI MURGHI
2 tbsps. ginger-garlic paste.

<u>Coarsely Grind:</u>
1 tbsp. black peppercorns
1 tbsp. cumin seeds
1 tbsp. coriander seeds
1 tbsp. fennel seeds
3 tbsps. almonds
3 tbsps. cashew nuts
salt
ghee or oil

- When buying the leg of mutton ask the butcher to remove the vein in the leg.
- Wash the leg well and apply salt and ginger-garlic paste. Poke the tines of a fork into the flesh so that the juices run out. Rub the tandoori masala along with the jalebi colour and the yoghurt into the flesh. Marinate overnight in the refrigerator.
- Thaw the leg well and coat it with ghee. Place it over an iron grid or jali over hot coals. Turn the leg over from side to side as it begins to cook. After 2½ hours pierce the thickest part of the leg with a skewer and test to see if the mutton is done. If not, baste with more ghee repeatedly. Sprinkle the leg with hot water. Once the mutton is done, press the coarsely ground seeds and nuts onto its surface. Cook for a further 10 minutes and serve.

BADAMI TANDOORI MURGHI

Preparation Time: 20 mins. • Marinated Overnight • Cooking Time: 30 mins.
• Serves: 6

8 chicken breasts
120 gms. large almonds, boiled and skinned
100 gms. malai or cream
200 gms. yoghurt
1 tsp. aji-no-moto
3 green chillies, finely ground
1 tsp. black peppercorns, powdered
1 tsp. cumin, powdered
½ tsp. sugar
salt
pure ghee

- Wash the chicken pieces well. Make three diagonal slashes on each breast. Apply salt and aji-no-moto and set aside.
- Grind the boiled almonds in ¼ cup water to a soft butter consistency.
- Mix the malai, yoghurt, ground almonds, green chilli paste, black pepper, cumin powder and sugar. Coat the chicken pieces with this paste and chill overnight in the refrigerator.
- Thaw the chicken and cook over an iron grid or on skewers till soft and light golden brown.

TANDOORI MUTTON "SEEK SOTI"

Preparation Time: 20 mins. • Marinated Overnight • Cooking Time: 30-50 mins. • Serves: 6-10

The "seek soti wallah" is a common sight on the street corners of Bombay after 6 p.m. in the evenings. He sells little bits of tandoori beef and liver. These take less time to cook than the genuine article – the mutton seek soti

2½ kg. boneless mutton, cut into 1" cubes
1 tbsp. mint leaves, finely chopped
1 tbsp. coriander leaves, finely chopped
14 Kashmiri chillies ⎫
2" piece cinnamon ⎪
8 cloves ⎬ Grind together in sour lime juice
2 large cloves garlic ⎪
2 mace flowers ⎪
1 tbsp. black peppercorns ⎪
1 tsp. mango powder (amchoor) ⎭

- Wash the mutton twice in clean water. Beat with a mallet. Add salt and keep aside. Marinate in the masala paste adding the chopped mint and coriander leaves and refrigerate overnight.
- Skewer the cubes of mutton after thawing, and place over hot coals in a sigdi. Turn the skewers so that the 'botis' cook evenly. Serve with 'brun-pav-maska' as soon as they are done.

TANDOORI SHAMMI-KABABS ON SEEKS

Preparation Time: 2 hrs. • Cooking Time: 45-50 mins. • Serves: 6-8

1 kg. minced mutton
300 gms. chana dal, soaked overnight
2 tbsps. ginger-garlic paste
2 medium onions, minced
4 tbsps. fresh coriander, minced
2 tbsps. mint, minced
2 tbsps. chilli powder
1 tbsp. turmeric powder
1 tbsp. dhansakh masala
1 tbsp. mango powder (amchoor)
1 tbsp. garam masala powder
salt
oil
If desired, add two whisked eggs.

- Wash the soaked chana dal twice and grind till soft on a grinding stone. Add salt and set aside. Grind the mince on the stone till soft and set it on a thala or a high-sided tray. Add the ground dal, minced onions, coriander, mint, the chilli, turmeric, dhansakh, amchoor and garam masala powders. Mix well, adjust salt and set aside for two hours atleast.
- When ready to eat, take thick skewers and taking fistfuls of the mince mixture fix onto the skewers. Take note of the size of your sigdi before forming the kababs, so that they can be cooked safely.
- Fill all the skewers and apply a light film of oil onto the kababs and place over hot coals. Keep turning the skewers to cook evenly on all sides. Serve hot with onion rings dipped in lime juice.

BARBECUED PORK CHUNKS WITH PRUNES

Preparation Time: 20 mins. • Marinated Overnight • Cooking Time: 50 mins.
• Serves: 8

3 kg. English pork of the best quality
25 deseeded prunes
1 tbsp. crushed garlic
1 tbsp. crushed ginger
1 cup soya bean sauce
½ cup tabasco or red capsico sauce
½ cup tomato sauce
2 tbsps. black peppercorns, coarsely ground
1-3 twigs fresh rosemary, or 2 sprigs fresh or 1 tsp. dried sage
salt
peanut oil

- Remove the rind and cut the pork into good-sized chunks, more than one inch square atleast.
- Slightly salt the pork and pierce with the tines of a fork.
- Place the ginger, garlic, tabasco or capisco sauce, tomato sauce, black pepper, rosemary or sage all into a glass bowl. Add the pork chunks, mix well to coat all the pieces. Cover and refrigerate overnight.
- Thaw the pork. Build a coal fire in a rectangular sigdi. Take several thin skewers and wipe them with a cloth dipped in oil.
- Insert one chunk of pork meat one piece of red onion, one prune and fill the skewer in this arrangement. Place the filled skewers on the hot sigdi and cook evenly turning as required. Baste with the leftover marinade ensuring that the pieces do not burn.
- Serve hot with vegetable and egg fried rice.

TANDOORI POMFRET

Preparation Time: 20 mins. • Marinated Overnight • Cooking Time: 25-30 mins.
• Serves: 8

4 large pomfrets
1 unit masala as given for TANDOORI MURGHI
3 green chillies
1 tbsp. mint, finely chopped
salt
oil

- Wash the pomfrets and scrub off the scales. Cut below the mouth and remove the entrails and wash the stomach cavity clean.
- Rub the fish with salt, a little aji-no-moto and lime juice and set aside to marinate for atleast 2 hours. Make 3 diagonal slashes on each side of the pomfrets.
- Grind the chillies and mint with the red masala, add yoghurt, mango powder and the jalebi colour to it. Mix well and coat the pomfrets with this paste. Leave to marinate overnight in your refrigerator.
- Thaw the pomfrets. Skewer each pomfret and cook over white-hot coals, basting with a fine dribble of oil when necessary. Remove from heat when golden brown in colour.
- Serve with finger chips, lime wedges and tomato slices.

TANDOORI GHOL FISH FILLETS

Preparation Time: 15 mins. • Cooking Time: 40 mins. • Serves: 6

12 large 4" thick fillets of ghol
juice of 3 sour limes
1 tsp. aji-no-moto
1 tbsp. black pepper powder
1 tbsp. chopped coriander
salt
oil

- Wash the pieces of fish and salt them. Sprinkle the aji-no-moto and the black pepper powder.
- Mix the lime juice with an equal amount of peanut oil and apply all over the fillets. Sprinkle over the coriander and marinate for 4-6 hours.
- Heat over hot coals basting the fish with extra oil and cook till tender and golden in colour.
- Serve hot with garlic-tomato sauce.

TANDOORI LOBSTERS

Preparation Time: 45 mins. • Marinated Overnight • Cooking Time: 40 mins.
• Serves: 5-7

10 large lobsters
juice of 2 sour limes
300 gms. thick yoghurt
salt
oil
6 Kashmiri red chillies
2 tbsps. garlic paste
1 tbsp. black peppercorns   } Grind in
1 tbsp. mango powder   ¼ cup
1 tsp. cloves   sugarcane
1 tsp. bits of cinnamon   vinegar:

- Trim the whiskers of the lobsters. Turn the lobsters over and, making a sharp cut, devein them. Remove the deadman's fingers and clean the lobster's heads. Wash thrice and apply salt and sprinkle aji-no-moto on the soft stomach portions of the lobsters.
- Grind the masala and mix it into the yoghurt. Whisk well and apply to the lobsters. Marinate overnight in the refrigerator.
- Thaw the lobsters properly. Place on a grid over hot coals and baste with oil to prevent drying. Cook over white-hot coals till tender.
- Serve with toasted garlic bread and a green salad.

TANDOORI TIGER PRAWNS

Preparation Time: 25 mins. • Marinated Overnight • Cooking Time: 25-30 mins.
• Serves: 6-9

20 large tiger prawns
juice of 2 sour limes
½ tsp. asafoetida, powdered
½ tsp. fried mustard seeds
200 gms. thick yoghurt
1 banana leaf cut in the shape of a lotus leaf
10 tomato skin roses
salt
oil
4 Kashmiri chillies
1 tsp. black peppercorns   } Grind to a
1 tsp. broiled coriander seeds   paste in ¼
1 tsp. broiled cumin seeds   cup vinegar

- Shell and devein the prawns and wash them thrice. Apply salt and aji-no-moto and the lime juice. Let this marinate for two hours.
- Grind the masala into a soft paste. Add the asafoetida, fried mustard seeds and the yoghurt. Mix well and apply to the prawns, coating well. Marinate overnight in the freezer.
- Thaw the prawns. Make roses out of the tomato skins of 10 hard tomatoes. Arrange these roses on the banana leaf placed on a glass dish or thali.
- Grill the prawns till cooked soft. Arrange the prawns between the roses on the banana leaf and serve with whiskey or rum as an appetizer.

TANDOORI STUFFED BRINJALS

Preparation Time: 40 mins. • Marinated Overnight • Cooking Time: 50 mins. • Serves: 8

4 large black brinjals
500 gms. yoghurt, well whisked
salt
oil

½ coconut, freshly grated ⎫
6 green chillies
6 reshampatti chillies
2 tbsps. cumin seeds
1 tbsp. coriander seeds
1 tsp. fennel seeds ⎬ Grind together with a little water
1 tsp. black peppercorns
½ tsp. cinnamon powder
½ tsp. clove powder
2 tbsps. garlic paste ⎭

300 gms. boiled green peas
200 gms. boiled cubed carrots

- Wash the brinjals and prick them lightly all over with a clean pin and cut into four, three-quarter way up the stalk. I however prefer to cut the top, hollow out the body, stuff it with vegetables and replace both parts together with toothpicks. This way, the stuffing does not leak.
- Apply salt inside and outside the brinjals.
- Broil the spice seeds and grind with the remaining masalas along with the coconut to a smooth paste. Mix in the whisked yoghurt with the masala paste and vegetables and then stuff into the slit brinjals. Coax in as much masala as possible and refrigerate to marinate overnight. Tie the brinjals to ensure that the masala stays within.
- After marinating, lightly oil the brinjals and place them on a hot iron grid over white-hot coals. Fan the coals and turn the brinjals to cook evenly on all sides. Insert a thin skewer to check if the brinjals are done. Serve immediately with soft rotis and fried fish.

GARLIC-TOMATO SAUCE

Preparation Time: 5 mins. • Cooking Time: 7 mins. • Serves: 6-8

2 cups thick fresh tomato juice
1 cup tomato sauce
¼ cup tabasco or capsico sauce
¼ cup garlic paste
salt
oil

- Heat ¼ cup oil in a saucepan. Add the garlic and fry for a minute. Add the tomato juice, the sauces and salt and bring to a quick boil. Serve with tandoori fish.

TANDOORI STUFFED COLOURED PEPPERS

Preparation Time: 15 mins. • Cooking Time: 20 mins. • Serves: 12-15

20 coloured peppers
1½ kg. paneer of the best quality
2 packets chives, chopped fine
½ bunch fresh coriander, chopped fine
8 green chillies, deseeded and chopped fine
6 curry leaves, chopped fine
2 tbsps. black pepper, coarsely grated
1 tbsp. cumin seeds, broiled and coarsely ground
1 tsp. mustard seeds
salt
oil

- Wash and dry the peppers. Make a small slit on the side and remove the seeds.
- Crush the paneer in a tray, with your fingers. Add the chopped chives, coriander and green chillies and mix well.
- Heat 3 teaspoons of oil in a frying pan and put the mustard seeds. Once they splutter add the curry leaves, cumin and black pepper and remove from heat. Pour this masala on the paneer and mix well. Taste for salt.
- Stuff the peppers carefully with a tiny teaspoon. Apply a thin film of oil on the peppers. Place the peppers on a grid over hot coals. Turn them over and cook on all sides. The skin will blacken slightly.
- As soon as the skin is spotted and the peppers turn soft lay them out on a flat dish and serve with a yoghurt sauce.

YOGHURT SAUCE

Preparation Time: 30 mins. • No Cooking • Serves: 12-15

500 gms. thick yoghurt
½ cup sugar
3 spring onions, finely chopped
2 tbsps. parsley, finely chopped
1 tbsp. mint, finely chopped
4 green chillies, deseeded and finely chopped
4 gherkins, finely chopped
10 olives, sliced (optional)
salt

- Whisk the sugar and yoghurt in a glass bowl.
- Add all the chopped herbs and mix well. Add a sprinkling of salt. Chill and serve.

LARGE STUFFED TANDOORI POTATOES

Preparation Time: 20 mins. • Cooking Time: 30-35 mins. • Serves: 15-20

25 large potatoes, washed and scrubbed
900 gms. yoghurt, whisked
salt
oil
foil

1 grated coconut
1 kg. washed and powdered fresh green peas
juice of 4 sour limes
2 tbsps. black pepper powder
1 tbsp. garlic paste
2 tbsps. ginger paste
2 tbsps. sugar
1 tsp. mango powder
} Mix well

10 red chillies
1" cinnamon stick
4 cloves
4 mace flowers
1 badian or star anise
} Grind in ¼ cup water

- Place a large dekchi of water to boil. Add coarse salt and when the water bubbles immerse the washed and scrubbed potatoes into it. Allow to cook for 10 minutes.
- Remove from the hot water and set aside for 15 minutes.
- Place each potato on a wooden board and halve horizontally. Scoop out some potato from each of the halves leaving the shell intact.
- Heat ½ cup oil and add the grated coconut-green peas masala paste and stir vigorously till cooked. Remove from the fire and add the lime juice and sugar. Set aside.
- Fill teaspoonfuls of the pea-mixture into the split potato cases and refit to form complete potatoes. Tie with string to keep them from splitting.
- Mix the second paste with the yoghurt.
- Place the potatoes on a straight-sided plate or thali and pour the yoghurt masala over them. Turn the potatoes and marinate for 2-4 hours.
- One hour before they are required wrap each potato, heavily rolled in the masala, in foil. Wrap securely so that no masala leaks out. Heat coals in a choola or tandoor, fanning them till they are red hot. Place the wrapped potatoes in the red embers and cover them with the hot ash. They should be cooked within an hour. In case required, cook further, adding hot embers upon the ash.

TANDOORI CAULIFLOWER

Preparation Time: 15 mins. • Cooking Time: 45 mins. • Serves: 8

4 cauliflowers approx 400 gms. each
juice of 2 sour limes
4 large banana leaves
salt
oil

½ coconut, grated
6 green chillies
1 cup coriander, finely chopped
1 tbsp. mint, finely chopped
1 tsp. mango powder
1 tsp. cumin seeds
1 tbsp. garlic paste
1 tsp. sugar

} Grind together into a fine pulp

- Remove the leaves and stalks from the cauliflowers and keep whole. Cut the stalk as near the florets as possible. Dip the cauliflower in water and drain well and apply salt and lime juice.

- Place the cauliflowers on a tray with the florets down and the stalk-side up. Stuff the gaps between the stalks with the ground masala. Wrap each cauliflower into a banana leaf and tie the packet with some thin cord.

- Roast over hot coals till the cauliflower becomes tender. Peel off the charred banana leaves and serve the cauliflowers with parathas.

BARBECUED WHOLE BANANAS OR FIGS SERVED WITH SWEET WHIPPED CREAM

Preparation Time: 5 mins. • Cooking Time: 10 mins. • Serves: 6-8

10 whole ripe bananas or,
20 whole ripe figs
200 gms. crushed almonds, pistachios or walnuts
900 gms. sweet whipped cream
thin rings of orange rind cooked in syrup

- Wash and dry the bananas or figs and lightly cover with a film of unsalted butter.

- Place on an iron grid over white hot coals. Turn evenly to cook on all sides. When the fruit is done place one banana or two figs on each plate. Cut the banana horizontally and serve immediately with sweet whipped cream.

- Cut each fig into four sections upto the stalk, do not separate. Spoon on some sweet whipped cream, decorate with orange rind and serve sprinkled with crushed nuts.

- If whipped cream is not available use cold vanilla blancmange.

SECTION 4

MIRROR FOOD

In India people eat food on plantain leaves, dried leaf plates, on aluminium, on enamel, on stainless steel, bone china and pure silver. They serve food in various metal and porcelain containers. Very rarely is the food served on round, rectangular, square, large or medium-sized mirrors.

Fifteen years ago I had this personal craze of displaying certain foods – cold foods – on mirrors. The displays pleased my clients no end so I thought I would include a chapter in this book on the various types of displays we created, using chickens, pomfrets, lobsters, ramas fish and boiled eggs.

Care is to be taken whilst dishing the food from the mirrors. Heavy cutlery should not be used and at all times, a butler should be there to do the serving. If a fork or serving spoon falls from a height, the mirror will crack immediately. So to avoid such accidents, care should be taken.

The mirror must also be kept in good condition. It should be washed with soapy water and dried and wrapped before being put away.

RUSSIAN SALAD

Preparation Time: 35-45 mins. • Serves: 15-20

1½ units mayonnaise (page 44)
1 kg. potatoes cubed small and boiled
1 kg. orange carrots cubed small and boiled
1 kg. french beans cut small and boiled
½ kg. tiny seedless grapes washed and dried
1-1½ kgs. red apples cored and chopped
4 fresh ripe pears (optional)
1-2 tins pineapple slices cut small with the syrup squeezed out
4 large cucumbers (gherkins) pickled or canned with their brine squeezed out
2 stalks celery cut small
1 bunch parsley chopped fine
salt and black pepper powder

- Place the boiled vegetables in a large vessel or tray. Add black pepper powder to taste.
- Gently mix in the seedless grapes, apples, pears, canned pineapples, gherkins, celery and parsley. Then mix in mayonnaise as required. Don't mix the whole lot altogether. First pour in half, mix well and then add the sauce as required. Chill in a refrigerator.

LOBSTER THERMIDOR ON A MIRROR

Preparation Time: 1-2 hrs. • Cooking Time: 40 mins. • Serves: 8-10

1 large lobster
6-8 medium sized lobsters
1 litre milk cooked into white sauce with butter and cheese
2 kgs. Russian salad prepared with apples and canned pineapples
associated fruits for decoration - red radish, canned peach halves from one tin
300 gms. paneer
2 eggs – whisked
1 celery
1 bunch parsley
black pepper powder
tabasco or capsico
salt

- Wash the lobsters and boil them in hot, salted water. When cooked, drain and keep aside.
- First of all, turn the lobsters upside down and remove the intestinal canal and all the portions one does not need. Place the lobster flesh in a glass bowl.
- Make the white sauce by heating 200 gms. butter in a saucepan. Add 3 tablespoons of maida and lightly fry till ivory coloured. Add 1 litre milk and make a thick sauce. Add salt to taste and 300 gms. grated cheese. Mix well and remove from the stove. Cool and mix into the lobster flesh.
- Clean the lobster shells by washing them. Leave the largest sized lobster shell intact and with the help of sharp scissors, cut the medium sized lobsters into half.
- Whisk two eggs into the lobster mixture, stir well and fill the lobster shells with the mixture. Pre-heat oven to 350°F when needed, and bake the shells till the roux is golden brown.
- Place the Russian salad on the mirror in the form of a slope – or a sloping hill side. Smoothen the slope with extra mayonnaise. Mount the large empty lobster shell in the top centre of the slope. Arrange the baked shells along the slope and on the mirror.
- Drain the peach halves. Crush the paneer, add salt and pepper powder and stuff the peaches with it. Stick a cherry in each centre. Arrange around the mirror along with the red radishes and cherries, grapes, and other fruits cut like flowers.

THE GEISHA'S FAN

Preparation Time: 20-30 mins. • Arranging Time: 45 mins. • Serves: 10

16 pomfret fillets from 4 pomfrets, each fillet rounded at the broad top end
juice of 2 sour limes
2 tsps. freshly grated black pepper
2 tsps. broiled, finely ground cumin seed
1 tsp. red Kashmiri chilli powder
1 tsp. turmeric powder
2 large yellow and 2 large red bell peppers
8 tbsps. flaked almonds
4 eggs
2 small papayas cut into flowers
2 small watermelons cut
4 lettuces, their leaves cut julienne
strawberries and black grapes for decoration
2 bunches spring onions
salt
peanut oil

- Wash the prepared fillets and keep 2 aside. We need 14 fillets only to make 2 fans of 7 fillets each.
- Marinade the fillets in the lime juice, black pepper powder, cumin powder and red chilli powder and set aside.
- When it is time to prepare the mirror, decorate it with all the cut fruits and thinly cut lettuce. Cut the yellow and red bell peppers into thin ribbons.
- Deep fry the fillets in hot oil in a kadhai half an hour before needed. We need to roll the fillets gently in beaten egg and then press them into the finely flaked almonds. Pick the fillets by the tails and carefully submerge each in the hot oil. Fry 3 to 4 at a time. Do not break the fish or lose the almond flakes.
- Make the fan arrangements diagonally opposite each other on top of the chopped lettuce on the mirror. Lay out 7 fillets in the shape of a fan. Make ribbons out of the yellow and red peppers and thread them in and out of the fillets. Tie the ends with the long greens of the spring onions into little bows. To make the ribbons extra long, fit two pepper ribbons to each other with wooden tooth picks.
- Arrange the fruits in their corners and decorate with strawberries and black grapes.
- Serve with green coconut chutney.

COLD RAMAS ON GLASS

One of the most beautiful items arranged on mirrors is the cold Fish. It is created on a base of Russian salad and reconstructed like a fish. The head, fins and tails are original ramas. The flesh is deboned mixed with finely chopped canned pineapple and butter and the scales are made up of cucumbers. The whole mirror is decorated with fruits.

Preparation Time: 1½ hrs. • Cooking Time: 30 mins. • Chilled: 4 hrs. • Serves: 50

1 large 5-6 kg. ramas
3-4 kgs. Russian salad with apples and pineapples
5 tins pineapple slices
2 tins gherkins
500 gms. butter
1 bottle tabasco or capsico
1 celery
1 bunch parsley
2 cos lettuce
2 endive lettuce
1 kg. cucumber thick, tender white ones
250 gms. black grapes
250 gms. green grapes
250 gms. fresh cherries
6 sweet limes, 6 malta oranges
1 small watermelon
2 ripe papayas
20 boiled eggs

- Scale the ramas, cut the head, tail and fins and wash them and place them in a separate pot and boil. Fillet the rest of the fish and place it in a large vessel along with water so that the fish is covered completely. Add salt, 20 black peppercorns, 6 deseeded green chillies, 1" fresh ginger-sliced, and 3 stalks of celery cut into 3" pieces. Cook over a high flame till soft. Drain the water and discard the peppercorns, chillies, ginger and celery.
- Chill the Russian Salad in the refrigerator.
- Keep the head, tail and fins carefully in a refrigerator.
- Debone the fish and mash the flesh and mix it with the butter and as much tabasco or capsico as you feel your guests will tolerate.
- Chop the gherkins and pineapple slices finely, squeeze the syrup from them by pressing with both your hands and mix into the buttered fish. Chill in a freezer as the fish should be cold when eaten.
- Three-quarters of an hour before the party begins, polish the mirror with a soft cloth and cover it with cos lettuce in the middle and the curly endive lettuce should be edging the mirror. Place the Russian salad in the centre of the mirror and level it and reconstruct the fish with the mashed mixture incorporating the head, fins and tail. Smooth the surface of the fish's body.
- Peel the cucumbers and cut thin slices. Cut each slice into 4 triangular pieces. Starting from below the head position, hold each tiny cucumber piece with the tip of the piece facing the head of the fish

and embed it into the flesh. Make overlapping lines with the cucumber whites facing you. Fill up the whole body down to the tail position. Make the eyes red with the cherries embedded into the eye socket.

- Surround the fish with fruits cut into flower shapes as in the illustration. Do not make a jungle out of the mirror. Arrange the fruits so the appearance is classy and calculated to please.
- Make three-coloured – orange-green-natural – devilled eggs, about 30-40 pieces and place around the fish.
- Serve with Melba Toast. This is bread cut thinly into triangles and toasted in the oven.

DEVILLED EGGS ON MIRRORS

Preparation Time: 45 mins. • Arranging Time: 60 mins. • Serves: 80-100

3 small round mirrors
500 gms. butter
50 boiled eggs cut into two horizontally
natural egg yolk colour
tomato sauce
tabasco or capsico sauce
1 bunch parsley
canned cherries
salt and pepper powder

- Place the eggs in a large dekchi of water and add 2 cups white vinegar. This will stop the egg shells from cracking. Boil. When cooked, allow to cool in the water. Drain the water, shell the eggs and cut horizontally into 2 pieces.
- Remove the yolks equally into 3 glass bowls. Place the whites of the eggs in cold water. Mash the yolks in all 3 bowls with 100 gms. of butter each. If the paste is not soft, add more butter. In one bowl add 3 to 4 tablespoons tomato sauce, in one add tabasco sauce to taste, and in one add black pepper powder. Taste for salt.
- Take 3 sets of piping bags and fill each with one coloured yolk mixture. Remove the whites from the water and arrange on the mirrors. Pipe the yolk into the egg white and decorate with half a canned cherry and a parsley leaf.

CRAB OR LOBSTER STUFFED GRAPEFRUIT COCKTAIL

Preparation Time: 45 mins.-1 hr. • Arranging Time: 45 mins. • Serves: 15

10 grapefruits each cut into 2 pieces
boiled crab meat from 14 crabs or lobster meat from 10 lobsters
2 large tins sliced pineapples
1 large tin gherkins
2 large cups mayonnaise
2 tbsps. tabasco or capsico sauce
1 cup tomato sauce
fresh fruits and vegetables for decoration:
4 sweet limes
2 oranges
1 papaya
1 watermelon
1 fresh pineapple
2 bunches green grapes
2 bunches parsley
1 small can cherries
2 tbsps. brandy (optional)
1 kg. shredded green cabbage
6 tomatoes
6 spring onions
salt and pepper to taste

- The first step is to assemble the salad mixture and chill it in the refrigerator. Half an hour before eating time you must place the grapefruit in a silver salver and start decorating the dish.
- Use live crabs and boil them in salted water. Remove all the unnecessary portion and retain only the soft, white flesh. Spread and place in the refrigerator.

  If using lobsters, retain the head pieces and empty tail shells for use as decoration. Dip the lobsters into salted boiling water and cook. They will turn red. Then save the heads and remove the white flesh from the tails. Discard the dead man's fingers.
- Cut the grapefruits into two pieces. Cut with a sharp penknife in a saw toothed design. Remove the pulp and make juice in a liquidiser and use as and when desired.
- Turn the grapefruit shells upside down on a tray and refrigerate.
- In a large glass bowl, place the crab or lobster meat. Add salt, freshly ground pepper, tomato sauce and the tabasco sauce. Cover with foil and chill.
- Cut the gherkins and pineapple slices into small strips and add to the flesh in the bowl. Mix in the mayonnaise sauce. Add the brandy if you are using it. Cover and chill.
- Cut the papaya and the watermelon into flower shapes. Do the same with the sweet limes and oranges. Shred the cabbage. Place the cabbage in iced water. Keep a steady hand while cutting the fruit. If necessary, draw the outlines in pencil on the fruit before cutting into it with a sharp penknife. Cut slices from the fresh pineapple.
- Place the cabbage on the mirror or salver. Decorate the edges with pineapple slices. Stuff the grapefruit cups with the mixed salad and decorate each with a

cherry and tiny parsley sprig. Arrange the cut papaya at one end of the dish and stuff with the green grapes. Place the cut sweet limes in between the grapefruit cups. Place the watermelon at the other end of the dish and decorate the rest of the dish with 6 roses made from the skin of the six tomatoes.

- Place the whole salver on another dish full of crushed ice in the centre of the buffet table and serve. One grapefruit for one person and some extra cups for doubles should always be taken into account. If using a mirror place directly on the table.
- If desired, decorate the dish or mirror with the lobster heads and tails. This is a very delicious item and the only difficulty is the arrangement of the fruits.
- Fruits can be cut in variety of ways. You can make a basket out of the watermelon and stuff it with black and green grapes.

Cold Ramas Fish on Mirror (pg. 53)

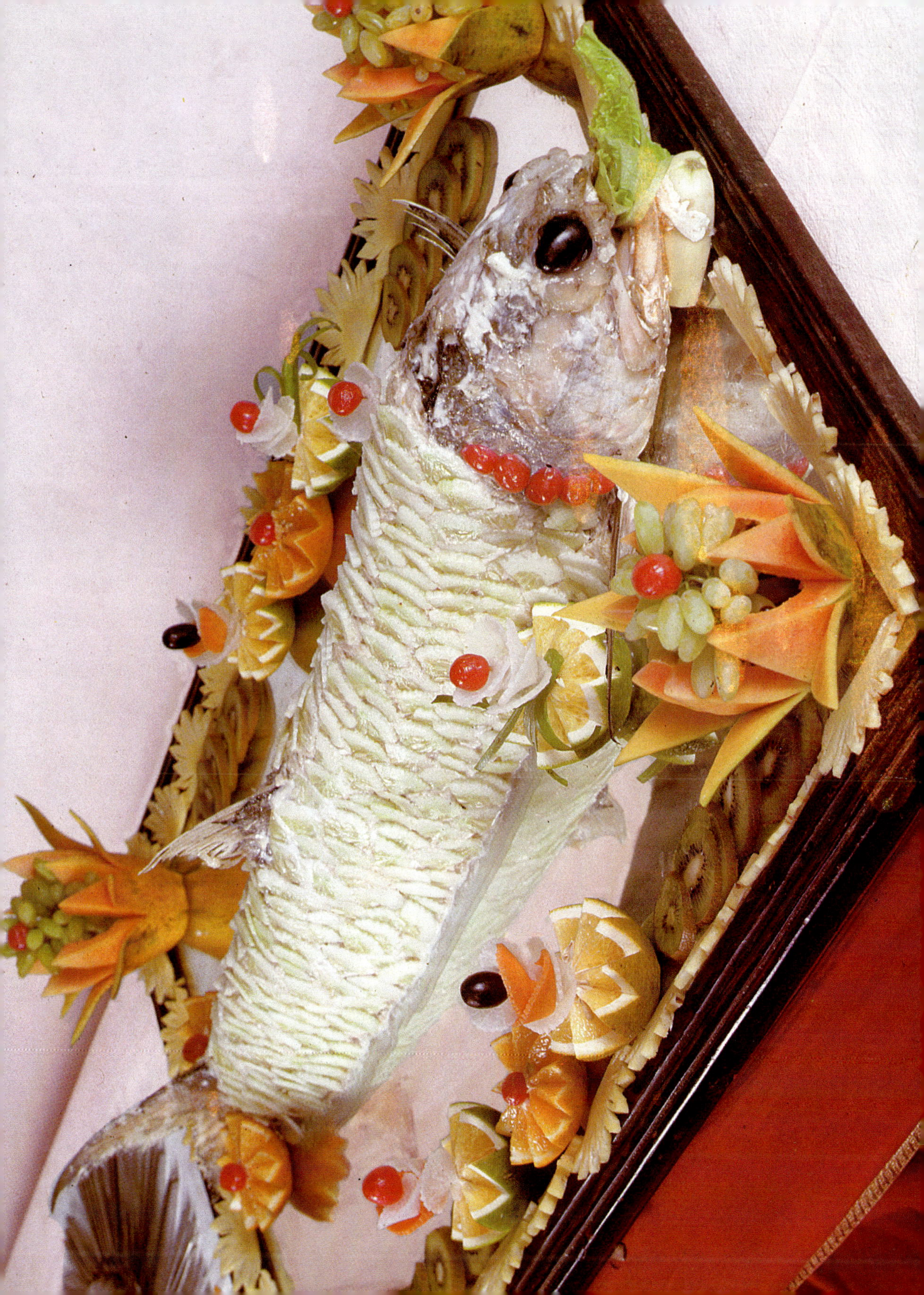

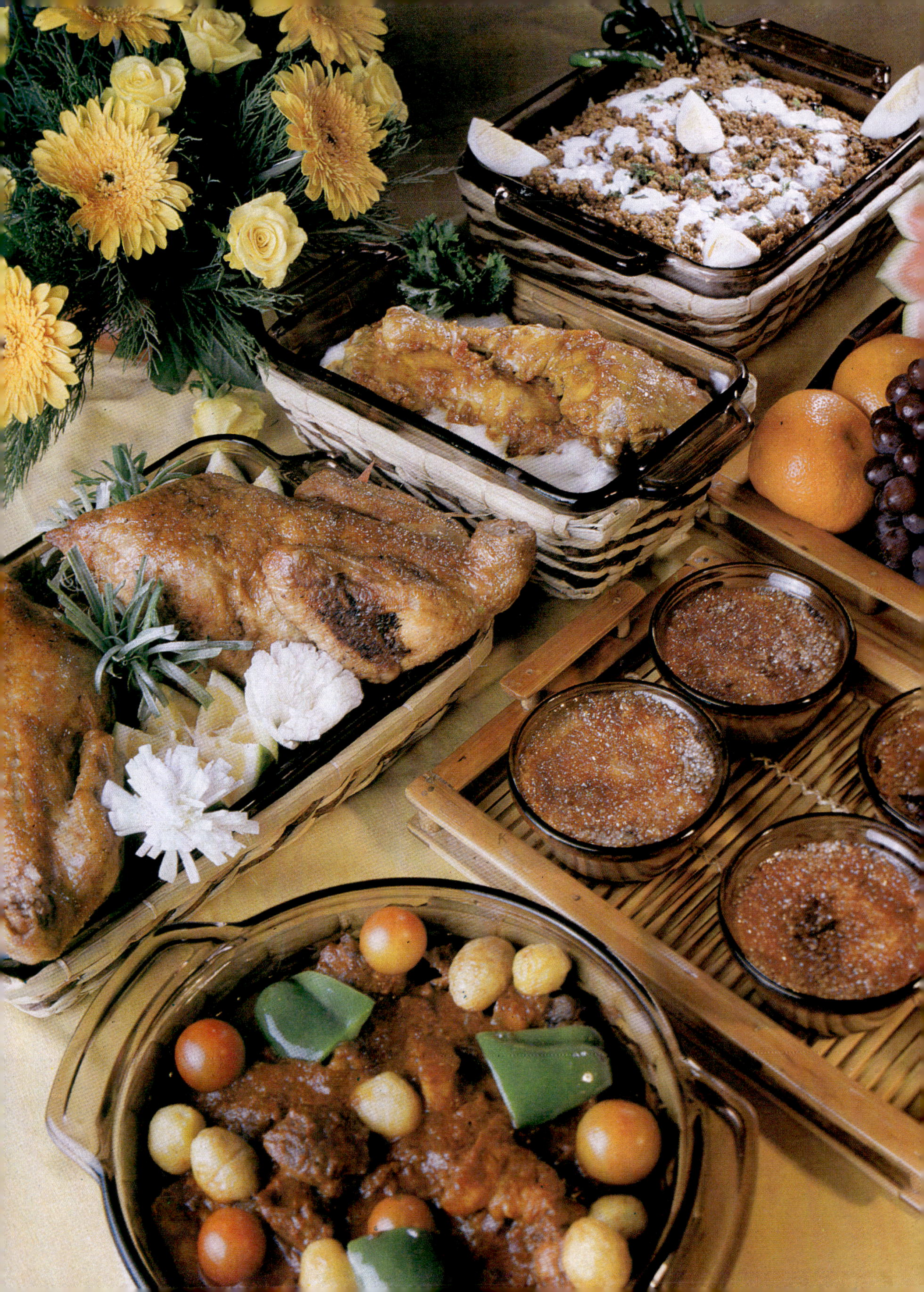

CHICKEN HAWAIIAN SALAD

This is a delicious cold salad and can be eaten as a main dish on its own. It's tangy, it's sweet and sour and cold and it's beautiful to look at. It's served in large pineapple halves and you must count one half pineapple for eight to ten people at a pinch. Otherwise I would suggest two halves for fifteen people.

Preparation Time: 55 mins. • Arranging Time: 45 mins. • Serves: 16

2 large pineapples with green shiny leaves
3 boiled chickens – 1 kg. each
3-5 cups mayonnaise
100 gms. cream
4 sweet limes
2 oranges
1 papaya
1 watermelon
2 bunches green grapes
1 bunch black grapes
2 cabbages – green and fresh
2 heads of fresh lettuce
1 bunch parsley
1 bunch spring onions
4 large red tomatoes
4 large capsicums cut julienne
2 large capsicums finely chopped into tiny squares
1 small can cherries
1½-2 tins cheese, frozen
2 large cans pineapple slices
1 stalk celery
½" ginger
1 large can gherkins
black pepper to taste
tabasco sauce or capsico sauce
salt to taste

Kheema Malai Pulao
Himalayan Murghi (pg. 176)
Stuffed Roast Chicken (pg. 158)
Sweet, Sour and Hot Pork (pg. 122)
My Apple Brulée (pg. 75)

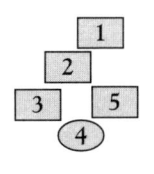

- Buy the largest pineapples you can find in the market. They should be firm – not over ripe and have glistening green leaves. Wash the pineapples and cut them horizontal with a very sharp knife. You should have two equal halves. Remove the pulp from the fruit and leave only the shells. Use the pulp to make pineapple jam. Then overturn the shells, cover and keep in a cool place.

- Boil the chickens in salted water along with 4 black peppercorns, 4 slices of fresh ginger and a stalk of celery. When soft, drain the water and remove the skin, bones and tendons and flake the flesh into strips and keep it in the refrigerator.

- Chop the canned pineapple slices thinly into fine strips. Open one tin of frozen cheese and cut into strips. Cut the capsicums into thin strips like potato shoestrings. Set all this in separate containers in the refrigerator.

- Prepare your mirror or silver salver for decoration one hour before the dinner begins.

Cut the cabbages into fine strips and soak in iced water for half an hour. Drain and spread over the salver. Wash the lettuce in iced water. When crisp, drain and dry. Trim the bottoms of the leaves and spread them over the edge of the salver so that they overlap each other. Cut four of the sweet limes into rings and then cut them into halves and decorate the edge of the mirror or salver over the lettuce leaves. Cut the watermelon into a basket shape and place a bunch of green seedless grapes with some canned cherries in it. Next, cut the papaya into two flower shapes as shown in one of the pictures. Place one bunch of black grapes into each of the papaya flowers. Make roses out of the skins of the four tomatoes.

- Finally, cut the spring onions julienne. Include the firm green portion above the white of the onions. In a large bowl mix the onions, chopped canned pineapple, gherkins, capsicum, cheese and chicken and blend in 3 cups of mayonnaise, two tablespoons of tabasco or more as required, one teaspoon of black pepper and salt to taste. Lastly, mix in one cup whipped cream. Chill this mixture for half an hour. Never put it in the freezer.

- When it is time to eat, put the salad mixture into the pineapple skin bowls and top it up into a mound. Decorate with the tiny pieces of capsicum and tiny pieces of cheese cut from the reserved half tin of cheese. Decorate with tomato roses and place in the salver. Then decorate the mirror or salver with the watermelon basket, the papaya flowers and segments of skinned orange.

- This is not a cheap dish by any means but it tastes so good and looks like a tropical garden that it will make your party a huge success.

MIRROR CHICKEN

Preparation Time: 45-60 mins. • Arranging Time: 45 mins. • Serves: 30

6 chickens roughly 800 gms. each
100 gms. ginger-garlic paste
3 bay leaves
2½" pieces of cinnamon
1 bottle best quality tomato sauce
soya bean sauce to taste
2 tsps. fresh black pepper powder
2 tsps. red Kashmiri chilli powder
6 raw beetroots grated
7 large red carrots grated
½ kg. each black and green grapes
4 grapefruits cut into flowers
10 tomato skin roses
1 pineapple, skinned, hollowed out and cored to accommodate a lit candle within cucumber and carrot flowers
2 small watermelons cut into flowers
4 lettuce
fresh cherries for decoration
salt
peanut oil or olive oil

- Remove the neck and wing portions of the chickens completely. Cut the chicken into 2 breasts and 2 legs and then cut each of the pieces into two. So you should get 8 pieces out of one chicken. That is 48 pieces in all.
- Wash the chicken pieces thrice. Apply salt and the ginger-garlic paste and sprinkle some black pepper on the chicken pieces. Set aside.
- Keep the mirror washed and dried till it sparkles.
- Take a flat bottomed large vessel and place half a litre oil, the bay leaves and cinnamon in it. Place on a stove on a medium flame. When the oil heats up, drop all the chicken pieces into the dekchi and stir them all well till they are coated with the oil. Gently roast the chickens in their own juice over a low heat. Cover, and place water on top of the cover. After 10-15 minutes, add the hot water from the cover and as much water as needed to allow the chicken to be tender.
- When the water has almost dried up, sprinkle half a cup of soya sauce on the chicken pieces. Stir for five minutes. Then add half the bottle of tomato sauce and chilli powder. The chicken pieces should all be well coated with the red sauce. If necessary, add some more sauce. Gently heat the chicken till it is dry. Cool.
- Half an hour before the party is due to start, begin arranging the chicken pieces on the mirror. Cover the edges with grated beetroot and red carrots and finely sliced lettuce. Arrange all the cut fruits tastefully and finally the fresh cherries and black and green grapes.

The whole mirror looks beautiful with this sort of decoration.

ROAST CHICKEN ON MIRROR

Preparation Time: 60 mins. • Arranging Time: 60 mins. • Serves: 20-30

5 whole chickens 1200 gms. each
100 gms. ginger-garlic paste
2 tbsps. freshly ground black pepper
½ cup cornflour
lettuce-cos – endive – iceberg
2 courgettes grazed with the tines of a fork
12 tomato skin roses
8 petals made out of green peppers
4 roses made out of yellow peppers
4 roses made out of red peppers
tabasco sauce
butter

- Wash the whole chickens, the front and back cavities three times. Marinate in salt, pepper powder and ginger-garlic paste.

- Deep fry the entire chickens in hot oil. Remove and cook in a large vessel after adding 2 litres of water. Add more water if necessary and cook till tender. Remove the chickens and allow to cool. Place in a refrigerator if you have the place.

- Remove all the left-over gravy into a large saucepan. Place on medium heat and whisk in the cornflour mixed in half a cup of water. Bring to the boil, stirring all the time. Add some tabasco sauce if you like.

- Arrange the green lettuces on the mirror. Take a sharp poultry scissors or an extremely sharp knife and cut each chicken into its breast pieces along with the wings, its thighs and drumsticks and arrange in the same shape as a live chicken on the mirror – neck between two breasts, then the thighs and drumsticks.

- Arrange four chickens in the four corners and the fifth one in the centre of the mirror. In each corner near the edge of the mirror where the two arms meet, make an arrangement of 3 tomato – skin roses and two petals made out of green capsicum.

- Make shapes out of the courgettes and arrange red and yellow peppers discreetly around the chicken formations.

- Serve the brown sauce, hot, in a gravy boat.

SECTION 5

COLD CUTS

Some of the most beautifully arranged food in the world will be seen on tables laid with Cold Cuts.

Primarily, a "cold cut" was a piece of meat which could be eaten without heating it. It still means the same, but now the word cold cut embraces more than just a piece of meat. It embraces cold, smoked, roasted game, poultry or duck, chicken, turkey, ham, mutton, beef, eggs, open sandwiches of non-vegetarian and vegetarian items. These are displayed in thin delicate sheets, cuts and in various forms such as cutlets, patties, mince pies and stuffed mince potatoes, tomatoes, gherkins, pork sausages, meat sausages, chicken sausages, cold prawns stuffed in celery stalks and avocados and pie shells stuffed with a variety of beans, egg mixtures, mushroom sauces, cheese sauces, fruit boats stuffed with fruits and sweet cream like strawberries, grapes, kiwi fruits, raspberries, mangoes, cherries, black berries, blue berries, papayas and citrus fruits. The list is endless.

What is very important is how this large list of items is served. It has to be beautifully decorated so as to catch the diners' eye.

Unfortunately, only two large photographs could be published on cold cuts.

You can clearly see how the sausages, luncheon meat, ham slices, salami slices, smoked chicken are placed on a silver salver, which is first filled with cabbage shreds and lettuce leaves on the sides of the dish. There should be a slight bulge at the head and centre. The pieces are placed in overlapping positions and then decorated with fruits, olives, bunches of red, black and green grapes. Sweet-limes, oranges, strawberries, papayas and water melons are lavishly used as also canned cherries.

Open cheese and asparagus sandwiches are a must. So also red and black caviar served with tiny bits of toast. Devilled eggs with various types and different coloured stuffings are laid out on circular mirrors or wooden trays, decorated with cherry bits and parsley.

Pies are filled with baked beans sautéd in butter, spring onions and celery. Akoori of several kinds can be served in the pie shells. Scrambled paneer cooked with a swish of green fresh chilli and fresh ginger can be very tasty. Some fillings to which I am very specially addicted are a heavy cream cheese sauce with tiny bits of celery or mushrooms, or ham or chicken. The list is endless. Just use your imagination and your taste buds.

Wonderful open and closed sandwiches can be made with roasted meats, masala meats, Thai dressings, Cajun style and a variety of white breads, brown breads and rye breads.

Tiny baby tomatoes are stuffed with pork mince. Baby potatoes are stuffed with a savoury vegetable mixture. Cucumbers are hollowed out and stuffed with a mayonnaise, chive and prawn mixture. Baby brinjals are stuffed with a paneer bhurji. Ripe mango cheeks are stuffed with sweet cream and raspberries. As you can see, I have given the recipe for grapefruit shells stuffed with crab or lobster meat. Empty lobster shells can also be stuffed with a mayonnaise sauce with pomfret bits.

Anyone who has never laid out a buffet with cold cuts, can first learn to make flowers out of sweet-lime, grapefruit and papayas. It's very easy. All you need are sharp, small knives and concentration and a picture in front of you. Leaves can be made from cucumbers and carrots. You can make plain ones and feathery ones by finely slicing the edges, and soaking them in cold water.

Different types of mayonnaise and savoury butters can be made. I have given a small list below as well as a recipe to make pies. You will find them very useful when entertaining your friends to brunch, high tea or cocktails.

TODAY'S PARTY FOOD

I have been to most countries of the world, but, the vast variety of food in America took my breath away. You can get Swedish food near the Great Lakes, French cuisine in Louisiana, hot Mexican food in Texas and so on. Each state has its innumerable varieties and tastes. When a buffet is laid out at a hotel or on a friend's patio, it consists of a number of dishes which run a gamut of colours and tastes. They include fish, chicken, turkey, beef, pork, mutton, fruits, vegetables, nuts, dips, breads and colourful unusual mixtures of salads which make you do a double-take. It's the wildly unlikely combinations which the hostess uses which enhances her party and makes it a success.

Where our Indian food is concerned, we do not go in for soups, except rasams, and the thali is attacked straightaway. Nowadays, every family has a member or two who has gone abroad and feasted their eyes on pizzas and finger-dip meals as well as elaborate banquets and it is but natural that they would like to bring some of their experiences into the family home. So whether you are a vegetarian or not, I suggest that at every party you include some of the fantastic looking but easy to make salads. There is no need to use asparagus and artichokes, just use simple items which are available in our markets, such as chinese cabbage, broccoli, bean sprouts, celery, parsley, red cabbages, nuts such as almonds, cashews, pistachios, walnuts, dried fruit such as apricots, figs, currants, raisins, pears, peaches and prunes.

Many European and American types of salad dressings would not appeal to Indians or blend with their cuisine, but at the Freemason's Hall, P.V.M. Gymkhana and the Ripon Club, I used various dressings. The most popular, however, were those with a mayonnaise base.

Olive oil is imported into India and is extremely expensive. So I use the best quality refined groundnut (peanut) oil. I normally make one large lot in my electronic mixer-grinder. The basic quantity is placed in a large covered vessel of glass or stainless steel and used as and when necessary. For one lot of mayonnaise I use:

MAYONNAISE

3 eggs
4 tsps. sugar
4 tsps. white vinegar or lime juice
½ tsp. pepper powder
½ tsp. mustard powder (optional)
1½ kgs. refined groundnut oil
salt to taste

- Place the eggs in the mixie along with the salt, sugar, pepper, mustard and vinegar. Mix well and add the oil in a slow trickle till the mayonnaise becomes thick and forms peaks.
- Place in a closed container. Chill.

FILLINGS FOR SANDWICHES

PRAWN MAYONNAISE

1 cup mayonnaise
1 cup boiled prawns – minced
1 tbsp. minced capsicums
1 tbsp. minced parsley
2 tbsps. tabasco or capsico sauce
salt to taste

- Mix all the ingredients well. Bottle and chill. Use fast. Use as a dip or sandwich filler. Do the same for all the combinations given below.

CHEESE AND MUSHROOM MAYONNAISE

2 cups mayonnaise
1 cup grated cheese
1 cup finely chopped, boiled mushrooms
½ cup finely chopped coriander or parsley
1 tbsp. lime juice
because of the cheese you will not need salt

HERB MAYONNAISE

1 cup mayonnaise
2 tbsps. tomato sauce
1 tbsp. finely chopped celery
1 tbsp. finely chopped chives
1 tbsp. finely chopped coriander
1 tbsp. finely chopped white cucumber flesh
1 tbsp. capsicum flesh
1 tsp. coarsely ground black pepper
salt to taste

MAYONNAISE WITH GREEN PEPPERCORNS AND DILL

1 cup mayonnaise
2 tbsps. green peppercorns – pickled
1 tbsp. chopped dill
½ tsp. powdered sage

. . . .

GHERKIN AND BOILED EGG MAYONNAISE

1½ cups mayonnaise
4 gherkins – finely chopped
4 boiled eggs – finely chopped
1 spring onion – finely chopped
1 tomato – peeled, deseeded and finely chopped
½ tsp. thyme
2 tsps. chopped parsley
1 tsp. coarsely ground black pepper
½ tsp. roasted ground cumin seeds
salt to taste

. . . .

MAYONNAISE WITH WALNUTS, APPLES, CELERY AND OLIVES

1 cup mayonnaise
½ cup finely chopped, peeled apples
½ cup chopped celery
½ cup sliced olives
2 tbsps. crushed walnuts
½ tsp. fresh thyme

PINEAPPLE MAYONNAISE

1 cup mayonnaise
1 cup, chopped, canned pineapple
2 tbsps. parsley
2 tbsps. chopped spring onions
2 tbsps. capsicums, cut julienne
1 tbsp. chopped basil
½ tsp. black pepper powder

. . . .

HAM MAYONNAISE

1 cup mayonnaise
1½ cup chopped ham
½ cup chopped prunes
2 tbsps. celery
1 tbsp. chives finely chopped

. . . .

ORANGE AND CHIKOO MAYONNAISE

1 cup mayonnaise
1 cup orange flesh skinned and flaked
1 cup sweet lime skinned and flaked
1 cup chikoos peeled, chopped

. . . .

CHERRY AND APPLE MAYONNAISE

1 cup mayonnaise
1 cup chopped apples
½ cup canned cherries, deseeded
1 tbsp. celery cut diagonally

SANDWICH FILLERS – SAVOURY BUTTER FOR SANDWICHES

(All the butter should be used within three days. Mix in a food processor and chill.)

BUTTER WITH CHICKEN

300 gms. salted butter
350 gms. chicken, boiled, finely chopped
2 tbsps. lime juice
1 tbsp. pepper coarsely ground
1 tbsp. tabasco sauce
1 tbsp. parsley finely chopped

. . . .

FISH BUTTER

300 gms. salted butter
350 gms. white fish flesh boiled, deboned
2 tbsps. parsley - minced
1 tbsp. mint - minced
1 tbsp. prepared mustard
1 tbsp. chopped thyme

. . . .

HAM BUTTER

300 gms. salted butter
350 gms. ham finely chopped
250 gms. finely chopped canned pineapple
1 pinch paprika or mustard powder

. . . .

CRAB BUTTER

300 gms. salted butter
350 gms. fresh crab meat
2 tbsps. celery, chopped
2 tbsps. red or green peppers
1 tsp. black pepper, coarsely ground
2 tsps. sour lime juice

CHEESE-GHERKIN-DILL BUTTER

350 gms. salted butter
350 gms. cheese – grated
6 gherkins – squeezed and chopped
2 tbsps. dill – minced
2 tbsps. green pickled peppercorns
1 tbsp. finely chopped chives

. . . .

CHEESE AND WALNUT OR ALMOND BUTTER

400 gms. salted butter
400 gms. cheese
200 gms. crushed walnuts or salted almonds
3 tbsps. chopped spring onions
3 tbsps. chopped olives
1 tbsp. chopped fresh coriander

. . . .

PRAWN AND CHILLI BUTTER

400 gms. butter
400 gms. prawns deveined, salted boiled and finely chopped
2 tbsps. coriander, chopped
4 green chillies de-seeded and finely chopped
2 tbsps. lime juice
2 tbsps. chives, chopped

GREEN GRAPES AND ONION BUTTER

300 gms. salted butter
200 gms. tiny onion rings, pickled overnight in white vinegar
200 gms. seedless grapes, sliced
2 tbsps. almonds, coarsely ground
2 tbsps. parsley, chopped
2 tbsps. chives, chopped

MUSHROOM BUTTER

350 gms. butter
350 gms. mushrooms, salted, boiled and finely sliced
2 tbsps. tomato sauce
1 tbsp. tabasco sauce
1 tsp. green chillies, deseeded and finely chopped
1 tsp. thyme or fresh coriander, chopped fine

USES FOR MAYONNAISE MIXTURES AND SAVOURY BUTTER

- As sandwich fillings
- As tartlet fillings
- As a dip with potato chips
- As a dip with garlic bread
- As toppings for cutlets, fried fish fillets, roast mutton or fried chicken legs
- As dips with wafers or raw vegetable crudities
- As an accompaniment to salads and boiled vegetables or meats
- As an accompaniment for hamburgers, patties, and samosas

PIE CASES

Preparation Time: 10 mins. • Baking Time: 36 mins. • Makes: 40

100 gms. cornflour
250 gms. self-raising flour
250 gms. butter
50 gms. sugar
6 eggs
¼ tsp. baking powder
1 tsp. salt
2 tbsps. extra butter

- Lightly mix all the above ingredients and knead gently into a ball. Cover and refrigerate for 20 minutes
- Grease 40 small pie cases with butter and preheat the oven to 350°F.
- Roll out the dough. Cut small circles of the dough and even out the edges with a knife. Prick the bottom of the cases with a fork. Place the tins in an aluminium tray and bake for 12 minutes in 2 or 3 batches. When cool, tip out the pie cases and store in an air-tight container.
- Fill the cases with masala paneer, mushrooms in cheese sauce, mayonnaise prawns, Russian salad, savoury butters or a long list of mayonnaise based spreads included in this book. You can also serve sliced fruits with a custard sauce or jams and blancmanges as sweet fillings.
- This same recipe can be used to make larger tart cases and quiches.

SECTION 6

AN ENGLISH TEA IN YOUR ROSE GARDEN

During January and February my Lonavala garden is aglow with flowers. After the long monsoon and cold spell, the trees are eager to greet the sun and this is the period I like best when we can take the table and chairs into the garden, put up the sun umbrellas and enjoy the company of my friends at tea time. The light breeze wafts the aroma of the roses around the garden and the jasmine flowers, small and white like little stars add their own perfume to the atmosphere with every breeze that ripples through its creepers.

I normally have one luscious fruit cake, baked two days before, strawberry shortcake with cream, a cherry-filled black forest cake, a sponge cream and, fresh fruit cake and little boats with cream and soft fruits. Then I serve 2 to 3 types of tiny tarts or bouchees made with ham, chicken or mushrooms and cheese. Some unusual sandwiches with fillings like Russian salad, crab meat, prawn butter or a celery, apple and nut mixture. I almost always serve an apple pie with fresh cream or a glacé custard of pouring consistency and two types of ice creams. I find that my guests enjoy the Peach Melba we make with Australian peaches and the Melba Sauce which is cooked in the peach juice. Another sweet greatly appreciated is our chilled apricot and crystallized ginger ice cream.

Sometimes I make almond and butter biscuits and sometimes scotch bread. All in all, the parties are always a success as every time the guests never find any item repeated unless asked for by their demand.

It was the Memsahibs who came into India by the boat loads during the British Raj who introduced us to cakes and biscuits. The most prominent cook book on the shelves of all Indians was the popular Mrs. Beeton's "Pudding And Pies". My grandmother had one in her house and it was one of the first books with photographs of how to make the sweet dishes and biscuits.

Nowadays we have beautifully illustrated books from all over the world. Nobody can say he or she has discovered a new recipe because thousands of books have been published around the basic original recipe. What we can change are the measurements of commodities, the amount of cream, the type of decoration, the creams for sandwiching and decorating meringues and sponges and marzipan cakes. Amongst these hundreds and thousands of recipes, a particular one captures your eyes and turns out wonderfully well when cooked. Then this is the recipe you should return to again and again, and make it perfectly so that it's a joy to serve and eat. This is how I selected many of my cake and biscuit recipes. There are some fruit cakes like the Dundee Cake and glacé fruit cakes which are a pleasure to eat because of their lovely crunchiness and I have given several versions of them. You can make whichever one you like, depending on your pocket and your fondness for chopped fruit and peels.

There are many recipes for Tarte Tatin which was accidentally created by two French sisters in Paris. I have given the version I liked best. This is an upside down baked tart and all its ingredients are simple and available to every Indian housewife. Formerly we had only a limited crystallized fruit range but now all the major cities and towns in India keep a variety of prunes, orange peel, raisins, sultanas, cherries, green crystallized papaya, ginger, pears, apples and the favourite angelica. I don't know if we grow angelica in India or not, but it is most famous in France where it grows all over the Loire Valley. The stems of the plant are crystallized. Although you can eat the leaves as a salad, and the tree grows six feet high, it's the younger plants which are harvested for crystallization and exported all over the world.

I have always maintained that if one or two items in a recipe are not available, you can still go ahead and try it out. Unless, the whole meal revolves along the item you can't acquire.

In one of the beautiful cake books I have in my possession, a light sponge cake was topped with a fantastic collection of berries not available in India. So I substituted the berries with peaches, apricots, plums and black and green grapes.

Where making light cakes is concerned, you can make the simplest cake look positively grand by using your imagination into decorating its top with colourful fruits and chocolate shapes.

Cakes, more or less, originated in Europe and Great Britain and thence to the U.S.A. The earliest evidence we have is of bread baked with honey and then it went onto bread baked with honey and dried fruits and nuts. It was the monks who made this sweet to be dispensed on festival days. Slowly, the courts and rich merchants also bought the expensive white sugar to make delightful desserts with different creams. However, it was with the advent of traders from the Mediterranean who brought flower and fruit essences, delicious dried dates and dried figs and crystallized citrus fruits that cake making took a serious and trendy turn. The Dark Ages did not see such a spurt of interest in cake making because all these items were then not available, but after the crusades and much contact with the Arab world, the increase in trade of spices, traders' Guilds sprang up in Europe and Great Britain. Bakers' Guilds popped up and marzipan called "marchpane" by the Elizabethans and their compatriots became a very popular sweet item.

But it is in the end of the 15th century and the 16th and 17th centuries, that the French and Italian aristocracy gave an impetus to this creative art. Small pastry shops came into existence in sophisticated quarters. In Vienna, "cafes" came into being. It became the fashion to drink coffee and eat tiny little cakes with it.

The stodgy cakes with sugar, honey, nuts and berries had given way to light, airy, cream filled confections. A cake rage occurred in Europe. England was not far behind this revolution taking place in sweet making. Afternoon tea became an important part of Great Britain's life. Matrons would invite each other's families and friends to drink Indian, Ceylon or China tea, from delicate porcelain cups. Alongside, tiny, paper thin sandwiches of cucumber and watercress were served with little cream cakes on tea stands very much like the one in our photograph. Silver tea urns, milk jugs and sugar bowls with elaborate designs came into creation along with a special small "pastry fork" with which to eat your cake. With the passage of time, tea became cheaper and the lower middle class and the poorer people also took to tea drinking until it became an afternoon ritual. "High Tea" came into being at about 6 o'clock in the evenings when father returned from work and the school children and elders gathered around the dining table to partake of tea, ham and cheese sandwiches, fruit cakes, sausages, pasties and mango chutney, all swallowed down by delicate, hot, sweet tea.

From England, the Memsahibs brought the tea ritual to India. Their maids or ayahs, butlers or khansamas, cooks or bawarchis earned more than the average person if he or she knew the ritual of tea making.

Similarly, the Dutch people, the Swedes and Germans brought their culinary expertise to whosoever wished to learn and create in America. This huge country soon took up coffee drinking along with cake eating and "coffee mornings" grew up and so did the habit of eating "coffee cakes".

In all the chief cities of India and even in the vast interiors, cakes have become a way of life. In sophisticated cities like Calcutta, Mumbai, Chennai and Delhi, Italian confectionery shops began to mushroom. Today, Mumbai city boasts of thousands of women cake makers. Most of them Parsi women. I know of two Parsi men, one is Mr. Iranpour of the Taj Mahal Hotel, Mumbai, the premiere hotel in India, and the other is a young man called Mehernosh Khajotia. Both of them have been trained in Switzerland, and make the most delicious cakes. After eating Mehernosh's cakes you will refuse to eat any other. Mr. Iranpour being in charge of such a huge, commercial "patisserie" is tied up by rules and regulations and still manages to produce a fantastic array of exquisite snacks and cakes, flans and pastries you would never tire of.

What makes cakes such a popular item is that they are made of the choicest items the world produces. Sugar, butter, cream, honey, the best of wheat flour, dried and crystallized fruits, fresh fruits, essences, flower waters, saffron, vanilla, roses and lavender. All sorts of liqueurs are used nowadays to enhance the taste of the flour-made layers.

We have to follow a few rules. All the necessary items must be ready on the table before you. Do not be in a hurry. Follow your cake book. Use your own discretion also.

FRESH RASPBERRY AND STRAWBERRY CREAM CAKE

Preparation Time: 10-15 mins. • Cooking Time: 30 mins. • Serves: 8

For the Sponge:

180 gms. icing sugar
60 gms. fine flour
60 gms. potato powder
5 eggs, separated
2 tsps. orange juice
½ tsp. orange essence
a pinch of salt

For the Cream Filling:

450 ml. double cream
250 gms. fresh strawberries
250 gms. fresh raspberries
7 tbsps. cherry liqueur
150 gms. icing sugar

- Grease an 8½" round cake tin and line it with greaseproof paper.
- Sift the flours together and set aside.
- Take 3 tablespoons of icing sugar and set aside. Whisk the remaining sugar and the egg yolks. Whisk the whites with the reserved icing sugar.
- Fold the flour, orange juice and the essence into the yolk mixture. Carefully fold in the egg whites. Stir gently and pour the mixture into the prepared tin and bake at 180°C.
- Remove sponge from the oven and let it cool. Remove the paper and slice horizontally into three layers. Sprinkle the lower two layers with cherry liqueur. Place the third layer on a fancy dish or silver tray.
- Put aside ten of the best raspberries and strawberries for decoration. Slice the rest of the fruit or cut them into quarters. Sprinkle with some icing sugar. Whip the cream with the rest of the icing sugar. Spread the strawberries over the bottom layer of cake and spread over ⅓ of the cream. Cover with the middle layer of sponge. Spread the raspberries and cover with another ⅓ of the cream. Place the topmost layer of cake on this and spread the remaining cream on it. Decorate the top of the cake with the reserved fruit and dust with icing sugar. Chill for two hours before serving.

STRAWBERRY SHORTCAKE

Preparation Time: 12 mins. • Baking Time: 30 mins. • Serves: 4-6

100 gms. butter
75 gms. flour
45 gms. cornflour
60 gms. castor sugar
2 eggs
1 tsp. baking powder
1 punnet strawberries
200 ml. double cream
1 egg white
30 gms. castor sugar

- Place butter and sugar in a bowl and beat lightly. Beat the eggs and add to the creamed mixture.
- Sift the flour, cornflour and baking powder and add to the creamed batter. Mix well.
- Grease a 7" cake tin and line the bottom with greaseproof paper. Pour the batter in and bake in a moderate oven, 180°C or 350°F., for 25-30 minutes. Remove to a wire rack and cool.
- Slice the cake horizontally into two pieces. Whisk the cream with 30 gms. castor sugar till stiff. Reserve 8-10 strawberries for decorating the top of the cake. Slice the rest of the fruit. Fold in the egg white into the beaten cream. Mix half of the cream with the sliced strawberries and spread onto the lower half of the cake. Cover with the top slice of the cake and spread the rest of the cream on the top. Decorate with the remaining strawberries, halved or sliced, as desired.

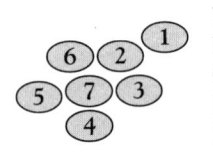

Chef Nowzer Iranpour
Apple Tart (pg. 107)
Pavlova (pg. 73)
Black Forest Cherry Cake (pg. 74)
Mixed Fruit Creme Brulee (pg. 90)
Croquembouche with Spun Sugar Net
Strawberry Shortcake (pg. 72)
Mixed Fruit Cheese Cake (pg. 89)

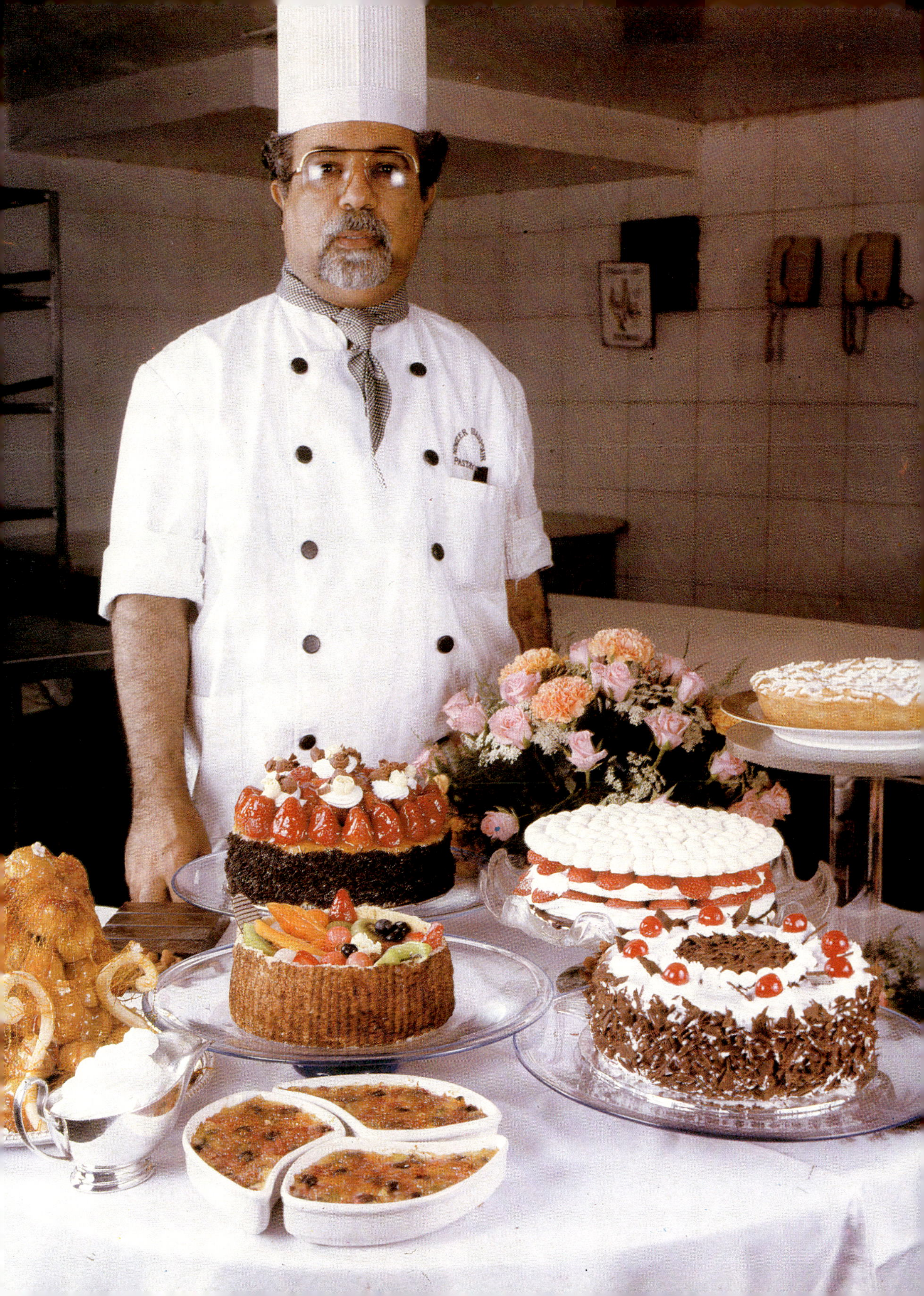

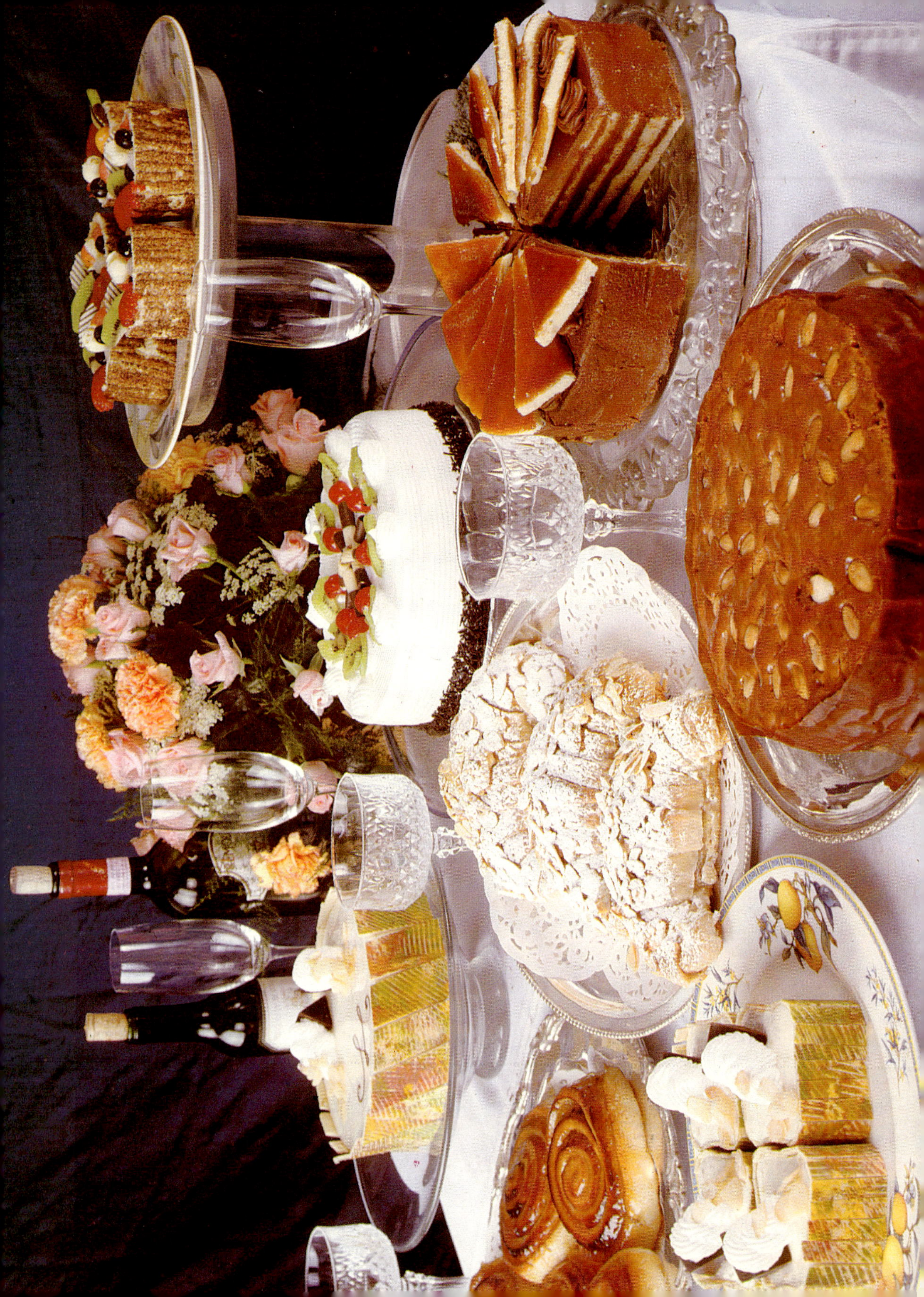

PAVLOVA

Preparation Time: 10 mins. • Cooking Time: 3-4 hrs. • Serves: 8

225 gms. castor sugar
225 gms. canned fruits including fresh strawberries
1 tsp. cornflour
1 tsp. vanilla essence
½ tsp. white synthetic vinegar
300 ml. double cream
4 egg whites

- Draw a circle on greaseproof paper, 20 cm. (8 ins.) in diameter. Oil the sheet and place it on a greased baking tray.
- Place the egg whites in a bowl, add the vanilla essence and whisk until stiff.
- Very gradually add half the sugar and continue whisking the whites. Then add the rest of the sugar, vinegar and the cornflour.
- Place the mixture in a piping-bag fitted with a star nozzle. Pipe along the outline of the greaseproof paper and then fill up the inside upto a height of 2½-3".
- Bake in a moderately warm oven, 110°C, for 3-4 hours until completely dry.
- Place in an air-tight tin. When needed, whip the cream with sugar and fill the meringue cases with cream and fruit. Decorate with the strawberries.

Individual Fruit Cheese Cakes (on Stand) (pg. 89)
Dobos Cake
Dundee Cake (pg. 78)
Individual Amaretto Mousse
Chelsea Buns
Amaretto Mousse (pg. 90)
Cream Cake with Fruits
Almond Crescents

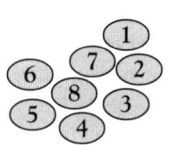

BLACK FOREST CHERRY CAKE

Preparation Time: 25-30 mins. • Cooking Time: 40-60 mins. • Serves: 10

For the Cake:

230 gms. castor sugar
100 gms. melted butter
75 gms. self-raising flour
60 gms. cocoa powder
1 tsp. vanilla essence
6 eggs

For the Filling and Decoration:

600 ml. cream
70 gms. icing sugar
80-100 gms. plain grated chocolate
100 gms. chocolate curls
2 small cans or one large can cherries
10-12 tbsps. kirsch liqueur

- Grease, flour and paper a 9" round cake tin.
- Whisk the sugar, eggs and vanilla in a bowl and put it over a saucepan of simmering water and whisk until the mixture thickens. Remove from the saucepan and cool. Fold in the flour and cocoa powder and mix it gently and thoroughly. Finally mix in the melted butter and pour the cake batter into the prepared tin.
- Pre-heat the oven to 375°F or 190°C and bake the cake for 40-60 minutes. Cool for 5 minutes in the tin.
- Two hours before you begin to bake your cake, open the cherry cans, drain the fruit and reserve the sweet liquid. Place the cherries in a glass bowl and add 10 tablespoons of kirsch and mix the cherries well and set aside till needed.
- Turn out the cake onto a wire rack and when cool, cut into 3 horizontal layers.
- Drain the cherries once more and sprinkle all the 3 layers with the kirsch flavoured syrup.
- Whip the cream, add the sugar and the remaining liqueur. Divide the cream and mix the cherries into one half of it and fill the 2 bottom layers with the cream and cherries. With the other half of the cream, cover the sides and the top of the cake. Press the grated chocolate into the sides of the cake.
- Pipe the remaining cream into swirls on the edge of the cake and decorate with maraschino cherries if available.
- Use the canned cherries, they will do beautifully as well. Chill the cake for an hour or two before serving it. Do not keep any food which has a sharp smell, in the refrigerator. The delicate aroma of the kirsch will be lost.

MY APPLE BRULÉE

Preparation Time: 15 mins. • Cooking Time: 25-30 mins. • Serves: 5

400 gms. cream
4 apples – tart ones – skinned, cored and sliced
200 gms. castor sugar
5 egg yolks
40-50 gms. brown sugar
1 tsp. vanilla essence
70 gms. extra castor sugar

- Place the extra sugar and apple slices along with 2 cups of water in a saucepan. Bring to a boil. Cool. Drain the apple and divide them between 5 ramekins.
- Place the cream on a low flame and heat it. Do not allow to boil. Cool. Beat the egg yolks and castor sugar with a whisk and mix into the cold cream. Add the vanilla essence. Stir and pour into 5 small ramekins.
- Pre-heat oven to 350°F or 180°C. Bake the ramekins till the custard turns golden brown. Remove from the oven.
- Place the oven shelf a little higher and turn the heat from 350°F to 400°F. Spread a layer of brown sugar on top of the custards and heat for 4-5 minutes till the sugar has melted. Remove from the oven and cool. Cover. Chill overnight before serving.
- STRAWBERRY BRULÉE: Cut 15 large strawberries into half. Place in a saucepan with 70 gms. castor sugar and half cup water. Bring to a boil. Cool and drain. Divide the strawberries amongst the ramekins and proceed as above.

LEMON MERINGUE PIE

Preparation Time: 45-55 mins. • Cooking Time: 35 + 10 mins. • Serves: 8

For an 8" Pie:
170 gms. self-raising flour
110 gms. unsalted butter, cold and diced
30 gms. castor sugar
1 egg yolk
a pinch of salt
2 tbsps. cold water

For the Filling:
280 ml. water
200 gms. castor sugar
50 gms. unsalted butter
2 egg yolks
40 gms. cornflour
grated rind of two sour limes
juice of three sour limes

Meringue Covering:
150 gms. castor sugar
3 egg whites

- Take a bowl and sift the flour and salt into it. Add the sugar and the diced cold butter and mix with your finger tips and aerate the flour. Beat in the egg yolk and cold water and make a firm dough. Add more water if necessary and chill for 15 minutes.
- Knead the dough on a floured board and roll out to cover a 10" pie dish. Let the pie dough extend a little bit over the side of the pie.
- Prick the bottom of the pastry case and chill for another 10 minutes.
- Pre-heat the oven to 400°F or 200°C and bake for 15 minutes after placing a piece of foil in the pie case with cooking beans or ceramic beads.
- Place the lime juice and water into a saucepan. Add the cornflour and stir briskly. Add the rind. Place on a stove and bring to the boil. Stir until the mixture thickens and beat in the egg yolks and the sugar and lastly the butter. Cool and pour into the pastry case.
- Whisk the egg whites till stiff and satiny. Gently add the sugar and whisk again. Spoon the egg whites over the lemon filling. Cover it completely.
- Bake the pie at 350°F or 180°C for about 20 minutes till the meringue topping is firm and golden brown.

BABA AU RUM OR SAVARIN

- One of the nicest sweets I ever made and ate was a baba au rum or savarin; I don't know if you can call it a cake or a pudding. Its soft, sweet and juicy and full of fruits and cream.
- I am giving several recipes choose the one you like most.
- What you need is an 8" or 9" ring mould or eight small ring moulds for individual babas. The most important ingredient in this recipe is fresh or dried yeast.
- There is a very thin line between a baba or savarin. Most people use both names for the savarin which is cooked in a ring mould. The baba was baked in "bucket shaped" individual "clariole moulds" according to Linda Collister and Anthony Blake. The individual baba, not made in ring moulds includes currants and is heavily doused in Kirsch or rum and the ring moulds were flavoured with lemon or orange zest or candied fruits and then soaked in lemon or orange syrup.
- Anyway, whatever you do, whether it's a baba or savarin, you will enjoy this sweet immensely. Grand Marnier and Cointreau are favourites for soaking savarins. Freshly whipped cream, sliced strawberries, raspberries, green and black grapes, pineapple pieces, kiwi fruit slices are used to decorate the centre.

Preparation Time: 4½ hrs. • Cooking Time: 30-35 mins. • Serves: 8

Cake:
220 gms. self-raising flour
30 gms. sugar
18 gms. fresh yeast
3 eggs
50 gms. unsalted melted butter
pinch of salt

Syrup:
250 gms. sugar
130 ml. dark rum

Glaze – Fruit Filling:
50 gms. apricot jam
250 gms. cream
30 gms. icing sugar
1 tsp. vanilla essence
3 tbsps. dark rum
sliced fresh or canned fruits

- Grease an 8" savarin ring mould.
- Sift flour and a pinch of salt in a bowl. Add the sugar. Mix the yeast into 2 teaspoons of warm water and pour it onto the flour. Whisk the eggs and add them to the flour as well as the softened butter. Mix well into a sticky dough.
- Put the dough on a lightly floured board and knead it for 5 minutes until it becomes smooth. Roll it into a ball shape and place it in a flour-smeared bowl. Cover the dough and place it in a warm spot for about 2 hours until it has doubled in size.
- Replace dough on the board and form into a thick rope. Press it into the prepared mould, cover loosely and set in a warm place again for 2 hours until the dough becomes as high as the mould.
- Pre-heat the oven to 375°F or 190°C, and bake for 30 minutes till the savarin is well browned. Cover with foil for the last 10 minutes.

Rum Syrup:

- Put the sugar and 400 ml. water in a saucepan and allow to boil without stirring the mixture. Cool a little and add the rum.
- Strain the apricot jam and heat with 2 tablespoons of water.
- Place the still warm savarin on a serving dish and prick all over with a long large needle and dribble the rum syrup on it so it soaks up all the syrup.
- Cover the savarin with the sieved apricot liquid and refrigerate.
- Just before serving, whip the cream well with the sugar and vanilla and pipe it at the top and base of the savarin. Fill the centre with sliced strawberries, papaya, peaches, cherries, kiwi fruit and canned pineapple.

DUNDEE CAKE

Preparation Time: 35 mins. • Cooking Time: 2-2½ hrs. • Serves: 10-12

175 gms. butter
175 gms. castor sugar
250 gms. self-raising flour
450 gms. crystallized fruits such as pineapples, cherries, currants and raisins and a little crystallized ginger
50 gms. orange and papaya peel
50 gms. ground almonds
50 gms. whole almonds, boiled and skinned
4 eggs
2 tsps. nutmeg-cardamom powder
½ cup milk
1 egg white, whipped; to glaze the cake
1 tsp. baking powder
1½ tsps. salt

- In a large bowl whip the sugar and eggs together and slowly beat in the butter. When smooth, add the spice powder, flour and then the ground almonds. Add the salt, baking powder and milk. Mix.
- Sprinkle flour on the dried fruits and peel so that they don't sink to the bottom of the cake.
- Mix the fruits into the mixture and stir gently.
- Grease an 8" (20 cms.) round cake tin and pour the batter into it. Arrange the blanched almonds on the top in concentric circles, starting from the centre.
- Glaze the top with the whipped egg white and bake in a preheated oven at 350°F or 180°C for 2-2½ hours. Check if the cake is done by inserting a skewer into the centre. It should come out clean.

A ROYAL FRUIT CAKE – DUNDEE CAKE

It seems this rich fruit cake was baked especially for Mary, Queen of Scots. She had come from a fashionable court, that of Henry IV, Diane de Poitiers and Mary de Medici. The grey Scot weather and the uncouth and wild behaviour of her noblemen drove her to unhappiness and confusion. It is good to know that her confectioners encouraged her sweet tooth by making sweets with difficult to obtain items. She did not like cherries, therefore there are no cherries in this cake. Use an 8" cake tin with high sides.

Preparation Time: 25-30 mins. • Cooking Time: 2½ hrs. • Serves: 10

250 gms. brown sugar
280 gms. self-raising flour
180 gms. butter
340 gms. sultanas
250 gms. currants
120 gms. chopped candied peel
75 gms. ground almonds
80 gms. vanaspati ghee
5 eggs
2 limes – grated zest
25-30 boiled, skinned whole almonds
2 tsps. vanilla essence
2 tsps. nutmeg and cardamom powder

- Grease the cake tin well. Place 3 pieces of butter paper around the inside and 3 circles of paper on the bottom of the tin. Cover the outside of the tin with 3 sheets of butter paper to form a high collar.
- Pre-heat the oven to 350°F or 180°C.
- Take a large mixing bowl and place the sugar, butter and vanaspati into it and beat until soft.
- Add the lime rind or zest to the eggs in a separate bowl and whisk together. Add this to the sugar mixture very, very slowly beating all the time.
- Spray the currants, sultanas and finely chopped peel with a little flour so the fruit does not sink to the bottom of the cake.
- Add the flour and ground almonds a little at a time. Do the same with the fruit until both, flour and fruits have been mixed well into the butter-sugar mixture. Add the vanilla and spice powders. Mix one last final time and put the cake mix into the cake tin. Press your knuckles on the top of the cake and level it. Place the boiled almonds in neat circles on top of the cake and press lightly.
- Place a stack of 4-5 newspapers below the cake and place both on a baking tray. Bake at 350°F or 180°C for 40-45 minutes, after which bake the cake at 325°F or 170°C for another 1½ to 1¾ hours.
- Cool the cake overnight in the tin. Wrap it next morning in butter paper and place in an air tight tin.

CHOCOLATE FUDGE CAKE

Preparation Time: 40-45 mins. • Cooking Time: 35 mins. • Serves: 8

180 gms. plain chocolate
80 gms. plain chocolate grated
180 ml. cream
80 gms. castor sugar
5 egg whites
2 egg yolks
50 gms. unsalted butter

- Prepare a round 7" cake tin by greasing and papering it inside.
- Place the 180 gms. of plain chocolate together with the butter in a sauce pan and allow to melt very gently. Cool.
- Whisk the egg yolks with 1 tablespoon of castor sugar until sugar has melted and pour it into the melted chocolate.
- In a large bowl whisk the egg whites until they rise in peaks. Add sugar and beat till stiff. Take a metal spoon and place 2 spoonfuls of whisked egg white into the melted chocolate. Mix gently and then slowly add all the egg whites and mix gently into the chocolate mixture.
- Pre-heat the oven to 350°F or 180°C. Place the mixture into the greased and papered tin and bake for roughly 30-35 minutes. Remove from the oven and cool. Ten minutes later, remove from the cake tin and cool further on a wire rack.
- Place the cake on a glass dish. Whip the cream and spread it over the cake top. Decorate evenly with the grated chocolate.

FRENCH APPLE TART

Preparation Time: 25 mins. • Cooking Time: 25-30 mins. • Serves: 8

250 gms. flour
185 gms. butter
1 tbsp. powdered sugar
1 egg yolk
1 tbsp. iced water

For the Apple Filling:

2 large green apples
150 gms. ground almonds
100 gms. unsalted butter
70 gms. powdered sugar
2 large eggs
1 tbsp. flour
1 tsp. vanilla essence

- Place the flour in a bowl and rub in the butter till the mixture resembles breadcrumbs. Add the sugar and mix well. Beat egg yolk and water and add to the flour. Mix to form a firm dough. Wrap in plastic film and chill in the refrigerator for an hour. Roll out the pastry on a floured board and line a round 23 cm. flan tin.

- To make the filling, cream the butter and sugar and beat in the eggs, flour and the almonds. Add the vanilla and mix well. Peel, halve and core the apples. Slice each half thinly, keeping all the slices touching each other in a group. Pour the almond cream into the pie-case and place each sliced fruit-half carefully in four cardinal directions.

- Place the tart into a pre-heated oven at 400°F or 200°C and bake for 10 minutes. Then reduce the heat to 325°F or 160°C for 25 minutes until the tart is golden brown.

BANANA BREAD

Everyone in the family loves this bread. It's so delicious that it can be eaten plain. Topped with butter it's really woozy. It's very simple to make and the ingredients are to be found in every house. You can make it on the spur of the moment. I have three banana bread recipes but this is my favourite one.

Preparation Time: 10-15 mins. • Cooking Time: 1-1¼ hrs. • Serves: 12

400 gms. skinned ripe bananas
250 gms. self-raising flour
130 gms. butter
130 gms. brown sugar
3 eggs
3 tbsps. honey
2 tsps. orange rind, grated
1 tsp. nutmeg-cardamom powder
a pinch of salt

- Mash the bananas in a glass bowl.
- Place the flour, butter and salt in another bowl and rub together with your fingers till it resembles breadcrumbs.
- Stir in the brown sugar, beaten eggs and honey with the mashed bananas. Also stir in the orange rind and nutmeg-cardamom powder.
- Place the mixture in a rectangular 1 kg. loaf tin and bake in a preheated oven at 180°C. It will take about 1¼ hours. When ready, cool a little, (5 mins.) remove to a wire rack and cool completely.

WALNUT BROWNIES

Preparation Time: 30 mins. • Cooking Time: 25 mins. • Serves: 8-10

180 gms. brown sugar
130 gms. butter
130 gms. small walnut pieces
70 gms. plain chocolate
70 gms. self-raising flour
3 eggs
1 tsp. vanilla essence

- Sieve the flour in a bowl.
- Place the butter and chocolate in a saucepan and melt the chocolate over a gentle heat.
- In a large bowl whisk, the brown sugar and eggs till sugar melts. Add the melted chocolate and vanilla.
- Gradually add the flour and walnuts in small amounts. Mix well and pour into a greased, papered, 8" square or rectangular aluminium tin.
- Pre-heat the oven at 350°F or 180°C. Bake the brownies for about 25 minutes. The brownie should be a little soft in the centre. Place on a wire rack to cool. Cut into even squares and serve.

ALMOND AND BUTTER BISCUITS

These delicious sweet morsels are known as Bienenstich in Europe. I find that they taste better with a teaspoon of vanilla essence and a strong pinch of nutmeg-cardamom powder.

Preparation Time: 45 mins. • Cooking Time: 35-40 mins. • Serves: 8

For the Base You Need:
200 gms. self-raising flour
125 gms. castor sugar
125 gms. unsalted butter
1 egg
zest of 1½ sour limes
1 tsp. vanilla essence
½ tsp. nutmeg-cardamom powder
1 tsp. baking powder

For the Toffee Topping:
250 gms. almonds, boiled, skinned and flaked
100 gms. butter
100 gms. castor sugar
2 tbsps. brown sugar
2 tbsps. milk

- Grease a 9" square cake tin with butter and spread a double layer of greaseproof paper so that the bottom of the biscuits do not burn.
- Beat the butter and sugar for the base till the mixture is light and fluffy. Whisk the egg and add to the mixture. Lightly mix in the flour, vanilla essence, nutmeg-cardamom powder, lemon zest and the baking powder and mix well.
- Spread the mixture onto the greased cake tin. Level the top.
- To make the toffee topping, place the butter in a heavy-based pan. Add the castor sugar and brown sugar and let them melt. Add the milk and as soon as the mixture boils remove the pan from the heat. Add the sliced almonds and mix vigorously so that all the almond flakes are covered with the toffee mixture. Cool.
- Pre-heat the oven for 10 minutes, at 180°C or 350°F. Spoon the cool toffee mixture evenly over the biscuit and bake till golden or done. This should take about 35 minutes.
- With a sharp tipped knife cut the biscuits into pieces while still hot. Allow to cool a little before lifting them out.

STRAWBERRY FRESH PANEER TART

Preparation Time: 15 mins. • Cooking Time: 1 hr. • Serves: 6-8

330 gms. full cream best quality paneer
200 gms. large fresh strawberries
4-5 tbsps. orange juice for the tart case
8-9 tbsps. orange juice for the cream
200 gms. best quality self-raising flour
50 gms. castor sugar for the tarts
200 gms. castor sugar for the cream
110 gms. butter unsalted, for the tart
1 tbsp. butter unsalted for the tart case
3 eggs well beaten for the cream
3 tbsps. apricot jam for glazing

- Mix the self-raising flour, butter, sugar and salt in a bowl with your fingertips till crumbly. Add the orange juice and bind together. Place in foil and chill for 10 minutes.
- Roll the dough out to fit a 10" flan tin. Prick the bottom, place a foil piece over the pie, cover it with cooking beans and bake at 220°C for 10 minutes. Remove the foil and bake for a further 10 minutes at 180°C.
- Make the cheese mix in your mixer. Crumble the paneer and place it in the mixer along with the sugar, eggs and orange juice and beat till smooth and glossy.
- When the tart case is cool, pour in the whipped cheese mixture and bake at 180°C for 20-30 minutes.
- Slice the strawberries and lay them in concentric rings on the baked cheese cream. Brush with hot, strained apricot jam.

A PURE CREAM TART

Preparation Time: 20 mins. • Cooking Time: 1 hr. • Serves: 6-8

Filling:

1 kg. pure cream – preferably from Parsi Dairy
200 gms. castor sugar
5 egg yolks, beaten
1 tsp. vanilla
1 tsp. cardamom-nutmeg powder

Puff Pastry:

220 gms. best quality self-raising flour
60 gms. chilled white vanaspati ghee
60 gms. chilled unsalted butter
one pinch salt
6-7 tbsps. of very cold water

- Place the flour and salt in a bowl. Chop the vanaspati and butter into small squares and crumble into the flour. Add the cold water and knead the dough lightly into a long, broad band. Take the top of the band and fold it halfway up. Do the same with the lower flap so they both meet in the middle and fold the roll into half. Knead twice in the same way so the pastry fluffs out. Chill the dough for 15-20 minutes before rolling out.
- Roll out the pastry and place in the pie case. Prick the bottom with a fork and allow to bake for 15 minutes till light golden brown. Cool.
- Heat the cream and sugar over a very low flame stirring all the time till it comes to a low boil and the cream evaporates, at least for 15-20 minutes. Remove from the stove and add vanilla and the cardamom-nutmeg powder. Cool. Add the 5 egg yolks well whisked.
- Pour into the tart case and bake for a further 14-18 minutes. Keep an eye on the colouring of the tart. It should be golden brown. Trim the tart edges and serve after it settles down, an hour later.

TARTE TATIN

I just love the taste of this delicious sweet. All the goodness lies in cooking the apples in sugar and butter to a dark plum-like colour just short of dark brown. This little tart has a history. It seems there were two sisters who ran a restaurant in Sologne in France. Hurried and tired, one day one of the sisters placed the fruit in the pastry pan without placing the pastry base. So she hurriedly placed the pastry on top of the fruit and baked the pie and then overturned it. To her surprise, the sweet crust with the hot trickle of apple syrup and caramellised apples became an immediate success. It became most popular when introduced at the famous restaurant MAXIMS.

For the tart, you need a thin pastry crust. I took a 10" pastry case or fruit flan made of aluminium.

Preparation Time: 35 mins. • Cooking Time: 1 hr. • Serves: 6-8

For the Pastry:
200 gms. self-raising flour
100 gms. unsalted cold butter
35 gms. castor sugar
1 pinch salt
7 tbsps. cold water
11 apples
200 gms. castor sugar
120 gms. unsalted cold butter

- Place the flour and salt in a bowl. Add the castor sugar. Chop the cold butter into tiny squares and then with the fingertips of both your palms, run the flour through as well as mash the butter, and from a height, try and aerate the flour. When the flour is crumbly, gather it altogether and add the cold water and make it into a ball. Wrap it in foil and chill for 10-15 minutes.

- Peel, core and cut the apples into 4 pieces each. Take the pan in which you are going to bake the tart. Spread it with slices of cold butter. Spread a layer of the sugar on top of the butter and cover the sugar with a layer of hard packed apples. The apples should be placed slice down. The round side should not be underneath or on top. Place over a very low fire and allow to cook till the apples are soft and gooey and the juice of the apples has dried up and only a thick syrup is left.

- Remove the pan from the fire and allow to cool for a few minutes. Then pre-heat the oven to 350°F, apply the pastry cover on top of the cooked apples and tuck in the extra pastry to form a case for the apples. Cook for 30 minutes till golden brown. Remove from the oven and carefully overturn the tart whilst still hot. If you allow it to cool, the apples will stick to the pan.

- Serve warm with tea.

ALMOND BRITTLE

Preparation Time: 10 mins. • Cooking Time: 30 mins. • Serves: 10

2 cups powdered sugar
1 cup golden corn syrup
½ cup water
1 cup very cold water from freezer
1½ cups blanched almonds
2 tbsps. butter
½ tsp. baking soda
½ tsp. salt

- Put the sugar, corn syrup, and half a cup of water in a heavy-bottomed pan and place it over medium heat and boil for 5 minutes. Lower the heat a little and cook without stirring for about 15 minutes. At this point it should reach a soft-crack stage.
- Add butter and salt and keep stirring for 5 minutes. Now you should have reached the hard-crack stage. To verify, drop a little of the syrup into the chilled water from the freezer. When removed from the water, the toffee should snap. Add the almonds remove the pan from the heat, stirring all the while.
- Add the baking soda into the pan, stir and quickly spread over a flat, greased tray in a thin layer. Cool.
- Break candy into the required size of pieces and store in an air-tight jar.

BREAD AND BUTTER PUDDING

Preparation Time: 20 mins. • Cooking Time: 30-40 mins. • Serves 4-6

1 litre milk
1 cup sugar
4 eggs
4 sandwiches made out of bread, butter and jam, each cut into four triangle
50 gms. raisins
½ tsp. vanilla
½ tsp. nutmeg powder

- Heat the milk. Cool. Add the sugar and bring to a boil. Cool.
- Beat the eggs well and add to the cool milk. Add the vanilla and nutmeg powder and mix well.
- Place in a shallow pyrex dish. Add the sandwich pieces gently to the milk mixture. They will float on top.
- Place in an oven at 350°F. After 15-20 minutes the pudding should set. Open the oven door and sprinkle the raisins and allow to cook for a further 15-20 minutes till golden brown.

A SPOTLIGHT ON NOWZER IRANPOUR

My friend Nowzer Iranpour grew up in Nasik and – you are not going to believe this – lived above a Bakery – the Meher Bakery. Every day his young nose was assailed by the wonderful aromas emitting from it. When it became time for him to decide upon a career, after he passed his S.S.C., he told his father, rather tremblingly, that he wanted to become a Baker. His father, who had a transport business of his own, was horrified. He burst out and asked his son "BAWARCHI KAI THAVA MANGECH?" "Why do you want to be a cook?"

The upshot of this argument was that Nowzer went and joined the catering college at Prabhadevi. Thirty years ago there was no hassle regarding admissions and after his course was over, he joined the Taj Mahal Hotel in Mumbai as a Trainee Cook at Rs. 75 per month.

In 1974, he was sent to Goa as Pastry-In-Charge and called back to Mumbai in 1975 and sent to Switzerland where he got his training in the Swissair Flight Kitchen. When he came back to India from Zurich, it was as Pastry Chef in the Taj Flight Kitchen.

In 1981, Nowzer became the Pastry Chef at the Taj Mahal Hotel, Mumbai. In 1983 he was sent to Düsseldorf and Munich to work at the Intercontinental Hotel. The reason was that he should gain new ideas.

In 1984-85, the Taj Mahal Hotel, Mumbai, held a European Pastry Festival at its shop, La Patisserie. It was a thundering success.

With foreign travel so common, the world had become smaller. Our Indians were requesting for different types of pastries which were available in U.K., Europe and America.

In 1990, between 29th January and 4th February, the All India Hotel Federation held a pastry competition at Pragati Maidan in Delhi. All the major hotels in India participated in the event. The chefs came from Jaipur, Bangalore, Calcutta and other major cities. My friend easily carried the day, getting three Gold Medals. One for "Presentation of Plated Desserts", a second one for "Petit Fours" and the third one for "Wedding Cake".

"Baker" and "Bawarchi" are no words to describe the job that Nowzer does. His job requires a great deal of discipline, hard toil and sweat. But it requires more important characteristics. A vivid imagination, and an almost perpetual search in order to present new and fresh items. It required the baker to be an "artist" in the proper sense of the word. He had to create sensational pastry items such as the Sugar Crown he turned out for Sushmita Sen after she was crowned Miss Universe.

Nowzer revels in creating desserts which use a lot of piped cream in various colours and designs. He himself expressed the view that it was difficult to last in this industry if one could not turn out new ideas or creations every few months. One of the nicest desserts at "La Patisserie" is the Prune and Walnut Pie. There

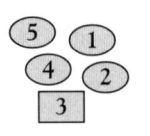

1. Strawberry Paneer Tart (pg. 84)
2. Crême Caramelle (pg. 114)
3. Bread and Butter Pudding (pg. 87)
4. A Pure Cream Tart (pg. 85)
5. Tarte Tatin (pg. 86)

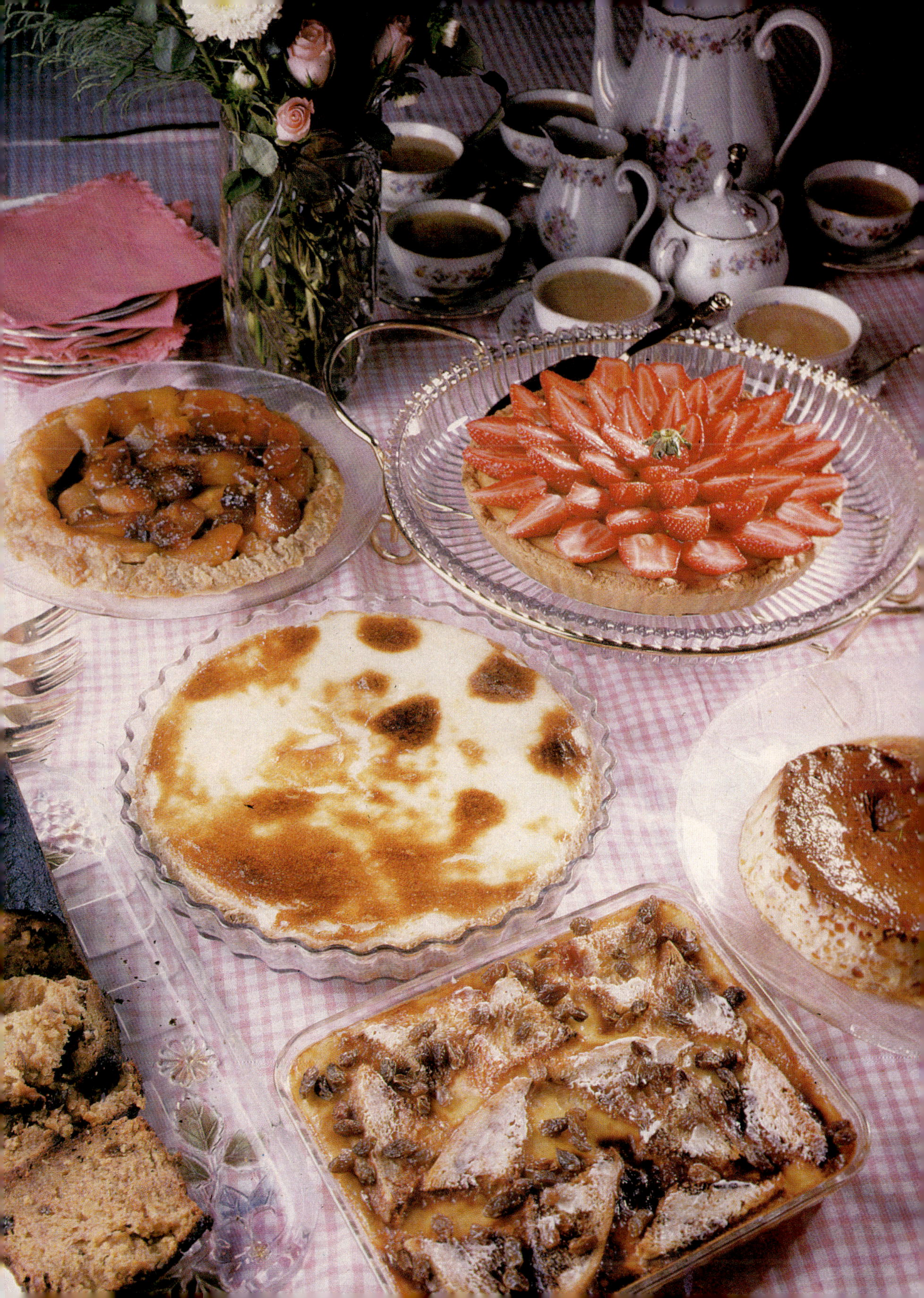

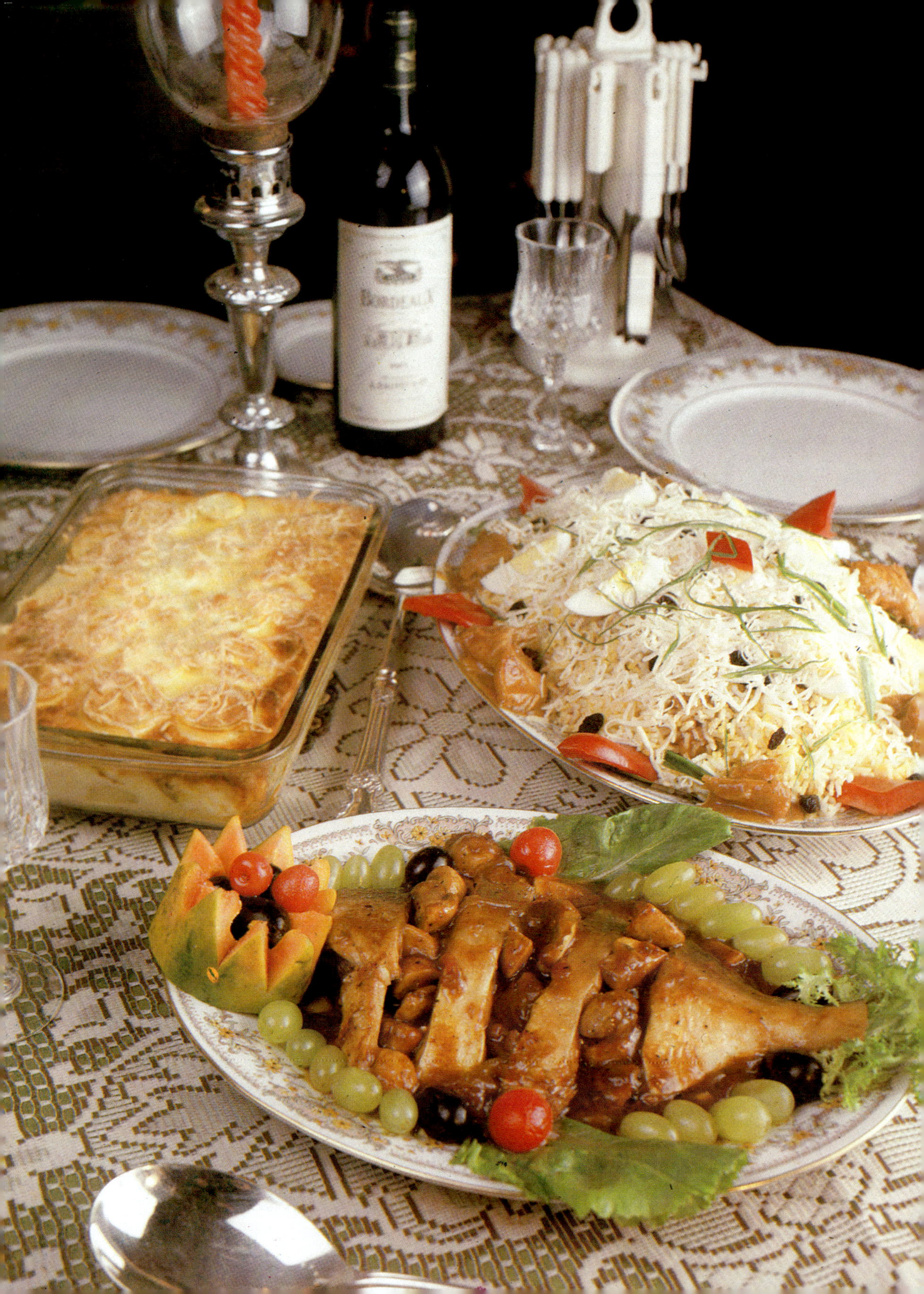
BORDEAUX

are various types of cheesecakes which are in heavy demand, especially the ones containing Passion Fruit and Blueberry. Many items in the kitchen are imported, the most important one being Calibo chocolate from Belgium.

Nowzer has been a loyal employee of the Taj Mahal Hotel for almost 30 years. Today, Nowzer has reached the top of his profession and we can proudly say that he can be counted as one of the world's greatest Pastry Chefs. About his job, he says, "I am happy and satisfied with my job. I have put in hard work to reach my position. There were no Godfathers for me."

We have an untapped treasure in Nowzer Iranpour. I am grateful to him for allowing us to photograph his sweet delights and thus give thousands of us a chance to see his tremendous calibre.

He was married in 1981 to a sweet girl called Villoo Elavia and has a very happy marriage.

Nowzer has very kindly given three of his delicious recipes for the readers of this book who, I am sure, will not only take pleasure in reading them, but I wish they will be sufficiently heroic, and try them out.

. . . .

MIXED FRUIT CHEESECAKE (16 portions)

Preparation Time: 25 mins. • Cooking Time: 45 mins. • Serves: 16

1 cup passion fruit pulp
1 cup mango pulp
20 strawberries
4 limes
100 gms. sugar
25 gms. gelatine
500 gms. mascarpone cheese
400 gms. whipped cream

Sponge Fingers for Lining

6 egg whites
6 egg yolks
180 gms. sugar
180 gms. sieved self-raising flour
1 tsp. vanilla essence

Spanish Rice (pg. 127)
Pomfret slices with buttered Mushrooms
Ramas Fish Baked with sliced Potatoes (pg. 184)

- Cook passion fruit pulp, mango pulp, strawberries, lime and sugar to boiling consistency. (Reduce).
- Add melted mascarpone cheese, and soaked gelatine to the batter. Cool down the batter to setting consistency. Add the whipped cream.
- Prepare the sponge fingers by whisking half the sugar with the egg yolks and half the sugar with the egg whites. Then blend them together in a bowl and add the sieved flour to it as well as the vanilla essence.
- Then take a thick Savoy Nozzle (1 cm.) and pipe the mixture onto a lined, baking sheet into fingers. Dust with sugar and cocoa powder. Bake at 230°C for 10-12 minutes. Remove and cool.
- Pour the mixture into the ramekins lined with sponge fingers. Allow to set in the freezer.
- Next day, just before serving, apply a jelly glaze and garnish with the mixed fruits.

AMARETTO MOUSSE

Cooking Time: 40 mins. • Serves: 12

½ litre milk
5 egg yolks
75 gms. sugar
120 ml. amaretto liqueur
150 gms. almond flakes, roasted
30 gms. gelatine
400 ml. whipped cream

- Boil half of the milk with sugar. Add the remaining milk to the egg yolks. Mix it well and add to the warm milk. Cook it gently until you get a custard coating consistency. Stir in the soaked gelatine and allow to cool.
- When the custard begins to set, stir until smooth. Add the liqueur and the roasted, flaked almonds and gently fold in the whipped cream. Carefully pour it into the necessary moulds.
- Place in the freezer to set. Garnish with cream designs and almond flakes.

MIXED FRUIT CRÊME BRULÉE

Preparation Time: 30 mins. • Cooking Time: 30 mins. • Serves: 16

1 litre cream
8 egg yolks
2 whole eggs
150 gms. sugar
1 tsp. vanilla essence
60 gms. brown sugar
gooseberries, blueberries – cut into half
raspberries, strawberries – sliced

- Place the cream in a large saucepan and add vanilla essence. Bring the cream to a boil. Remove from heat.
- Whisk eggs and egg yolks with sugar until the sugar has completely dissolved.
- Slowly whisk the cream into the egg mixture until well blended. Transfer to a clean vessel and place on a low flame, stirring constantly. Cook the mixture over very low heat until the custard thickens and coats the back of a wooden spoon.
- Divide the mixture into small ramekins. Bake for 30 minutes in a Bain Marie at 150°C. When the brulees are half done, sprinkle mixed berries on top and allow to bake firm. Remove from the oven.
- Sprinkle brown sugar over the cream and place under a hot grill to caramelise. Chill overnight.

SECTION 7

A WHIFF OF FRENCH FOOD

No French meal is complete without the addition of herbs. Just as we Indians cannot complete our meals without the use of ginger, garlic, chillies, coriander and curry leaves, the French feel their meals are incomplete without thyme, sage, rosemary, tarragon, celery, parsley, fennel and lavender. In the South of France there is a region called Provence where herbs grow wild on the hillsides right upto this day. Many herb gardens in Provence are built into the hillsides and are protected by rock walls so that the herbs don't suffer from the mistral winds.

Many herbs were grown in the olden days by monks in their monastery gardens. Beside culinary herbs, medicinal herbs were also grown. In many old gardens where generation after generation of French farmers have inherited their lands from father to son, this practice of having two types of herbs, still survives. A quiet walk in these gardens is a heart-warming experience. Innumerable scents invade the nostrils. A quiet, calm descends on one's body and soul. Many country kitchens have bundles of dried herbs such as Basil (tulsi), bay leaves (tamalpatta), oregano (ajwain), rows of garlic hanging in bunches tied together by their stalks. Bunches of red and white baby onions also hang from raftered ceilings, as they do in Indian country kitchens.

In France, in many farms and private homes, the housewife has only to step into her kitchen garden to procure the herbs she wants, depending on whether she is cooking pork, beef, mutton, poultry or fish.

My deep interest in French cooking led to my growing the herbs. In Lonavala I grow aniseed, parsley, celery, thyme, sage and marjoram in flat, round, shallow baskets filled with red earth and animal manure. You can likewise grow these herbs in pots. Place them in the sunniest place in your garden. When the celery seedlings grow 4 to 6 inches high, transplant them in the earth, 4" apart. They will grow over a foot tall and keep you in green salads and soup dishes for months. In Lonavala, sometimes the monsoon lasts till the tenth of November. After it is over, I plant the herb seeds, which come from France. The plants survive until March-April and then they die. A fresh batch is planted every November. The monsoon rains come down in torrents and only the hardiest plants survive. Chives grow well in India and is used in the cooking of all egg dishes and cream and cheese sauces as well as salads. Coriander and cumin are also used in France and are favourites of Indian housewives from Delhi to Kanyakumari. In India, cumin is grown in Saurashtra and Rajasthan. Dill is a widely used herb in France as well as India where it is known as suva or khatti bhaji. I have not grown fennel so far. This is our badi saunf. In France, fennel bulbs are boiled and eaten as vegetables. Specialised farms in India have taken to growing and selling them and I once cooked them for some French guests. The bulbs are small in size and not plump like the ones in France.

Garlic is used a great deal in France as it is in India. It is grown abundantly in the south of France. When the garlic is harvested, the stalks are cut long and after they are dried the stalks are braided and allowed to be collected in long bunches which are hung from wooden rafters in huge airy barns. The result is that they survive for a couple of years without spoiling.

Mint is lavishly used in France as well as India and none of us Parsees would be caught without having mint beds and lemongrass bushes in our gardens. We need both these herbs plus peppermint leaves to make our tea twice a day. Peppermint however is difficult to obtain in any local market in India. Only specialised shops carry it. The amount grown is small and the demand heavy. My friend Gustad Farhadi got me the plants with roots from his farm in Dahanu. Great care has to be taken to allow them to survive.

The French use a great deal of mushrooms and we get any amount in the city markets in 200 gm. packets. The green and black olives have to be imported into India. French dried herbs are sold all over France in terracotta pots and little cloth bags or see – through plastic bags and most are labelled "Herbes de Provence". This mixture of herbs includes basil, fennel, rosemary, thyme, sage, mint and oregano.

The French use edible flowers and leaves. No cuisine in the world did this until French influence crept to Europe, U.S.A. and Great Britain. Many of these flowers grow in India but we would think twice about eating them in our salads. Some of these flowers are heartsease, pansies – which are found in many gardens and parks in India and the common marigold – galgotas – yellow-golden blossoms from which garlands are made and which decorate every Hindu home, especially during Diwali, Festival of Lights. Indeed tons of flowers must be used each day. Even the leaves of these flowers are eaten in salads. Thyme, nasturtium and lavender flowers, violets are used in salads. In fact, violets, lavender flowers and rose petals are crystallized by covering them lightly with beaten egg-whites and powdered sugar sprinkled over the flowers which are then kept in a cool, dry place. These are used to decorate cakes, pastries, puddings and desserts.

Sometimes these aromatic petals are placed in layers between sugar in jars. The jar is kept in the sun for two weeks and every day it is shaken so that the petals shift and permeate all the sugar with their aroma. Vanilla pods can also be used in the same way to flavour sugar.

Salads are dressed not only with olive oil, but hazelnut and walnut oil which gives its own flavour to the greens and raw vegetables. Sometimes almond oil is also used as is pine kernel oil. The vinegars are flavoured with thyme, tarragon, balsam, raspberry, garlic, coriander seeds, baby onions and sorrel.

FLEMISH STYLE ASPARAGUS

Asparagus lovers in India will be pleased to note that all major city markets in India carry fresh asparagus. They will not have to depend on foreign, expensive canned asparagus. They come well wrapped in packages so that they don't get bruised during transport.

Preparation Time: 10 mins. • Cooking Time: 15-18 mins. • Serves: 6

1 kg. fresh asparagus
200 gms. good pink ham
150 gms. butter
4 boiled eggs
freshly ground black pepper to taste
parsley or celery leaves
2 green cardamoms
salt

- Trim the asparagus. Remove the thick outer skin so that it cooks quickly.
- Boil salted water along with the cardamoms and immerse the asparagus in it till soft and tender. Drain.
- Grate the eggs and melt the butter. Cut the ham into thin strips.
- Before serving, place the warmed asparagus on a flat dish. Sprinkle the ham strips and parsley leaves and place the grated eggs in the centre of the dish. Drizzle the asparagus with the melted butter. Serve immediately after sprinkling freshly ground pepper.

SOLE AU BEURRE DE CITRON VERT – DOVER SOLE
(Pomfrets Stuffed with Lime Butter)

Preparation Time: 12 mins. • Cooking Time: 25-35 mins. • Serves: 6

6 pomfrets whole
250 gms. butter
juice of 2 sour limes and zest of one
1½ tbsps. chives
1½ tbsps. parsley
black pepper freshly ground

- Remove the fins from the pomfrets. Make a cut from the lower side of the mouth and remove the entrails. Wash well inside and outside. Leave the side fins and the tails intact.
- Make 3 cuts on each side of the pomfrets. Lightly salt them.
- Mix the butter, chives, parsley, pepper along with the lime juice and zest. Stuff the butter in the stomach pockets and smear lavishly over the pomfrets.
- Place in a pyrex dish and bake in an oven until golden and tender.

NAVARIN OF LAMB

Preparation Time: 20 mins. • Cooking Time: 1½-2 hrs. • Serves: 6-8

1 kg. large mutton chunks
200 gms. baby onions
200 gms. baby potatoes in their skin
200 gms. baby carrots
150 gms. tender green frenchbeans
350 gms. red tomatoes, skinned
12 garlic cloves
1 tsp. fresh rosemary or ½ tsp. dried
2 cups chicken stock
2 cups red wine
freshly crushed black pepper to taste
butter
salt

- Clean and wash the mutton. Crush the garlic and apply along with salt to the mutton pieces
- Take a heavy based saucepan and add 3 tablespoons of butter to it. When hot, place the mutton pieces in the butter and cook for 10 minutes. Add the crushed black pepper and the stock and 4 cups of water and cook for 1½ to 2 hours till the mutton becomes tender. Indian meat takes a long time to cook so you can use a pressure cooker.
- Boil the onions, potatoes, carrots, frenchbeans stringed and cut into half each separately. Skin the tomatoes and liquidize them. Reserve the pulp.
- When the meat is soft, burn off the liquid and add the tomato pulp, and give a quick boil. Add the boiled vegetables and sprinkle over the rosemary and allow the mutton to simmer for 20 minutes till the meat has absorbed the aroma from the rosemary and vegetables. Pour over the red wine and serve immediately.

POISSON FLAMBÉ SEA BASS
(1 Large Ramas Barbecued)

Preparation Time: 10 mins. • Cooking Time: 25 mins. • Serves 6-8

1 large 2-2½ kgs. ramas
2 large whole garlic cloves, separated
½ cup parsley
2 tbsps. sage
1 tbsp. coarsely crushed coriander seeds
1½ tbsps. coarsely crushed cumin seeds
2 onions finely minced
juice of 3 sour limes
1 tsp. coarsely ground black peppercorns
lettuce leaves or banana leaves
olive oil or sunflower oil

- Start the coals burning in your sigri.
- Wash and scale the fish thoroughly. Keep the head intact. Remove fins and sides and leave the tail. Scrub well and wash the large stomach thoroughly. Salt the fish and keep it in a cool place.
- Crush the skinned garlic cloves and mix them with the minced onions, parsley, sage, lime juice, ground cumin seeds, ground coriander seeds and the peppercorns. Place in a bowl and add 4 tablespoons of olive oil or sunflower oil.
- Make diagonal cuts on both sides of the fish and smear it inside and out with the oil mixture. Allow to marinate for 2 hours.
- Wrap the fish with lettuce leaves or in tender banana leaves with the centre stalk removed. Tie the whole fish like a parcel with string. Pierce it in three places, near the tail, centre and below the head by thin iron rods or seeks.
- Wait till the coals are red and place the fish on top of the coal sigri and keep turning gently so that the fish does not get charred. Baste with oil. The leaves may char, but the fish will get cooked within 15-25 minutes, depending upon its thickness.
- Place the fish in a flat dish, remove the leaves and eat immediately so that you can enjoy the aroma of the leaves and coal have imparted to the fish.
- Serve with a green salad and hot, long French bread.

POULET À LA BOURGUIGNON
(A variation of Boeuf Bourguignon)

Preparation Time: 30-40 mins. Marinated Overnight • Cooking Time: 45-60 mins. • Serves: 8-10

1 kg. boneless breast pieces of chicken
400 gms. boiled mixed, chopped tiny cubed vegetables, such as carrots, onions, celery and spring onions (optional)
500 gms. baby button mushrooms, washed
500 gms. baby onions skinned
300 gms. best quality bacon – cut off the rind
2 cups tomato sauce
1¼ litres strong red wine
50 gms. garlic pulp
50 gms. ginger pulp
2 tbsps. freshly ground pepper
1 litre chicken stock or water
3 tbsps. self-raising flour or cornflour
350 gms. butter
200 ml. brandy

- Wash the chicken pieces and apply the ginger-garlic pulp to it. Add the black pepper and wine and marinate the chicken overnight.
- The next day take a heavy based wide mouthed vessel and put in the butter. Add ¾" pieces of bacon, cutting out the rind. Also add the whole washed mushrooms and the baby onions.
- Light the stove and cook on a medium flame stirring the contents with a wooden spoon till all three items get cooked. Take a slotted spoon and remove the bacon, mushrooms and onions into a tray.
- In the same large vessel put in the marinated chicken pieces and cook in 1 litre of chicken stock. If you do not have it, use water. When the chicken is tender, add tomato sauce and the wine marinade. Cook till the chicken boils.
- Mix the cornflower with ½ cup of the chicken gravy and when smooth, add it to the chicken and stir vigorously till you get a smooth glossy sauce. Add the bacon, mushrooms and onions and simmer for 10 minutes.
- Add the brandy, mix well and serve in a large dish.
- If you like you can serve with the boiled vegetables placed separately in a small dish.

POACHED PROVENCAL CHICKEN

Preparation Time: 25 mins. • Cooking Time: 1½ hrs. • Serves 4-6

1½ kg. fresh chicken
300 gms. mutton mince
200 gms. chicken liver mince
1 tsp. sage
1 tsp. ground black pepper
3 tbsps. best sherry
50 gms. carrots
1 onion studded with cloves
2 tbsps. thyme
2 tbsps. parsley
2 bay leaves
4 spring onions
2 tbsps. extra parsley
1" piece fresh ginger
1 star anise
rock salt

For the Sauce:

3 egg yolks
100 gms. butter
50 gms. flour
100 gms. thick fresh cream
2 tbsps. lime juice
1 tbsp. fresh black pepper powder
stock from the poached chicken

- Lightly cook the minced mutton and minced chicken liver over a low flame. Add the black pepper powder, parsley, sage, thyme and the sherry. Cook over a low flame for 20 minutes. Cool. Pound the fresh ginger and mix half of it into the minced mixture.

- Wash the chicken inside and out and rub in the rock salt. Stuff the chicken with the minced mixture and truss it up. Tie both the legs together and stitch up the flap at the neck.

- Place the chicken in a pot with an airtight lid. Pour in 3 litres of water. Add the sliced spring onions, half the pounded ginger, 2 sliced carrots, 1 onion studded with cloves, the bay leaves, star anise, extra fresh parsley about 2 tablespoons, and a little rock salt. Cover and cook over a very low flame for almost one and a half hours.

- Make the sauce just before sitting down to lunch. Melt the butter in a saucepan and add the flour and cook over a low flame. Remove from the fire and add 3 teacups of the stock in which the chicken has been poached. Add the black pepper powder and whisk well. Place on a low heat and cook, stirring non-stop, till the sauce thickens. Slowly add the cream and stir. Taste for salt.

- Mix the egg yolks and the lime juice and stir well and add to the sauce. Whisk. Lightly heat the sauce.

- Serve the chicken on a flat dish along with boiled frenchbeans. Serve the sauce separately.

RAVIOLI

Preparation Time: 50 mins. • Cooking Time: 45 mins. • Serves: 10

For the Ravioli:

300 gms. flour
5 eggs
3 tbsps. olive oil
salt to taste

For the Filling:

300 gms. mince preferably made out of tender, cooked mutton
200 gms. spinach, cleaned, washed and blanched
2 onions chopped finely
2 tbsps. crushed garlic
3 egg yolks
pepper and salt to taste
1 tbsp. olive oil

- Place the flour on a large tray or table top. Make a well in the centre. Break 5 eggs into it and add 3 tablespoons of olive oil and salt to taste.
- Knead the dough lightly for 5-10 minutes until it is elastic and keep covered for an hour.
- Mince the cooked meat and add the washed, cleaned, finely chopped spinach.
- Fry the onions in olive oil till soft and pink. Add the crushed garlic and cook till soft. Whisk the egg yolks. Add the onions to the meat mixture along with the whisked yolks, salt and pepper powder. Mix well.
- Roll out the dough on a floured surface to form square thin sheets $1/8$" thick.
- Cut each sheet into a 3" square. Divide the squares. On half these squares place 1 tablespoon of the filling at decent intervals. Cover with a plain square of dough. Seal the meat mixtures into little squares with your fingers and cut squares around the filling.
- Place a large pan of salted water to boil. Add a little olive oil. Cook the ravioli in the boiling water. Allow to float to the surface before removing them with a slotted spoon onto a dish. Drizzle lightly with olive oil and serve immediately.
- Sometimes, the ravioli, especially the ones with cheese and herb fillings are deep fried in olive oil after being gently poached, and served as snacks.

SAUSAGES AND SPAGHETTI

Preparation Time: 10 mins. • Cooking Time: 40 mins. • Serves 6-8

6 strips streaky bacon
400 gms. spaghetti
1 kg. tomatoes, skinned
8 garlic sausages
15 large garlic cloves
5 basil leaves, chopped
1 tsp. black pepper powder
1 lump sugar
butter
salt to taste

- In a non-stick pan, fry the garlic cloves and sausages in 2 tablespoons of ghee. When brown, add 6 strips of streaky bacon cut into small pieces. Lower the heat and allow the bacon pieces to cook.
- Cook the spaghetti in a large pan of salted water till tender. Drain.
- Chop the tomatoes. Remove the sausages and bacon onto another large vessel. Place the tomatoes, basil leaves, salt, pepper and sugar and cook over a slow fire for about 20 to 30 minutes.
- When a sauce is formed add the garlic, sausages and bacon pieces and simmer for 10-15 minutes.
- Serve separately or along with the spaghetti.

A DAUBE FROM AVIGNON

This dish was cooked in a traditional big, round pot called a daubiere. It was a glazed earthenware dish with a hole in the lid. A thick ribbon of flour and water was pressed between the lid and pot and the cooking done in a slow oven. We can now do the same by using a good covered pot in an oven or on top of a stove.

Preparation Time: 15 mins. • Cooking Time: 3 hrs. • Serves: 6-8

1 leg of lamb deboned and cut into 1" square pieces. Retain the leg bone.
25" piece of streaky bacon
2 onions chopped
2 carrots sliced
12-15 large unpeeled garlic cloves
2 bay leaves
3 pieces of dried orange peel
1 bottle of white wine
1½ tsps. nutmeg powder
1 tsp. black pepper powder
salt to taste
½ kg. wheat flour

- Place the leg bone and washed pieces of lamb into the daubiere. Cut pieces of bacon and add to the lamb pieces. Add all the other ingredients and allow to marinate for 2 hours.

- Place a ribbon of flour mixed with water on the rim of the pot to keep in all the steam. Allow to simmer in the oven for 3-4 hours.

CREPES AUX FRAISES
(Strawberry Pancakes)

Preparation Time: 7 mins. • Cooking Time: 25 mins. • Serves 5

For the Pancakes:
75 gms. fine white flour or maida
1 cup milk
2 eggs
1 pinch sugar
1 pinch nutmeg powder
1 pinch cardamom powder

For the Strawberry Filling:
500 gms. strawberries
180 gms. powdered sugar
1 tsp. finely chopped mint leaves
200 gms. thick cream or malai
1 tbsp. powdered sugar

- Heat the milk in a saucepan and cool it. Whisk the eggs and add them to the cooled milk. Mix in the flour, sugar, nutmeg and cardamom powders. Allow the batter to rest for an hour.

- Wash the strawberries. Remove the green stalks and thickly slice them. Place them in a frying pan along with the sugar and mint leaves on a medium flame. Stir the fruit and sugar till it becomes a sticky mixture.

- Butter a non-stick frying pan, heat, and pour 3 tablespoons of batter onto its base. Cook the pancake till it is golden brown on both sides. You should get at least 10 pancakes from this quantity of batter.

- Keep the pancakes warm. Just before serving them, place each pancake on a wooden board and cover half of it with the strawberry mixture and top with a tablespoon of cream or malai. Fold and fold again into a roll or keep it half folded in a half-moon shape. Pile the pancakes neatly on a flat dish and sprinkle with the powdered sugar. Serve at once.

OEUFS À LA NEIGE AUX ROSES
(Snow Eggs with Rose Petals)

Cooking Time: 40-45 mins. • Serves: 4-6

1 litre milk
200 gms. rose scented sugar
1½ tsps. rose essence
2-4 tbsps. raspberry or strawberry crush
OR
2-3 drops of red food colouring
crystallised rose petals
3 eggs separated

- Take a large-mouthed, heavy based, flat pan or dekchi. Pour in the milk and place pan on a moderate heat.

- Separate the yolks and whites of the eggs. Beat the whites stiff with a pinch of salt and 25 gms. of the scented sugar. When the milk comes to the boil, add tablespoons of the egg white mixture into the milk. Poach these oval egg-shaped meringues gently by pouring the hot milk lightly over them. This will take 1 to 2 minutes. With a slotted spoon remove each egg gently onto a flat dish. Repeat till all the egg-white mixture has been used up, and made into steamed egg meringues.

- Whisk the egg yolks with 70 grams of the scented sugar. Remove the pan of milk from the fire. Stir in the egg yolk mixture and whisk with a spoon. Replace over a low fire and keep stirring non-stop until the milk is slightly thick. Do not boil the milk.

- Remove the milk from the pan and add the strained raspberry or strawberry crush and the rose essence. Cool.

- Gently pour the custard into the dish containing the egg meringues until they are floating in the custard. Decorate with crystallised pink rose petals.

- To crystallize rose petals, brush both sides with whisked egg white and sprinkle with scented sugar and keep in a warm plate for several hours.

MOUSSE AU CHOCOLAT ET AU MENTHE
(Minted Chocolate Mousse)

Cooking Time: 20 mins. • Serves: 4

150 gms. dark dessert chocolate
5 eggs separated
3 tbsps. black coffee
2 tbsps. castor sugar
1½ tbsps. kirsch liqueur
1 tsp. finely chopped mint
150 gms. cream for decoration
¼ tsp. vanilla essence

- Place bits of chocolate, the black coffee and the kirsch in a double boiler or on a very low flame till the chocolate has melted. Remove immediately from the flame and mix in the chopped mint and sugar.
- Beat the egg yolks one at a time and add to the chocolate mixture.
- Whisk the egg whites with a pinch of salt till stiff and mix it with a metal spoon into the chocolate. Fold the mixture into a souffle dish, cover and chill overnight.
- The next day beat the cream with ¼ teaspoon vanilla essence and 1 teaspoon powdered sugar and decorate the mousse with cream rosettes.

FIG JAM PROVENÇAL STYLE

2 kgs. firm sweet figs
1½ kgs. brown sugar
1 glass rum

- Wash and prick each fig several times with a needle.
- Boil a huge vessel of water. Drop the figs into the boiling water for 1 or 2 minutes and drain.
- Place the blanched figs in a large pan or dekchi. Sprinkle the sugar onto the figs and cover the vessel and keep it like that overnight.
- Next day cook the figs and sugar water until the syrup thickens. Add the rum, cook for 5 more minutes and fill into sterilised glass bottles.

CARAMELISED APPLE CAKE

Preparation Time: 10 mins. • Cooking Time: 35-40 mins. • Serves 8

200 gms. flour
200 gms. caster sugar
4 tbsps. extra sugar
150 gms. melted butter
2 eggs
5 large apples
2 tsps. baking powder
2 tsps. vanilla essence

- Crack the eggs into a large bowl. Add the sugar and vanilla and mix well. Gradually add the melted butter and then the flour and baking powder.
- Take a large deep cake tin. Add 4 tablespoons sugar and place on a low heat till it caramelises. Turn the tin with both hands, wearing oven gloves, so that the liquid touches the sides also.
- Peel, quarter and core the apples and arrange in a circle at the bottom of the tin with the cut sides facing upwards.
- Pour the well whisked batter over the apples and bake in a pre-heated oven at 350°F for 35 minutes.
- Pierce a thin metal skewer into the cake to see if it's ready and quickly overturn onto a wire rack. If you allow the cake to cool, the caramel will become cool and the cake will not come loose off the tin.

CHOCOLATE CAKE

Preparation Time: Nil • Cooking Time: 1 hr. • Serves: 6-8

300 gms. dark chocolate
250 gms. butter
150 gms. sugar
80 gms. self-raising flour
1 egg – whisked

- Place the sugar in a saucepan along with 2 tablespoons of water. Lower the heat as soon as the sugar melts and add pieces of the chocolate and allow to melt.
- Remove from the heat, add the butter and whisked egg and mix in the flour.
- Turn the batter into a deep cake tin and place in a tray of water. Bake in the oven for one hour.
- Remove from the oven and allow to stand for 5 minutes. Invert directly onto the serving dish. The cake may split whilst being transferred to the dish. If this happens, smoothen the top with a flat knife and sprinkle with powdered sugar.

ALMOND BISCUITS

Preparation Time: 5 mins. • Cooking Time: 20 mins. • Serves: 9-12

325 gms. sugar
325 gms. blanched almonds
500 gms. wheat flour
4 eggs, whipped
a pinch of salt
100 ml. water

- Place a pan on the fire with water and sugar and allow to cook till the sugar has melted.
- Pour the syrup into a large bowl and add the blanched almonds. Keep in the syrup for 4 hours.
- At the end of 4 hours, place the flour onto a marble or wooden work surface. Make a well in the centre and pour the almond syrup. Add eggs, salt and mix well with fingertips. Knead till smooth.
- Roll it out into a rope, ½" thick and cut the dough into long strips.
- The cut strips should be 8" long (20 cms.) by 1¼" wide. Place them on buttered sheets of baking paper and bake for 20 minutes at 350°F.

FRUIT CAKE

Preparation and Soaking Period: 24 hrs. • Cooking Time: 45-50 mins. • Serves: 8

250 gms. self-raising flour
125 gms. butter
150 gms. caster sugar
125 gms. mixed glacé peel, peach and apricot ⎫
125 gms. whole red glacé cherries ⎬ *soaked in rum for 24 hours beforehand*
125 gms. golden sultanas ⎭
3 eggs
zest of half an orange
1 tbsp. rum in which the fruit was soaked
1 tsp. baking powder
a pinch of salt

- Lavishly butter a 9" cake tin and cover the bottom and sides with greaseproof paper.
- Mix the butter and caster sugar in a large bowl along with a pinch of salt. Mix till you get a smooth finish and add the eggs one at a time. Add the orange zest, flour and baking powder and stir well.

  No essence or spice powder is added but I suggest 1 teaspoon of nutmeg powder.
- Add the drained, soaked fruit to the flour mixture. Retain the rum liquid for another use, after adding 1 tablespoon of it to the cake mixture.
- Heat the oven at 350°F for 15 minutes before the cake is put in the oven.
- Gently place the batter in the greased and paper covered cake tin and bake for 45 to 50 minutes. Insert a skewer to test if cake is cooked. Remove from the oven if skewer comes out clean and remove from the tin. Cool and wrap in foil.

ORANGE CAKE

Preparation Time: 5 mins. • Cooking Time: 1 hr. • Serves 6-8

200 gms. self-raising flour
125 gms. caster sugar
125 gms. butter
juice of one orange
50 gms. candied orange peel
3 egg yolks
zest of one orange and one lime
2 tsps. baking powder

- Take a large bowl and mix in the butter, sugar, juice of orange, peel, flour, baking powder, egg yolks, zest, and if necessary, some milk. Make a soft dough and place it in a shallow buttered flan case. The layer should not be thick.
- Preheat the oven to 325°F and bake the cake for one hour.

APPLE TART

Preparation Time: 15 mins. • Cooking Time: 1 hr. • Serves: 6-8

250 gms. self-raising flour
150 gms. butter
125 gms. caster sugar
2 tsps. vanilla essence
a pinch of salt
1 egg
150 gms. butter
125 gms. caster sugar
1 egg
100 gms. flour
250 ml. cream
5 large apples, peeled, cored and sliced

- Place the flour, butter, sugar, vanilla and salt in a bowl and mix well till it looks like bread crumbs. Beat the egg and add to the mixture. Knead and place in a plastic bag in the refrigerator for half an hour.
- In a clean, large bowl mix butter, caster sugar and egg till smooth. Slowly add the flour and mix, add 250 ml. cream, well beaten, into the mixture.
- Grease and flour a tart case. Roll the pastry kept in the refrigerator. Peel, core, quarter and slice the apples and arrange them in a circular pattern at the bottom of the tart case.
- Pour the cream batter over the tart pastry and bake in a pre-heated oven at 350°F for almost an hour.

SECTION 8

A MEAL WITHOUT CHILLIES FOR EDMEE GUYON AND RONALD MACDOUGALL

My daughter Freny is a government registered Tourist Guide in Mumbai and she meets some wonderful people from all over the world. One day whilst she was at SANGAM near Pune at a GIRL GUIDES meeting, we received a phone call from Ronald saying that he and Edmee would be arriving in Mumbai from an anthropological trip in Gujarat and catching their plane home the same evening. Feroze my husband immediately invited them to our house for lunch upon their arrival and requested them to stay over till it was time to catch their aeroplane.

Ronald MacDougall was a young Scotsman living in Paris, a lawyer by profession and an artist and scholar of antiquities by inclination. Edmee was a sculptress and a student of ancient art. She was a grandmother but one couldn't believe it – she was so full of life and her face was like a book telling one of the pain and pleasure she had been through.

I flew into a panic as to what to cook for their lunch as Ronald had told Feroze he had been ill in Gujarat because it was very difficult for them to get really well boiled water to drink in the interiors. I believed them because to most Indians boiling drinking water was a waste of time. In the vast stretches of desert and semi-arid regions when I was on our archaeological digs, we used to add tablets to our drinking water.

I decided to cook food which would not upset their palates – tasty and yet without a single chilli or peppercorn. I decided that half the meal would be European and half of it Indian – Fish Cakes with Mushroom Sauce, Asparagus with Hollandaise Sauce, Boiled Mange Tout and Boiled Fennel Bulbs. This was to be followed by a Vegetable Au Gratin, and then a gravy chicken Parsi style with thick potato chips and an Indian pulao with saffron and boiled eggs. All this was to be topped up by a Crême Caramelle. I was against serving a heavy sweet which had a cream or mava in it.

Well, they came and enjoyed themselves and Ronald, who had been ill, was happy to see that there were no chillies and mustard seeds floating in any of the food. They enjoyed the meal and we had a wonderful afternoon with them. As if it was telepathy, Freny phoned up after the meal and our guests were delighted to speak to her. They were so loving and spontaneous in their invitation to her to visit them in Paris whilst she was in Europe.

FISH CAKES WITH MUSHROOM SAUCE

Preparation Time: 35 mins. • Cooking Time: 25 mins. • Serves: 8

500 gms. boiled white fish
350 gms. mashed potatoes
1 tbsp. fresh parsley, finely chopped
1 tsp. cumin seeds, coarsely ground
1 tbsp. minced fresh garlic
1 tbsp. minced fresh ginger
1 small onion, finely minced
½ tsp. pepper powder
1 tbsp. butter
6 eggs
juice of 2 sour limes
breadcrumbs
salt
oil for frying

Mushroom Sauce

200 gms. mushrooms
200 gms. fresh cream
4 tomatoes, skinned and deseeded
2 tbsps. tomato ketchup
2 small onions, minced
2 tbsps. parsley
butter

- Mix the potatoes, fish, parsley, pepper, salt and lime juice in a bowl. Cover and keep aside.
- Place the butter in a small frying pan. Add the cumin seeds, ginger, garlic and onion and cook till soft. Add this to the potato-fish mixture. Beat one egg well and add it to this too. Mix well and make 15-20 balls. Pat each ball into a flat round with the help of a knife and then coat with breadcrumbs.
- Fifteen minutes before serving the meal, place a frying pan half-filled with oil on a high flame. Beat 2 eggs at a time in a separate bowl, dip each fish-cake into the beaten eggs and coat once more with bread crumbs. When the oil smokes, fry about 4 cakes at a time till golden brown.
- Cook the onion in 3 tablespoons of butter, till soft. Wash and slice the mushrooms and add to the cooking onions.
- When the onion is soft (do not allow it to brown), pulp the tomatoes and add them to the onions along with the finely chopped parsley. When the mixture has softened, add salt to taste and the ketchup. Lower the flame and fold in the cream and mix gently. Pour the sauce into a gravy boat and serve with the hot fish-cakes.

BOILED ASPARAGUS WITH HOLLANDAISE SAUCE

Preparation Time: 10 mins. • Cooking Time: 30 mins. • Serves: 6-8

2 packets fresh asparagus
200 gms. butter
3 egg yolks
¼ cup water
juice of 1 sour lime
10 black peppercorns
1 tbsp. parsley or chives or sage finely chopped

- Trim the asparagus so that they are all of the same size. The lower ends are often thick and wooden, so cut them off and use a scraper to remove the skin which covers the asparagus.
- I do not steam my asparagus. Take a flat tray or a large frying pan and cover it half-way with water. Add salt. When the water boils add the peppercorns and the lime juice and place the asparagus in a line in the water. Indian asparagus is tough, so wait for 7-10 minutes before turning, and cook till soft and tender. Do not discard the water. Let the asparagus be wet and warm.
- Take a heavy-bottomed saucepan or a double boiler. Place the egg yolks in the pan and whisk them until you feel that the mixture is thickening. Cut the butter in squares and add a few at a time to the yolk sauce, whisking all the time. Let the butter melt before adding more and continue until all the butter is used up.
- Arrange the prepared asparagus on a plate and pour the Hollandaise sauce, sprinkling finely chopped parsley, sage or chives over the sauce.

VEGETABLES AU GRATIN

Preparation Time: 30 mins. • Cooking Time: 40-45 mins. • Serves: 6-8

100 gms. broccoli florets
250 gms. cauliflower florets
200 gms. carrots, finely cubed
200 gms. french beans, finely cubed
100 gms. potatoes, finely cubed
100 gms. baby onions
2 stalks celery
3 tbsps. parsley, finely chopped
150 gms. butter
300 gms. cheese, grated
4 tbsps. self-raising flour
1½ litres milk
salt

1. Boil all the vegetables separately in salted water till tender. Drain.
2. Place the butter in a heavy-bottomed sauce pan. Add the flour and cook over a low flame. When the flour becomes ivory coloured pour in the milk and whisk vigorously till no lumps remain. Cook till the white-sauce thickens. Taste for salt and remove from heat.
3. Add the vegetables and half the cheese to the sauce and pour this mixture into a greased baking dish. Sprinkle the remaining cheese on the top and bake in a pre-heated oven at 180°C or 350°F, for 35-40 minutes till the top is golden brown.

SAVOURY CHICKEN WITH CHIPS

Preparation Time: 20 mins. • Cooking Time: 40 mins. • Serves: 4-6

1 large chicken, 1200 gms., cut into 12 pieces
3 large onions
450 gms. tomatoes
500 gms. large potatoes, cut into chips
1 tbsp. ginger-garlic paste
3 bay leaves
3 star anise
3 large black cardamoms
2 large pieces cinnamon
½ cup coriander, freshly chopped
1 tbsp. mint, finely chopped
1 large capsicum, sliced
pure ghee, oil
salt

- Wash the chicken pieces well. Discard the neck and wing pieces and use for soup or stock. Marinate the chicken in ginger-garlic paste and salt.
- Chop the onions finely and cook in 3 tablespoons of ghee till pink and soft. Add the bay leaves, star anise, cardamoms and cinnamon and fry for 5 minutes before adding the chicken. Stir the chicken in the onion mixture and cover and cook in its own juices over a low flame for 10 minutes.
- Wash and pulp the tomatoes and add them to the chicken along with sliced capsicum and 2 cups of water. Allow to cook till the chicken is soft and tender. Taste for salt.
- Soak the potato chips in salt water and then fry in hot oil till golden brown.
- Serve the chicken on a flat dish and cover with the chips. Sprinkle chopped coriander and mint and serve with rotlis or parathas.

SAFFRON AND EGG PULAO

Preparation Time: 12 mins. • Cooking Time: 40 mins. • Serves: 6

250 gms. basmati rice
8 eggs, boiled and halved
2 large onions
4 large tomatoes
3 tbsps. coriander, chopped fine
1 tsp. cumin seeds, broiled and powdered
1 tsp. coriander seeds, broiled and powdered
1 tsp. mace, powdered
1 pinch turmeric powder
2 tbsps. fried raisins
2 tbsps. fried cashew nuts
1 sliced & deep fried onion
1 gm. saffron
2 cups fresh coconut milk
3 bay leaves
2 small pieces cinnamon
3 cloves
2 cardamoms, crushed
pure ghee
salt

- Cook the rice along with a pinch of turmeric powder, the saffron, salt, the whole dried spices, coconut milk and 2 tablespoons pure ghee. Make up the necessary liquid with water.

- Cut the onions fine and cook until pink in 2 tablespoons ghee. When soft, add the finely chopped tomatoes along with the powdered cumin, coriander and mace. Add 1 cup water and salt to taste. Cook till soft. Remove from flame, add the fresh coriander, stir and keep warm.

- When ready to serve, lay out half the rice in a warmed dish. Spread the tomato gravy on top of it. Cover with the halved eggs and the remaining rice. Top with crisp-fried onions, raisins and cashew nuts.

CRÊME CARAMELLE

Preparation Time: 30 mins. • Cooking Time: 35-40 mins. • Serves: 8-10

2 litres rich, creamy milk
2 cups sugar
½ cup condensed milk
3 tbsps. extra sugar
7 eggs
1 tbsp. vanilla essence
1 tsp. nutmeg-cardamom powder

- Boil the milk and sugar in a heavy-bottomed pan for about 15 minutes, till the milk thickens. Add the condensed milk and whisk well for a further 10 minutes. Remove from the fire. Add the vanilla and the nutmeg-cardamom powder and whisk again. Allow the milk to cool.
- Take a shallow vessel with a tight fitting lid. A stainless steel round dabba (vessel), 3"-4" in height and 7" in diameter would be ideal.
- Place the dabba on a low flame and melt the extra sugar till it turns golden. Take a tea-towel in each hand and tilt the vessel to coat the bottom and sides with the liquid caramel. Cool.
- Whisk the eggs well till they are frothy and add them to the cold sweetened milk. Mix well. Pour the milk into the caramel-coated dabba. Close it tightly and place it in a large pan of water. Place this over a medium flame. Cover the pan and cook for 35-45 minutes. If necessary, top up the water in the pan. Remove from the fire and cool. Chill overnight in the refrigerator.
- To serve, open the dabba and pass a snub-nosed knife around the edge of the custard and then invert the custard gently onto a plate. Do this very carefully ensuring that the custard does not break.
- Serve with fresh raspberries or strawberries or with sweetened whipped cream.

A SPRING BREAKFAST IN LONAVALA

From January to March we bring the tables and chairs out into the garden to catch the mild sunshine in the mornings. The leaves and the grass still have dew on them and a soothing perfume pervades the air. The children all help to set up the table. Since they are usually down in Lonavala only for a couple of days I try to cook something different everyday. The normal items like various types of jams, marmalades, bread, butter, cheeses and ham or sausages are there, but I try to cook one major item to make the breakfast memorable.

So we sit among the colourful flowers and aromatic plants and chat our precious time away, together. Each one is totally relaxed and reminiscences float around. This is how it came about that when we were all sitting relaxed after a wonderful breakfast, Daraius, who was lounging on the swing on the verandah said, quite out of the blue, "Mother, couldn't you write some totally new and original recipes in your book? I know that you are avoiding common items like samosas and batata wadas." It is difficult to say that one's recipe is original because in this big wide world, who knows what has been written and by whom. Yet I have to tell you that I have never heard of several recipes which were included in my book, JAMVA CHALOJI, for instance, Prawns in cream, Prawn and Banana Skin gravy, or Fried Masala Lobsters.

"Mother, have you ever thought of creating a recipe which could be used at breakfast, lunch and dinner? It has to be versatile and of universal appeal, and simple at the same time. The ingredients should be easily available and affordable too." "You are asking too much of me" I said with a laugh. "Let me think for a while. I cannot promise you an original creation but I can promise you a brand new combination of ideas which would meet your requirements." Thus was born the recipe – A Magical Mouthful.

It consists of soft, delicious crepes made of cream, milk and saffron, stuffed lavishly with minced chicken cooked in a tomato gravy with the tiniest of baby onions, and spiced with thyme, basil and a splash of sweet, red wine. The crepes were to be covered by a cheese sauce containing finely chopped chives, parsley and minced buttered mushrooms. This was topped with lightly fried eggs sprinkled with finely chopped coriander and powdered black pepper.

For vegetarians, the crepes were stuffed with a wine and tomato filling and covered with a spinach sauce with cream, sugar and sour lime sauce topped with slices of fried paneer.

FRESH BOMBAY DUCKS FRIED

Preparation Time: 20 mins. • Cooking Time: 25 mins. • Serves: 4-6

36 fresh Bombay ducks
500 gms. gram flour (besan)
2 tbsps. chilli powder
1½ tbsps. turmeric powder
4-6 sour limes
36 long green chillies
salt
oil

- Clean and wash the Bombay ducks thrice. Apply salt on them. Marinate with 3 teaspoons turmeric powder and 4 to 6 teaspoons chilli powder. The masala should be added according to the taste and colour you require when serving the Bombay ducks. Set aside.
- Fifteen minutes before you sit down to eat, heat two non-stick frying pans half filled with oil. Stuff each Bombay duck with 1 whole green chilli.
- Spread the gram dhal flour on a sheet of old newspaper and roll the Bombay ducks in it. When the oil starts smoking, lower the flame a little bit and holding the ducks by the tail, immerse them in the hot oil. Turn over when one side is cooked and golden brown. Serve at once with slices of sour lime.

A MAGICAL MOUTHFUL

Preparation Time: 40-50 mins. • Cooking Time: 1 hr. • Serves 4-6

For the Pancakes
½ litre milk
½ gm. saffron
200 gms. cream
7 eggs
275 gms. self raising flour or maida
4 tbsps. oil
100 gms. melted butter
butter
salt to taste

For the Chicken Mince:
800 gms. fresh chicken mince
1 tbsp. ginger-garlic paste
1 tsp. paprika
½ tsp. freshly ground black pepper
2 chopped basil
2 tbsps. chopped fresh thyme
If using dried herbs, use half the quantity
200 gms. baby onions
1 cup strong red wine
2 cups pure tomato juice
1 cup chopped onions
butter
salt

For the Sauce:
1¼ litres milk
400 gms. sharp grated cheese
250 gms. washed and minced fresh mushrooms
3 tbsps. cornflour
2 heaped tbsps. butter
salt to taste

For the Topping:
1 egg per person
fresh coriander
black peppercorn powder

- Whisk the eggs, melted butter, oil and salt to taste. Add the flour gradually along with small quantities of cream.
- Warm the milk. Heat the saffron on a griddle and mash into the warm milk. Add the egg mixture. Then whisk well and set aside for 1-2 hours.
- Butter the non-stick frying pan and pour a small ladleful of batter at a time on its hot surface. Turn the pan to spread the liquid evenly.
- Turn the crepe once and remove onto a sheet of butter paper.
- Place 3 tablespoons of butter into a heavy based frying pan. Gently heat and add the baby onions. Cook over a low heat and when soft, lift out the baby onions and set aside.
- Place 1 more tablespoon of butter in the frying pan and cook the chopped onions until soft and pink. Add the ginger-garlic paste, the paprika, black pepper, basil and thyme. Add the mince and allow to cook in its own juice, on a low speed, for 10 minutes. Add the tomato juice and salt to taste and cook till the mince is tender. When the mince is soft and dry, add the wine and cook till the gravy has almost dried out. Add the cooked baby onions.
- Place 2 heaped tablespoons butter and 3 tablespoons of cornflour in a saucepan. Cook for 3 minutes. Add the mushrooms, the milk and cook stirring all the time till you get a thick smooth sauce. Add the grated cheese. Stir. Taste for salt.
- Before serving, warm the mince and spread it in the centre of each pancake, roll it lightly and place on a flat dish. When all of the pancakes have been stuffed, warm the cheese sauce and pour it over them.

For the Vegetarian Filling:

300 gms. coarsely chopped tomatoes
200 gms. potatoes, finely chopped
200 gms. finely chopped onions
1 tsp. paprika
1 tbsp. minced fresh garlic
1 tbsp. celery
½ cup sharp red wine
butter
salt

For the Vegetable Sauce:

2 bunches spinach (palak bhaji) washed and finely chopped
200 gms. fresh cream
½ tsp. nutmeg powder
2 tbsps. cornflour mixed in ½ a cup milk
2 tbsps. lime juice
2 tbsps. sugar
butter
salt
topping of slices of lightly fried golden paneer

- Fry one egg per person and top the crepes with the egg, sprinkle fresh coriander and black peppercorn powder over.

FOR THE VEGETARIAN "MAGICAL MOUTHFUL"

- Place 3 tablespoons of butter in a non-stick frying pan. Add washed, finely chopped potatoes and onions, cover and cook over low heat till soft. Add the tomatoes, paprika, garlic, celery and salt to taste. Cook till soft. Add the wine and allow the mixture to dry. Fill the pancakes with this mixture.
- Heat the butter in a saucepan and add the spinach and cook for 5 minutes over low heat. Add the nutmeg. Remove from the fire.
- Place half a cup of milk and 2 tablespoons of cornflour in a small saucepan. Whisk well. Mix and add to the spinach. Cook till you get a smooth sauce.
- Mix the lime juice and sugar and add to the spinach sauce. Pour over the vegetarian pancakes.
- Fry flat thin pieces of paneer. Spread over the sauce before serving the crepes.

SAUTÉED PRAWNS

Preparation Time: 30 mins. • Cooking Time: 15 mins. • Serves 4-6

300 gms. large prawns deveined and washed
100 gms. finely chopped onions
200 gms. tomato pulp
2 green chillies deseeded and finely chopped
2 tbsps. freshly chopped coriander
½ tsp. mustard seeds
½ tsp. sugar
butter
salt

- Wash the prawns well and salt them. Place a saucepan with 2 tablespoons of butter on a medium flame. Add the chopped onions and cook till soft. Add the mustard seeds, allow to cook for 2 minutes – covered. Add the prawns, the tomato pulp, chillies and fresh coriander and cover and cook over a very low flame for 10 minutes.
- Serve with parathas.

MAMMA'S BANANA FRITTERS

Preparation Time: 10 mins. • Cooking Time: 20 mins. • Serves: 6

4 ripe mashed bananas
3 eggs
150 gms. maida
30 gms. yoghurt
150 gms. sugar
2 tsps. vanilla essence
1 tsp. caraway seeds
1 tsp. baking powder
1 tsp. cardamom and nutmeg powder
oil or ghee for frying

- Mix the sugar and eggs in a bowl till frothy and pale. Add the yoghurt, whip, then gradually add the maida, mashed bananas, caraway seeds, vanilla, baking powder and cardamom and nutmeg powder. Mix well. If the mixture is very tight, add 2 to 4 tablespoons milk. Mix well and allow to rest for 1 to 2 hours.

- When ready to eat, heat half a small kadhai of ghee and drop in teaspoonfuls of the mixture. It will swell in the hot oil. Allow to turn golden brown. Remove from the hot ghee when well-fried and serve warm with tea.

KANDA-PAPETA-PER-EDA

(Eggs on savoury potatoes and onions)

Preparation Time: 14 mins. • Cooking Time: 25 mins. • Serves: 4-6

8 eggs
400 gms. finely chopped potatoes
300 gms. finely chopped onions
½ bunch fresh coriander chopped finely
5 green chilles deseeded and chopped finely
½ tsp. black pepper powder
¼ tsp. cumin powder
ghee
salt to taste

- Finely skin the potatoes, chop into very tiny squares and soak in salted water. Finely chop the onions, coriander and chillies.

- Place 2 full tablespoons of ghee in a non-stick fry pan. Add onions. Drain the potatoes and add them to the pan. Add salt and stir cook covered for 15-20 minutes. Cook till soft and tender in their own steam. Add the chillies, coriander, black pepper powder and the cumin powder. Stir and remove from the fire. Taste for salt.

- If you are eating immediately, then do not remove the pan from the fire but make 8 depressions in the onion potato mixture. Crack one egg into each depression and cover and cook over a very slow flame. Serve immediately with hot toast or rotli.

SECTION 9

AL FRESCO LUNCHES

The weather being wonderfully cool and crisp from January to February, we take advantage of it by having lunch in the garden in Lonavala. Freny normally has five to seven friends over for the weekend and I have many friends coming over from Mumbai to stay in their bungalows. I love having people over when the flowers are blooming and so it's a pleasure to sit outdoors and eat a leisurely meal with people I like and respect. I love to have my friend Roda Dastur and her niece Jini Daruwalla for lunch. They exude such warmth and affection and when they leave, it's after giving me their blessings. For them, I always serve a bland lunch. Otherwise I cook the food according to the likes and dislikes of those I am entertaining. I remember once serving Roda, Jini and their guests chicken breasts stuffed with chopped ham, cheese and green peppers which they greatly enjoyed. Its nice to know these things so you can repeat the items since they were so heartily appreciated.

The curried lunch is normally prepared for the children's young friends who enjoy hot food.

OLD FRIENDS' REUNION

RIPE MANGO SALAD

Preparation Time: 15 mins. • Arranging Time: 20 mins. • Serves: 6-8

6 ripe mangoes, peeled and sliced
2 iceberg lettuces – washed
3 sliced gherkins
8 slices canned pineapples – halved
4 sliced tomatoes
2 sliced boiled beetroots
4 sliced capsicums
2 avocados thinly sliced
2 cups mayonnaise
2 tbsps. tabasco sauce
1 tbsp. roasted sesame seeds
black pepper powder
salt

- Arrange the mango slices and vegetable slices on a platter. Sprinkle salt and pepper and refrigerate. Just before serving sprinkle the roasted sesame seeds.
- Mix the mayonnaise and tabasco sauce. Chill in a fancy bowl and serve along with the salad.
- If you like, use ripe papaya and apple slices also.

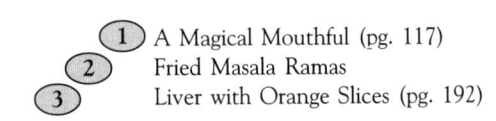

1. A Magical Mouthful (pg. 117)
2. Fried Masala Ramas
3. Liver with Orange Slices (pg. 192)

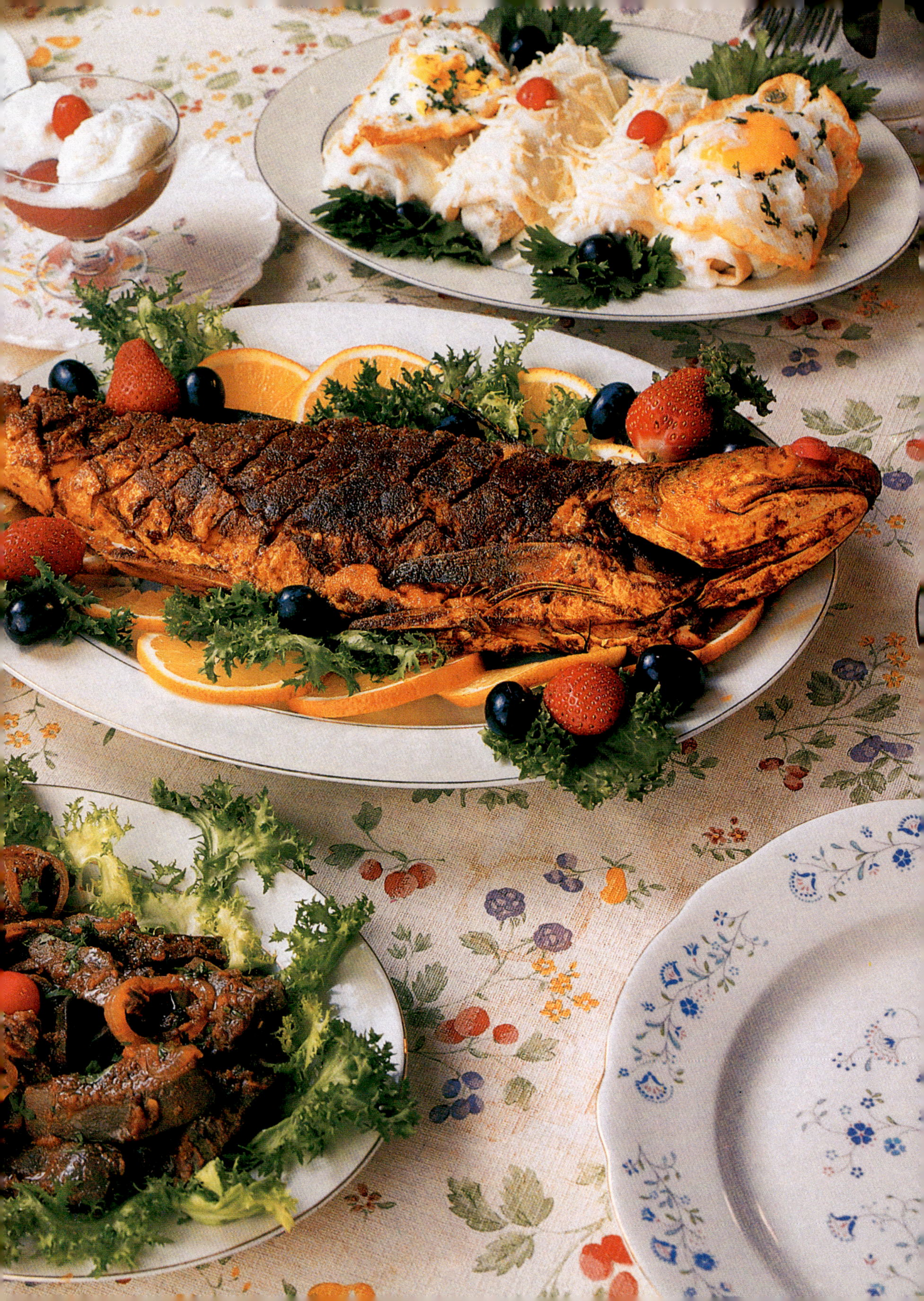

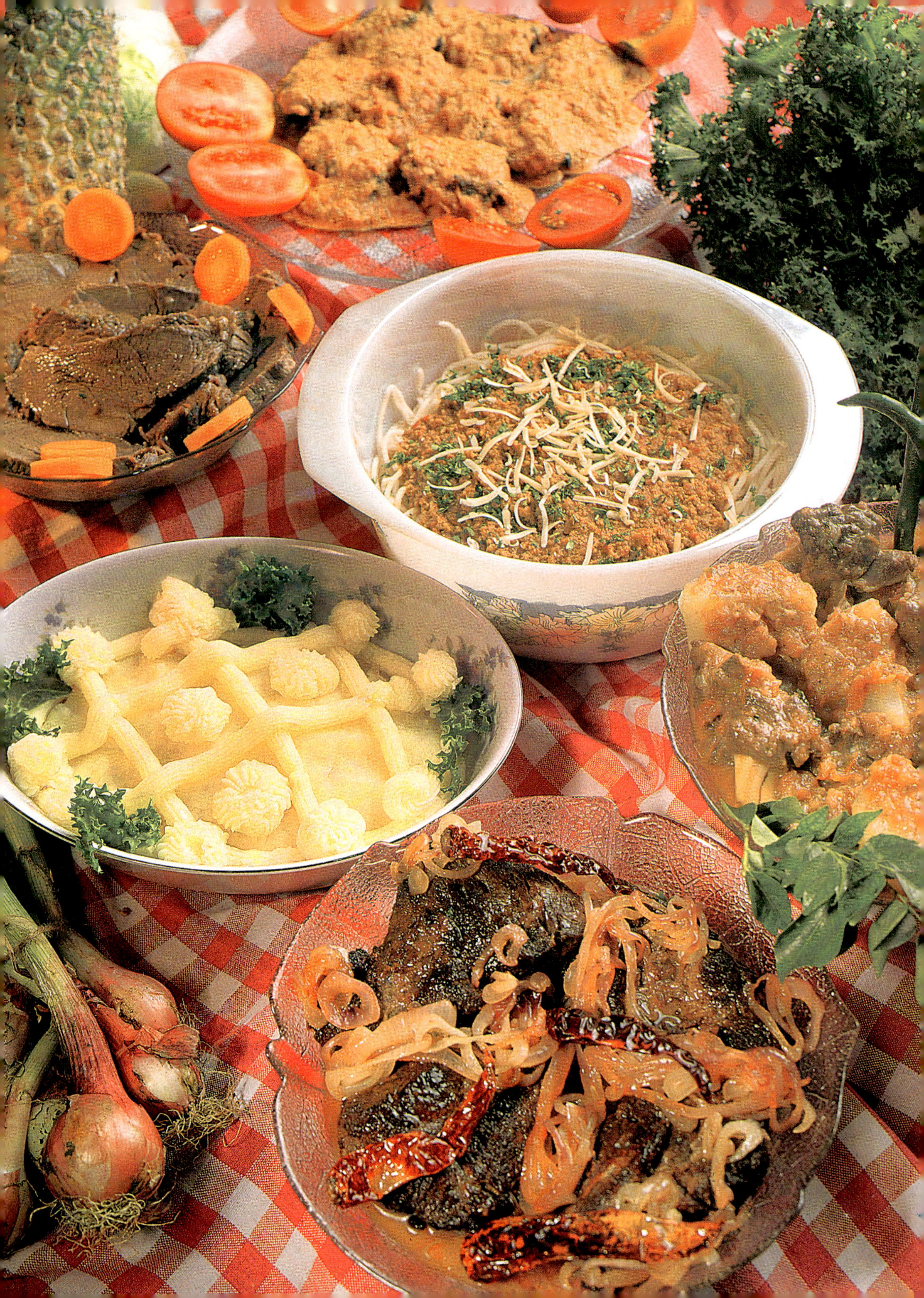

POMFRETS STUFFED WITH CHEESE AND PRAWNS

Preparation Time: 30 mins. • Cooking Time: 45 mins. • Serves: 6

6 medium sized pomfrets, filleted from head to tail – but intact on one side
1 cup shelled deveined prawns
½ cup grated cheese
tooth picks
1 cup chopped tomatoes
4 eggs
1 cup bread crumbs
1 tsp. fennel powder
2 tbsps. chilli powder
1 tbsp. turmeric (haldi) powder
1 tsp. black pepper powder
juice of two sour limes
salt
oil

P.S. : Use one whole pomfret per person and a few extras. My recipe is for six stuffed pomfrets.

- Wash the fish well and salt it inside out. Apply the lime juice, chilli and turmeric powder on the outside and set aside.
- Cook the deveined, shelled prawns in 1 cup chopped tomatoes, fennel powder and salt. Once the prawns are cooked, mix in the grated cheese and black pepper.
- Divide the prawn mixture into 6 parts and stuff the pomfrets. Seal the cut side of the pomfret with toothpicks or tie string around the cut portion.
- Place 2 large fry pans or iron skillets with ½ cup oil to heat on your stoves. Beat the eggs, cover the pomfrets with the beaten eggs and crumb them.
- When the oil is hot, lower the pomfret by its tail and fry slowly till golden on both sides. Serve immediately with chips, green salad or a lightly cooked vegetable. The pomfrets should be well fried.

Variation: POMFRETS STUFFED WITH CHEESE AND MUSHROOMS.

- Cook exactly as in the above recipe. The mushrooms – atleast 1 packet of fresh ones – should be washed, sliced and sautéed or cooked in 2 tablespoons of butter. When soft, 1 cup grated cheese should be mixed and the mixture stuffed into the pomfrets. If you wish you can mix 2 tablespoons of sweet marjoram with the stuffing or chives.
- In this recipe the pomfrets should be marinated only in salt, 1 tablespoon black pepper powder and the juice of 2 sour limes.

Spaghetti Bolognaise (pg. 131)
Papeta-ma-Gosht (pg. 173)
Poor Man's Steak
Roast Beef
Fluffy Mashed Potatoes
Hyderabadi Pasande Gosht (pg. 138)

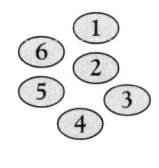

PRAWN MASALA TOASTS

Preparation Time: 10 mins. • Cooking Time: 20-25 mins. • Serves: 8

6 large bread slices
2 eggs
1 cup deveined washed prawns
1 cup grated cheese
1 tbsp. chopped coriander
1 tbsp. cornflour
1 tsp. red chilli powder
salt
oil

- Chop the prawns roughly, apply salt and place them in a bowl. Add the cheese, coriander, cornflour and chilli powder and the two eggs well beaten. Mix and taste for salt and apply on one side of each of the six bread slices. Cut each slice into four triangles.
- Heat a kadhai half full of oil and when the oil is hot, deep fry the triangles, prawn side down. Turn the triangles once when golden brown and remove from the oil.

SWEET, SOUR AND HOT PORK

Preparation Time: 40 mins. • Cooking Time: 40 mins. • Serves: 8-10

1½ kgs. good English pork
2 tbsps. ginger-garlic paste
15 Kashmiri chillies
1 tiny piece fresh turmeric
6 black pepper corns
¼ tsp. cloves
1 tsp. black mustard seeds
1 tsp. cinnamon
1 pod garlic
1 tbsp. cumin seeds
2 cups sugarcane vinegar
75 gms. jaggery

} Grind together in sugarcane vinegar

- Wash the pork and remove the rind. Leave the fat on the flesh. Cut into 1" bits. Wash, salt and marinate in the ginger-garlic paste for 2 hours.
- Grind the masala in good sugarcane vinegar, about 2 cups or so. When soft to the touch, smear all over the pork pieces.
- Place with 2-3 cups water and the jaggery in a pressure cooker and cook till soft in its own fat.
- Serve with fried potatoes, diced capsicum, baby tomatoes and gotli bread.

APPLE MOUSSE WITH BRANDY

Preparation Time: 15 mins. • Cooking Time: 40 mins. • Serves: 6

4 large golden apples
½ cup cream
2 eggs
2-3 tsps. gelatine
4 tbsps. orange juice
2 tbsps. apricot jam
30 gms. butter
5 tbsps. sugar
praline
½ cup brandy
extra ½ cup cream

- Skin, core and slice the apples finely. Place in a heavy based saucepan with the butter, jam and 3 tablespoons sugar. Cook over a low flame till soft. Mash well.
- Melt the gelatine in the orange juice and when dissolved, cool and add to the apple mixture.
- Whisk the eggs with a tablespoon of sugar and cook in a double boiler till the egg thickens. Cool and add to the apple mixture. Add brandy and mix.
- Take half a cup of cream. Beat lightly and stir into the apple. Mix well, taste for sugar and pour into an attractive glass bowl. Chill overnight.
- Next day, before serving, whip the extra cream with a tablespoon of powdered sugar and make swirls over the mousse with a piping bag. Decorate with praline.

BAKED PEACHES AND STRAWBERRIES

Many desserts are made with canned and fresh fruits and since I had a number of peach tins with me, I decided to pair them with large fresh strawberries and bake them in a cream sauce. The result was surprisingly good. The experiment paid off!

Preparation Time: 10 mins. • Cooking Time: 30-40 mins. • Serves: 6-8

1 can peach halves
200 gms. large strawberries
250 gms. caster sugar
700 gms. cream
10 egg yolks
1 tsp. vanilla essence
extra 50 gms. brown sugar

- Place the peaches in a large rectangular pyrex dish and sprinkle brown sugar on top. Wash the strawberries and slice in half and place them on top.
- Place the cream over a low fire. Do not boil. Add the caster sugar and allow it to melt on a slow heat. Remove, cool and add the vanilla essence. Whisk the egg yolks and blend into the cool cream.
- Preheat the oven to 350°F for 10 minutes. Pour the cream over the fruit and bake until golden brown.
- Chill overnight and serve.

SECTION 10

NEW YEAR'S DINNER AT TWILIGHT

For the New Year we normally light candles on the dining table. The beautiful pair of glass candle sticks was given to us by Feroze's aunt, Lois Pochkhanawala. They really look beautiful and add to the elegance of the table laid out with bone china and flowers. The items served on this day are less than the ones I serve normally because they are heavy and take a long time to make.

. . . .

POTAGE A LA MARQUISE

This soup is easy to make but requires a number of items to be prepared and assembled, before hand. I suggest that you make the tomato base, white sauce, chicken flakes and meatballs in the morning and keep them in separate containers in the refrigerator. You can heat everything gently, when your guests arrive.

Preparation Time: 40 mins. • Cooking Time: 1 hr. • Serves: 10

For the White Sauce

1 litre full cream milk
3 tbsps. butter
½ thick stem celery, sliced
2-4 tbsps. cornflour
thickly ground fresh black pepper
salt

For the Tomato Base:

1 kg. ripe red tomatoes
1 bunch parsley
1 large white onion
2 tbsps. or more sugar per taste
salt
½ cup tomato ketchup or sauce for colour
zest of half a lime
1 cup grated cheese
10 cups soup and chicken flakes from boiled chicken

- Place the milk in the saucepan and boil it. Allow to cool.

- Take the cornflour, mix it with a little water and make a smooth paste. Mix it in the warm milk along with the butter, celery and salt to taste. Cook. Once it comes to a boil remove from the fire. Keep aside.

- Remove seeds and skin of the tomatoes. Chop roughly and place in a pan with at least 4-6 cups of water and 1 chopped onion. Bring to the boil and pass through a moule legume or a mixie. Add the lemon zest and half cup of tomato sauce and the finely chopped parsley. Keep on one side after reducing it by almost half.

- Boil 1 small chicken with salt, pepper, 2 pieces of celery and a little fresh ginger. When cooked, strain the liquid and reserve. Debone the chicken and flake the pieces. Discard the skin.

Meatballs in their Own Soup

½ kg. meat mince
1 chopped onion
1 tablespoon finely chopped mint
salt/pepper
2 eggs
oil

- Take the mince, add salt, pepper, fresh mint to taste and a small finely chopped onion. Mix well along with 2 well-beaten eggs. Dampen your hands and make small balls. Put the chicken soup to boil. Add the meatballs to the boiling soup and allow to cook over a high flame till soft. Remove the scum from the soup.

- Assemble all the items 10 minutes before serving the soup. If you wish you can toast triangles of bread in an oven to serve along with the soup. Taste all three soup gravies. If you wish, add one teaspoon of sugar or more to the tomato soup. Put the tomato gravy, the white sauce and the meatball gravy over a low fire till they are simmering.

- When your guests are seated at the table, place the required number of soup plates 4-8 in a row on a table. Use separate ladles for all 3 items. Bring the tomato soup to a boil and fill all the soup plates with equal amount of soup. In the centre of each plate, place dollops of thick white sauce and chicken flakes. Take a slotted spoon and place 3-4 meatballs in the centre of the white sauce. Get somebody to help you spread cheese over the meatballs and chicken and quickly serve your guests the assembled soup. Do not allow it to get cold.

- Prepare the next course with thought. Do not serve the next dish in a greasy, masala gravy. Serve a lightly tossed green salad, chicken farchas and a light pulao. For dessert, serve a fruit salad or simple ice-cream.

HEAVENLY CHICKEN-BREASTS WITH APPLES AND CREAM ACCOMPANIED BY FLUFFY POTATOES

Preparation Time: 30 mins. • Cooking Time: 40-45 mins. • Serves: 6-8

8 skinless and boneless chicken breasts
250 gms. bacon cut into small rindless pieces – optional
8 apples
1 tsp. caraway seeds
1 tbsp. coarsely ground black peppercorns
1 tsp. grated fresh ginger
¼ tsp. red chilli powder
2 tsps. cornflour
1 tsp. minced garlic
2 cups thick cream
½ cup brown demarara sugar
6 bunches spinach
6 potatoes – boiled and mashed with ½ cup milk
grated nutmeg
½ cup sweet wine – (optional)
1 cup red wine
butter
salt

- Fry the bacon pieces and keep aside.
- Apply salt and pepper to the chicken and then gently saute in 2 non-stick fry pans in 3 tablespoons of butter. Sprinkle the ginger and garlic over the chicken pieces. Sprinkle occasionally with water and allow to cook till golden brown and soft.
- Peel and cut each apple into 8 pieces and place in a frying pan. Dot with butter and cook till soft. Sprinkle the brown sugar on the apples as well as the carraway seeds. Add wine if using it.
- Arrange the chicken breasts on a pyrex dish. Scrape the frying pans with quarter cup of water. Combine water from both frying pans into one. Toss in 2 teaspoons of cornflour and the chilli powder and cook over a medium flame stirring all the time. Taste for salt and when cooked, pour some over the chicken pieces. Decorate with the bacon pieces. Place the cooked apples in the centre of the dish.
- You can pop the dish into the oven and heat it or you can place it in a decorative vessel and heat it on top of the stove.
- When ready to eat, whip the cream lightly, add a little grated nutmeg and pour it over the chicken and apples.
- Lightly boil the spinach in salted water. Puree in a liquidizer. Heat 2 tablespoons butter. Toss in the pureed spinach and serve separately.
- For The Fluffy Potatoes:
- Mash the potatoes with half a cup of milk. Add salt. Whip lightly and serve, dotted with butter.

SPANISH RICE OR PAELLA

This is a delicious dish to serve at parties. First of all, its combination is unusual and it is very colourful besides being tasty. It consists of chicken, chicken livers, prawns, eggs, raisins, capsicum and cheese and is a very popular dish amongst my clients.

Some of my clients like the rice to be cooked along with ham and bacon. It tastes good with or without these items.

How you serve this dish is important. Always lay it out in two flat dishes instead of one large dish so that the rice does not cool before everybody is served.

Preparation Time: 45 mins. • Cooking Time: 1¼ hrs. • Serves: 15

2 gms. saffron,
½ tsp. saffron colour
1 kg. old basmati rice
10 chicken breasts, deboned and cut into chunks
500-700 gms. shelled and deveined prawns
10 fried prawns with their shells intact
1 pomfret, filleted and cut into small pieces
200 gms. bacon (optional)
200 gms. ham (optional)
300 gms. chicken livers each cut into 2 pieces
2 kg. large ripe tomatoes, skinned and deseeded
2 tbsps. sugar
400 gms. capsicums, cut julienne
500 gms. finely chopped onions
10-15 black olives (optional)
4 green chillies finely chopped
2 tbsps. parsley
½ cup raisins
400 gms. grated cheese
whole spices such as black peppercorns, cinnamon and cloves
2-3 tbsps. fresh ginger-garlic paste
2 tsps. ground mace
1 tsp. ground cloves

- The first step is to divide the rice into two portions.
- Puree the tomatoes in a liquidiser after washing them. Place the tomato liquid on a stove with salt and 2 tablespoons of sugar. Bring to a boil and set aside 2 cups of the tomato liquid.
- Wash the two portions of rice separately. Cook one portion with ghee, 3 bay leaves and whole spices and a pinch of saffron colour and the bacon if you are using it. Cook the other half with 3 bay leaves and whole spices in the tomato juice. Use the tomato liquid a little at a time. An electric cooker is best suited for cooking this rice.
- Cook the chopped onions in 1 cup or more of oil. When golden coloured, set aside one third of the onions. Add the chopped chicken pieces along with 1 tablespoon of ginger-garlic paste, ground mace, ground cloves and coarsely ground cardamoms and 1 tablespoon chilli powder and 1 tablespoon black pepper powder. When the chicken is well mixed in the spices, add 1 cup of the thickened tomato liquid. Cook until the chicken is soft and tender. Heat the saffron and add it to the chicken.
- Take a saucepan, place half cup oil and heat it. Add the reserved onion and the washed and deveined prawns along with 4 finely chopped green chillies and 1 tablespoon chilli powder. Cook in the tomato liquid till the prawns are soft. Taste for salt.

3-4 coarsely beaten cardamoms
6 bay leaves
2 eggs – raw
4 eggs – boiled
breadcrumbs
2 tbsps. red kashmiri chilli powder
1 tbsp. or more freshly grated black pepper
oil for cooking
salt to taste

- Wash the chicken livers and cut each into two. Salt them and add a little ginger-garlic paste. Cook in a fry pan with a little oil till tender.
- Fry the raisins and capsicums lightly and set aside.
- Beat the two eggs and toss into the filleted crumbed cut pomfret pieces. Add salt and pepper and deep fry the pieces and set aside.
- Now to assemble the paella:
- Keep the two rice, chicken and prawn gravies hot.
- Lay the red tomato rice on the bottom of the dish. Place the chicken gravy on top of it, then lay out the prawn gravy on top of the chicken. Sprinkle with the fried pomfret pieces. Cover with the saffron rice and top with the raisins, chopped parsley, fried prawns with shells intact and capsicums. Top with the black olives (and ham pieces, if used), sliced boiled eggs, fried liver and cover with the grated cheese. If you have an oven, heat the dish for fifteen minutes at 350°F.

PEACH MELBA

Serves: 15

2 blocks vanilla ice-cream packs
2 large cans Australian peaches halved
1 bottle raspberry jam
½ cup cornflour
mint leaves (and blanched almonds – optional) for the decoration

- Place the syrup from the peach cans into a heavy bottomed saucepan. Beat the jam till smooth and add it to the syrup. Mix the cornflour in 1 cup of water and add it to the jam mixture and stir vigorously, over a high flame. When the mixture boils well and becomes clear, remove from the fire. Cool and refrigerate. Refrigerate the peach halves.
- When it is time to serve the dessert, put two scoops of vanilla ice-cream into champagne glasses. Cut each peach half into two and place it on the ice-cream scoops. Drench with raspberry sauce and top it with two blanched almonds and two mint leaves.
- Since the jam sauce contains the peach syrup, the taste will be doubly enhanced.

SECTION 11

SUMMER SHADES AND SPLASHES

Kurush has his birthday on the second of May, closely followed by Daraius' on the fifth of June. By this time the weather becomes warmer and is redolent with the smell of the santoor berries (mulberries), which cover three trees in the corner of the garden. The roses add to the scent of the fruit and so does the grass as it slowly turns yellow and then brown. By June the garden is waiting for the rains to fall. The hills in front of the house have turned brown and you feel the palpable beat of the earth as it waits restlessly for the first drops of rain to cool its parched surface. The mosquitoes start harassing, so it is safer to have parties indoors.

Kurush prefers meaty dishes hence I normally include a dish like Hyderabadi Pasande Gosht for his birthday spread. Daraius prefers pulaos with dhansakh dal, so I had cooked Golden Pepper pulao for him along with his favourite dal. As for Feroze, he doesn't have any strong likes or dislikes — but he does like steak and has a sweet tooth so it is the dessert which he favours above all else.

PEACH, BROCCOLI AND ALMOND SALAD

Preparation Time: 15 mins. • Serves: 4-6

8 fresh peaches
12 small florets broccoli, boiled
10 almonds, boiled, skinned, sliced and golden fried
100 gms. cheddar cheese, or any sharp Indian cheese, grated
½ cup mayonnaise
½ cup cream

- Arrange the boiled broccoli florets in a bowl. Skin the peaches and cut each into six slices. Arrange them above the broccoli.
- Mix the mayonnaise, cream and the cheese into a smooth paste. Pour over the peaches. Sprinkle with the fried almonds. Chill and serve.

FISH FILLETS CHILLED AND SERVED WITH PRAWN MAYONNAISE

Preparation Time: 35 mins. • Cooking Time: 20 mins. • Serves: 6-8

1 iceberg lettuce
1 sliced orange
8 fillets of ramas or pomfrets, 2 inches long × ½ inch thick
1 cup mayonnaise
1 cup boiled, salted prawn
2 tbsps. parsley, chopped
1 tsp. garlic, minced
½ tsp. ginger, minced
½ tsp. grated orange peel
2 tbsps. orange juice
1 tsp. pickled green peppercorns, coarsely ground
½ tsp. roasted coriander seeds, coarsely ground
butter

- Place 3 tablespoons of butter in a large skillet. Wash the fish fillets, salt them and cook them along with ginger-garlic gently in the butter till tender and white. Remove them carefully onto a glass dish and chill them in the refrigerator.
- Chop the cooked prawns finely or pass them through a mincer. Place the minced prawns in a glass bowl. Add the rest of the ingredients barring the lettuce and the orange slices, and mix well. Chill.
- Serve the fish in 8 individual plates. Decorate each plate with lettuce leaves and a slice of orange on one side. Place one fillet carefully on one side and smoothen it with the prawn sauce.
- Serve as a first course with triangles of buttered toast or garlic flavoured french bread.

SPAGHETTI BOLOGNAISE

During my research years at Deccan College, Pune, I had made friends with a group of Italians who lived in Pune. Antonio, who worked with Bajaj Scooters, had brought his entire family from Italy. His wife, a cheery buxom lady, would cook the most delicious pasta and invite me and my friend Anna Radicchi for dinner. I used to enjoy the food as did everyone else, which included her two sons and a number of Italian friends. One major attraction used to be a dumb green parrot in a cage, which the younger child had unimaginatively christened "Poona"! Well, here's the way I make the sauce for the spaghetti for my children. I use mutton mince though most people prefer veal or beef mince.

Preparation Time: 10 mins. • Cooking Time: 35 mins. • Serves: 6-8

1 packet spaghetti
500 gms. mutton mince
750 gms. tomato pulp – no skin or seeds
1 cup grated cheese
2 large onions
1 tsp. garam masala
1 tsp. chilli powder
1 apple, chopped
1 stalk celery
½ cup mushrooms, sliced
1 tsp. ginger-garlic paste
½ tsp. nutmeg, freshly grated
1 tbsp. sugar
butter
salt and pepper

- First make the sauce by chopping the onions, slicing the celery and mushrooms and preparing the tomato pulp. Marinate the mince with salt, pepper and ginger-garlic paste.

- Place the chopped onions and 3 tablespoons butter in a large vessel. When the onions turn golden put in the mince and stir vigorously. Add the garam masala, nutmeg powder and the chilli powder and stir briskly Add the tomatoes and half a cup of water, stir and close the vessel. Keep checking so that it does not burn and add more water to the mince if needed. When the mince is soft enough (approx. 30-40 mins) add the sliced celery, one skinned and chopped apple and the sugar. Remove from the fire when the apple turns soft.

- Heat salted water in a large vessel and put in the spaghetti when it boils. Allow to cook and drain. Quickly place the spaghetti in a glass bowl or dish and toss the thickened mince sauce on top. Sprinkle the cheese on top of the mince and serve it.

CHICKEN STUFFED TOMATOES

Preparation Time: 25 mins. • Cooking Time: 35-40 mins. • Serves: 6-8

6 chicken breasts, boiled
8-10 large red tomatoes
1 large onion
½ cup parsley, chopped
1 tsp pepper, freshly ground
2 egg yolks
1 tbsp. sugar
2 tbsps. ghee or butter
salt

- Shred the boiled chicken breasts and set aside.
- Chop the onion and cook it in a saucepan over a low fire with 2 tablespoons of ghee or butter.
- Wash and dry the tomatoes. Take a sharp penknife and cut a small circle on top of the tomatoes and remove it. Then with a small teaspoon remove the pulp into a bowl. Sprinkle salt on the tomatoes and overturn them on a tray. Remove the seeds from the pulp and add the chopped pulp to the onions over a slow flame.
- When the tomatoes are soft add the chopped parsley, shredded chicken, sugar and black pepper. Thicken the mixture and fill in the tomato shells. Place the stuffed tomatoes on a buttered tray. Heat the oven to 350°F.
- Whisk the egg yolks and dot each opening in the tomatoes with the egg mixture and place the tray into the hot oven. When the eggs brown, remove the tomatoes and serve immediately.

RUM AND MACAROON TRIFLE PUDDING

1 cup rum or sweet sherry
100 gms. macaroon biscuits
1 litre milk
4 eggs
1 sponge cake – cut into 15 slices
1 small can fruit cocktail
1 can peaches
some canned cherries
sugar to taste
1 large bar chocolate
raspberry jam
1 tsp. vanilla essence

- Empty all the canned fruit in a glass bowl and reserve the syrup in a separate container. Cut peaches into small pieces after reserving four large pieces for decoration.
- Heat the milk in a saucepan and add sufficient sugar to sweeten it. Bring it to a boil and add the vanilla essence. Cool. Whisk 4 eggs well and add to the cooled milk. Mix well and place on a low heat. Stir non-stop till the milk heats and thickens and coats the back of a spoon. Do not allow to boil. Cool and chill in a refrigerator.
- Place the macaroons on a large plate and dampen with the sherry. Place the cake pieces on the bottom and sides of a large crystal or glass bowl. With a teaspoon take the sherry and dampen all the cake. Put dollops of jam on top of the cake.
- Reserve some peaches and cherries for the decoration and place all the fruit in the bowl. Top the fruit with the macaroons reserving some for decoration purposes.
- Then pour the glacé custard over the fruit and level the top. Decorate with the reserved fruits, macaroons and chocolate curls made from the chocolate bar. Chill for at least 2-4 hours.

KATY DALAL'S MOUSSAKA

Preparation Time: 10-15 mins. • Cooking Time: 45-50 mins. • Serves 8

For the Brinjals:
2 large black brinjals
½ tsp. turmeric powder
Juice of 2 sour limes
Salt

For the Mince:
600 gms. mutton or chicken mince
500 gms. fresh tomato puree
1 cup readymade tomato ketchup
1 large onion, finely chopped
1 tsp. crushed garlic
1 tbsp. freshly chopped parsley
½ tsp. oregano
½-1 tsp. paprika (sweet red chilli flakes)
1 tsp. black pepper powder
1 tbsp. sugar
Salt
Olive Oil

For the Cheese Sauce:
2½ heaped tbsps. maida
½ litre full cream milk
150 gms. butter
200 gms. sharp cheese, grated
2 eggs
Salt

- Wash the black brinjals. Thinly slice off from top and bottom and cut into ¼" thick round slices. Wash them and pierce them with the tines of a fork. Apply salt and turmeric powder on them and then sprinkle the slices with lime juice.

- Place the chopped onions along with 2 tablespoons of olive oil in a large saucepan and cook still soft. Add the mince and the crushed garlic paste, along with the oregano, paprika flakes and black pepper powder and stir for 3 minutes. Cover and allow to cook on a medium flame for 5 minutes. Then add the tomato puree and the sugar and cook till all the gravy has dried up.

- When the mince is tender, add the cup of tomato ketchup. Check that the mince is well cooked. If not, add some water and cook till you get the required softness.

- Whilst the mince is cooking, fry the brinjal slices and make the white sauce.

- Place the butter in a saucepan over a low heat. When melted, add the maida and stir well and pour the milk into the pan. Stir vigorously so that no flour balls remain, as the sauce has to be as smooth as silk. Taste for salt. The butter will automatically be salty, so be very careful. The cheese will add its own salt.

- When the sauce thickens to a strong pouring consistency, add 100 gms. of grated cheese to it and whisk the sauce rapidly and remove from the fire.

- Take a 1-litre rectangular pyrex dish. Cover the bottom with the smaller slices of fried brinjal. Then pour the thick mince sauce over it and cover it with the larger brinjal slices.
- When your sauce is cool, whisk in 1 egg. Mix the sauce well and pour it over the brinjal slices. Whisk the remaining egg and spread it with a new paint brush or your fingers, over the surface of the sauce.
- Next, sprinkle the remaining cheese over the egg covered sauce.
- Bake in an oven at 350°F until golden brown.
- Serve with French bread, butter and a green salad with plenty of different types of lettuce and cucumbers.

BRINJALS BAKED WITH CHEESE AND PRAWNS

Preparation Time: 20 mins. • Cooking Time: 45-55 mins. • Serves: 8

2 tbsps. coriander, chopped
2 eggs, well beaten
2 egg yolks
4 large black seedless brinjals
2 sour limes
2 cups prawns, deveined and boiled
½ litre milk
350 gms. butter
2 cups cheese, grated
4 chillies, deseeded and chopped
2 large tomatoes, skinned and deseeded
¼ tsp. mace powder
¼ tsp. nutmeg powder
1 tsp. chilli powder
4 tbsps. self-raising flour
salt

- Take 100 gms. butter and put it on a hot skillet. When it begins melting add the tomatoes, boiled prawns, green chillies, nutmeg, mace and chilli powders. Cover and cook over a slow fire. Taste for salt, add the coriander, stir and set aside.
- Make a roux out of the remaining butter, flour, cheese and milk, reserving a cup of cheese and 2 tablespoons of the butter.
- Wash the brinjals and slit them into halves horizontally, keeping the stalks intact. Scoop out some of the flesh and make a little hollow in each half of the brinjals. Squeeze out the lime juice and mix with a little salt. Apply this to the inside of the brinjals. Steam in a colander with the soft, scooped outside facing downwards. Cook till the brinjal is almost done but still firm.
- Grease a rectangular pyrex dish or aluminium tray with butter. It is always better to do this in a pyrex dish as you can take it to the table directly. Sometimes things get spoilt whilst being transferred from oven to serving dish.
- Beat the eggs well and mix into the prawns along with the roux or white sauce and fill the hollow brinjals with this mixture. Do not flatten the mixture but let it bulge out. Smoothen the surface with the beaten egg-yolks and sprinkle with the reserved cheese.
- Bake in a preheated oven at 350°F till the top is golden brown.
- Make sure that the baking dish is lavishly greased so that the outer skin is cooked crisp.
- Serve immediately as this dish will not taste as good if prepared beforehand and the bake is allowed to lose its fluffiness.

SHAHJAHANI MURGHI

Preparation Time: 15-20 mins. • Cooking Time: 50 mins. • Serves: 4-6

1 chicken, cut into 8 portions, discard neck and wings
2 gms. saffron
½ cup almonds, boiled and skinned
½ cup raisins
2 large onions
4 large tomatoes, skinned and deseeded
2 star anise
1 tsp. ground cloves, cinnamon, black pepper and nutmeg
1 tsp. chilli powder
2 bay leaves
1 tbsp. ginger-garlic paste
1 cup fresh curd
3 tbsps. sugar
1 fresh lettuce, preferably iceberg
6 large potatoes
2 tbsps. fresh coriander
refined groundnut oil or ghee
salt

- Wash the chicken and marinate in salt and ginger-garlic paste.
- Peel the potatoes, cut into chips and soak them in salted water.
- Heat the saffron on a tava and then crumble it into a cup of hot water.
- Chop the onions finely and fry in 3 tablespoons of ghee or ½ cup oil till soft. Add the star anise, bay leaves, garam masala and chilli powder. Stir and add the chicken pieces and allow to cook for 5 minutes over a low flame. Cut the peeled tomatoes into large wedges and mix well so that the pieces blend well with the chicken. Pour 2 cups of water along with the saffron water and cover the chicken and cook over a low fire till soft and tender.
- Fry the raisins and the skinned almonds in a little ghee or oil and set aside.
- Wash the lettuce leaves and allow the water to drain. Whip the curds with the sugar and set aside. Fry the potato chips in hot oil and keep aside.
- Arrange the lettuce leaves on a flat dish. Place the chicken pieces in the centre of the dish and top with the chips and the fried almonds and raisins. Pour the whisked curds over and sprinkle with the chopped coriander leaves.
- This dish was very popular with a number of clients at the PVM Gymkhana.

HYDERABADI PASANDE GOSHT

Preparation Time: 25 mins. • Cooking Time: 55 mins. • Serves: 6-8

2 legs of lamb
1½ tbsps. ginger-garlic paste
4 onions, sliced, fried and ground to a paste
1 tsp. each cardamom seeds, cinnamon and shahjeera, ground dry
2 tbsps. each, almonds and charoli, boiled and ground to a paste
2 tbsps. fresh coriander, finely chopped
1 cup thick curds, without whey
10 dried red chillies ⎫
4 green chillies ⎬ Grind together
1 tsp. poppy seeds (khus-khus) ⎬
1 tsp. turmeric ⎬
1 tsp. black pepper powder ⎭
salt
pure ghee

- Request your butcher to remove the vein in the leg. Ask him to fillet 2½"-3" round or square cutlets about ½" thick. You can use the remaining meat and the bones for mincing and stewing.
- Wash the mutton fillets well. Beat them with a mallet and marinate in ginger-garlic paste and salt. Place in a pressure cooker, sprinkle with the black pepper, add half a cup of ghee and fry till red. Add 2 cups of water and pressure cook over a gentle flame.
- Place ground onion in a kadhai and add the masala paste and fry well over a medium flame. Add the ground almonds and charoli. Stir and add a quarter cup of ghee and cook well for a couple of minutes. Whisk the curd and add to the masala. Remove the mutton from the cooker and drain in a colander. Use the resulting soup in another dish. Gently add the fillets to the curd mixture and cook over a low flame for 10 minutes shaking the pan from side to side. When a pleasing aroma emanates from the kadhai, adjust salt and add the powdered spices and the coriander on top of the meat. Serve with rotis or French bread.

CAULIFLOWER-NO-PULAO

Preparation Time: 15 mins. • Cooking Time: 40 mins. • Serves: 4-6

300 gms. basmati rice
300 gms. white cauliflower
50 gms. french beans, julienned
50 gms. carrots, julienned
50 gms. broccoli, sliced
25 gms. each, ginger and garlic, chopped
3 green chillies, finely chopped
1 bunch spring onion, julienned
2 tbsps. soya bean sauce
1 tbsp. aji-no-moto
½ tbsp. black pepper powder
salt
ghee

- Cut the cauliflower into florets and parboil them in salted water. Drain.
- In a wok fry the florets in 2 tablespoons ghee and set aside. Fry the other vegetables separately, too. Add salt sparingly.
- Boil the rice in plenty of water and drain in a collander when done. Spread out on a thali so that the grains separate. Heat 2 tablespoons of ghee in the wok and put in the chopped spring onions, ginger, garlic and green chillies, fry for 2 minutes and then add the rice. Sprinkle aji-no-moto, soya bean sauce and the pepper powder. Toss in the fried vegetables and stir well. Serve at once.

CHERRIES JUBILEE

Serves: 15

2 blocks vanilla ice-cream, family packs
1 large can red cherries
½ cup cornflour
1 cup raspberry jam
1 cup cherry or plain brandy, or rum
½ to 1 cup sugar

- Drain the cherries and pour the liquid into a heavy-bottomed pan. Add ½ cup sugar, 1 cup water and the raspberry jam and stir with a whisk. Mix the cornflour in ½ cup water, stir well and pour into the jam mixture.
- Place on a low flame and stir till a smooth sauce is formed. Remove from heat and mix in the cherries. Cool and chill. Place the cherries in a glass bowl.
- When ready to serve pour some brandy or rum in a small saucepan. Light the liquor with a match and pour over the cherries and serve immediately.
- Scoop the ice cream into little glasses or bowls and serve with the cherry sauce. If required, add some red food colour to the cherry liquid. It should be red.

PINEAPPLE MERINGUE PIE

Preparation Time: 20 mins. • Cooking Time: 10 mins. • Serves: 6

450 gms. crushed canned pineapple
120 gms. butter
200 gms. glucose biscuits
2 eggs, separated into yolks and whites
1/3 cup castor sugar
4 tbsps. cornflour
1/2 cup water
1/4 cup sugar
1 tsp. lemon rind, grated

- Crush the biscuits finely with a rolling pin. Mix in 60 gms. melted butter and press into the bottom of a 9" flan ring. Press the mixture into the bottom and sides of the flan ring with the base of a bottle or glass. Refrigerate.

- Crush the canned pineapple and measure out 450 gms. Keep aside. In a small pan combine half a cup of water, a quarter cup of sugar and 4 tablespoons of cornflour. Mix thoroughly. Add the rind and the pineapple and bring to a boil. Reduce heat and let it boil gently. Keep stirring for a couple of minutes. Remove from heat and quickly stir in 60 gms. butter and 2 well-beaten egg yolks. Mix well and allow to cool.

- Place the egg whites in a separate bowl, add a pinch of salt and whisk well till they are white and creamy. Gradually add 1/3 cup caster sugar and whisk till stiff.

- Pour the pineapple mixture into the prepared flan ring and cover it completely with the whisked egg white.

- Bake in a preheated oven at 375°F for 10 minutes or till the top is lightly browned. Remove from oven and cool.

BENGAL TOAST

Preparation Time: 30 mins. • Cooking Time: 30 mins. • Serves: 10-15

400 gms. shelled, deveined, washed prawns
1 small sliced bread
4 large onions minced
1 cup fresh coriander minced
¼ cup fresh mint minced
6 green chillies deseeded and minced
1½ tsps. chilli powder
1 tsp. turmeric powder (fresh pounded turmeric, if available)
1 tsp. dhansakh masala
¾ cup sugarcane vinegar
½ cup brown sugar
salt to taste
ghee or oil

- Deep fry the bread slices and set aside.
- Place the minced onion in a frying pan with ½ cup of oil and cook till pink over a low flame. If necessary, add one tablespoon of oil so the onions don't burn.
- Add the prawns and salt. Cover and cook for 10 minutes. When soft, add the fresh coriander, mint and green chillies as well as the chilli powder, turmeric and dhansakh masala. Stir well and keep covered over a low fire for 10 more minutes. Keep stirring so that the prawns don't stick to the pan.
- Add the sugar and vinegar and taste for salt. Keep stirring the mixture till it thickens. Spread on the fried toasts and serve hot.

CHEESE FISH FILLETS WITH HOT TOMATO SAUCE

Preparation Time: 30 mins. • Cooking Time: 35 mins. • Serves: 4-6

1 kg. ripe tomatoes, skinned, deseeded and pureed
2 large pomfrets, filleted
juice of 2 sour limes
2 cups cheese, grated
2 tsps. black pepper powder
1 bunch parsley
2 beetroots, boiled and sliced
2 lettuce, washed
2 cucumbers, skinned and sliced
2 cups toasted breadcrumbs
1 onion, sliced
4 eggs, whisked
1 tsp. cornflour
1 tbsp. mint, chopped
1 cup tomato ketchup
1 tbsp. capsico or tabasco sauce
1 tbsp. sugar
1 tbsp. cornflour
salt
oil, for deep frying

- Wash the fillets and marinate in salt, lime juice and black pepper powder.
- Whisk the eggs in a soup plate with 1 teaspoon cornflour.
- Heat oil in a large kadhai. Roll the grated cheese on the inner side of the fish. Dip the fillets in the egg mixture and coat with the bread crumbs. Deep fry 3-4 at a time and remove when golden brown. Tie 3 sprigs of parsley in bunches and deep fry.
- Arrange the fried fillets on a bed of lettuce on a flat dish surrounded by rings of onion, cucumber, beetroot and lemon wedges.
- To make the hot tomato sauce, place the pureed tomatoes in a saucepan with the mint. Add tomato ketchup, 1 tablespoon capsico or tabasco sauce, 1 tablespoon sugar and 1 tablespoon cornflour mixed in 3 tablespoons water. Stir over a high flame and bring to a fast boil. Stir till the sauce thickens. Taste for salt. Serve along with the fillets.

BOMBAY HOT POT

Our Hot Pot recipe was a great favourite with the Freemasons in Bombay. It is a change from the ordinary and goes well with green salad with a lime and sugar dressing. No bread or rotis are necessary along with this dish.

Preparation Time: 12 mins. • Cooking Time: 60 mins. • Serves: 6-8

1 leg of lamb (2-2½ kg.)
2 tbsps. ginger-garlic paste
6-8 potatoes, sliced very fine
6-8 carrots, sliced fine
4-6 medium onions, sliced fine
1 tbsp. pepper powder
½ tbsp. chilli powder
½ tbsp. garam masala powder (optional)
2 green chillies
2 large tomatoes
2-3 egg yolks
6 eggs, boiled and sliced
1 tbsp. cornflour
2 tbsps. tomato sauce
salt
oil

- Ensure that your butcher removes the large vein from the leg of mutton. Wash the mutton leg and then dry with a clean cloth. Apply salt, ginger-garlic paste, pepper and the chilli powder. Prick the meat with a fork so that the seasonings can be absorbed well. Keep it covered in a cool place for 2-4 hours.
- Heat half a cup of oil in a large flat bottomed pan. Roast the leg till it is well browned. Add chopped tomatoes, chillies and some garam masala. Transfer to a pressure cooker. Add enough water and cook till the meat is tender, or you can roast it in your oven. Keep adding a little water till the meat is done. Let it cool slightly and then slice it thinly. Reserve all the stock.
- In a rectangular baking dish, arrange the meat slices so that they overlap and thus fill the bottom of the dish. Place the stock in a small pan and heat over a slow fire. Blend in 1 tablespoon cornflour dissolved in ¼ cup water. Mix well and stir till the sauce thickens. Add 2 tablespoons tomato sauce and stir. Spread this over the meat.
- Deep fry or boil the sliced vegetables without breaking the slices. I prefer frying them.
- Arrange the onion, carrot and boiled egg slices over the meat. Cover this with a layer of potato and ensure that all the meat is covered.
- 20 minutes before serving, beat the egg yolks well and brush over the top of the potato layer. Bake over medium heat till the top is browned, about 20 minutes.

PURE NECTAR

Preparation Time: 45 mins. • Serves: 6.

1 victoria sponge, sliced into two
600 gms. cream
6 ripe alphonso mangoes
200 gms. powdered sugar

1. Beat the cream with the sugar till it rises in stiff peaks. Refrigerate.
2. Peel the mangoes and cut the cheeks. You will have 12 portions. Cut each into 4-6 slices according to the size of the mango. Chill.
3. Remove the pulp off the 6 seeds that remain. Mash into a pulp and gently mix into the cream.
4. Spread the cream on the cut side of the cake and cover it with the upper half of the cake.
5. Lightly spread the cream on the top and sides of the cake. Put the remaining cream into a piping bag and decorate the sides and top of the cake with lines and rosettes. Chill and serve.

SECTION 12

SOME POPULAR CHINESE ITEMS I COOK

Mumbai has innumerable fancy restaurants, modest eateries and footpath food stalls. Eating is a rip-roaring business in this fast moving metropolis. The most popular items on the roadway stalls are "pao-bhaji". Hundreds of Udipi restaurants have sprung up like mushrooms to serve the public "idlis" and "dosas" with "sambhar" and "rasam". "Pizza" parlours have opened up with a frenzy. Yet, the middle class and up market public prefer to go to high class Chinese restaurants.

My friend, Sem Tian Ling, known to everyone in Mumbai as "Baba", has been running one of the oldest Chinese restaurants in India. His father, Yick-Sen-Ling, came to India 60 years ago from Shanghai to Mumbai where he was sent to run a Chinese Museum. Today the same place houses our Cottage Industries shop at Apollo Bunder. Yick-Sen was an enterprising young man. He hired premises opposite the Chinese Museum and opened a Chinese Restaurant called NANKING which soon became a rage in Mumbai. After this, other Chinese restaurants came up, but none could excel Nanking's. In the year 1991 he opened an elegant restaurant called "Lings' Pavilion". This restaurant is looked after by Baba, his brother Nini, Sem-Mon-Ling and his son Jason, Boom-Chang-Ling.

There is a special reason why the "Pavilion" is filled to capacity in the afternoons and evenings. The food is very good and fresh and you get excellent, huge, steamed pomfrets, crabs cooked in various ways, large jumbo prawns and lobsters. There is a reason for the freshness and wholesomeness of the food. From "day one till today" the Lings have done their purchasing themselves from Sassoon Docks, Crawford Market and Grant Road Market. That's how Feroze and I met Baba years ago at Crawford Market, dressed in a safari suit and big black gumboots. All the largest, fresh pomfrets, the best of prawns and the largest crabs are reserved for Baba. No "maachhan" or fisherwoman will sell her crabs until Baba has selected his and gone. It is this personal supervision which results in tasty food and a top-notch reputation. No "kothmir-pudina" goes into any of his food. There is no Punjabi "chilly sauce" to pander his clients. He goes in for sauces made in his own factory under the name "Nanking". He makes his own soya bean sauce, chilli sauce, black bean paste, sesame oil and chilli oil.

I wanted to include some Chinese recipes in this book. I realised that whatever I wrote would be incomplete if I did not mention Baba. The two colour plates included here are of food that we cook for our clients which are their favourite items. My recipes are simple and very popular and enjoyed by a large number of people. All contain simple items, which are easily available. I have not included any recipes which require imported fish sauces that have to be bought in Singapore or Hong Kong.

LARGE POMFRET STEAMED AND LIGHTLY FRIED IN BLACK BEAN SAUCE HUNAN STYLE

Preparation Time: 20 mins. • Cooking Time: 20 mins. • Serves: 4-5

1 large pomfret
2 cups black bean sauce
2" fresh ginger sliced and cut into very thin strips
15 large garlic flakes, finely chopped
2 tbsps. soya bean sauce
4 small spring onions including 2" of the green portion cut into thin diagonal strips
6 green chillies deseeded cut into thin strips
8 parsley clusters
juice of 1 sour lime
sesame oil
salt to taste

- Wash the pomfret and clean the surface with a knife and scrape off all the tiny scales. Cut below the mouth and remove the stomach entrails. Leave the fins and tail on. Wash 3 times, salt and rub with the lime juice and place in a cool place.

- Take a steamer basket if you have one and steam the pomfret or lightly boil it covered in a large flat thali.

- Take a huge flat iron tava or griddle. Pour 1 cup of sesame oil on it and place on a hot flame. Add the ginger, garlic, chillies and spring onions in this order. Place the pomfret on top of these vegetables, sprinkle with soya bean, cover, lower flame and allow to cook for 7 to 10 minutes. Then turn over and cook the other side.

- Heat the black bean sauce. If you like, add half an onion finely chopped and allow to cook till soft.

- Take a large platter. Pour half the black bean sauce on the dish, place the pomfret on top, sprinkle with all the vegetables and oil left on the griddle and pour the remaining hot black bean sauce over the pomfret. Fry the parsley clusters and place them around the pomfret. Decorate the dish with flowers made out of spring onions and carrots and serve hot.

BLACK BEAN SAUCE HUNAN STYLE

Preparation Time: 15 mins. • Cooking Time: 25 mins. • Serves: 10

200 gms. dark rajma beans
3 tbsps. brown sugar
3 tbsps. Nanking soya sauce
6 large cloves crushed garlic
2 tbsps. cornflour
1½ tbsps. brown sugarcane vinegar
100 gms. sesame oil
salt to taste

- Cook the beans in salted water in a pressure cooker till absolutely soft. Drain. Crush the beans and mix in the sugar, soya sauce, garlic and vinegar.
- Mix the cornflour in ¾ cup of water and add to the beans.
- Heat the oil in a saucepan and fry the bean mixture for 3 minutes or so. Remove from the fire. Cool and refrigerate. The sauce will keep for 4 days at least. Dilute as and when you need it.

MANCHURIAN CHICKEN

Preparation Time: 20 mins. • Cooking Time: 25-30 mins. • Serves: 4-6

4 boneless chicken breast, each cut into 3 large cubes
2 tbsps. maida ⎫
1 tsp. aji-no-moto ⎪
½ tsp. salt to taste ⎬ For the chicken batter
2 tbsps. soya bean sauce ⎪
½ tsp. black pepper powder ⎪
1 egg ⎭
1 tbsp. finely chopped ginger
1 tbsp. finely chopped garlic
1 tbsp. finely chopped green chillies
200 gms. fresh mushrooms sliced
a pinch of black pepper powder
2 tbsps. cut chives

<u>For the Gravy:</u>
4 tbsps. maida
2 tbsps. sesame oil
2 cups chicken stock

- Place 2 tablespoons sesame oil in a saucepan and add 2 tablespoons maida, the ginger, garlic and green chillies. Mix for 3 to 5 minutes. Lightly brown. Then add 2 cups chicken stock and 1 tablespoon soya sauce. Add 2 tablespoons cut chives and the sliced mushrooms. Bring to a quick boil.
- Wash the chicken pieces well. Marinade in salt and black pepper powder for at least half an hour.
- Make the batter by placing the maida, aji-no-moto, egg, soya bean sauce, salt and black pepper powder in a bowl. Stir well and add the marinaded chicken pieces. Coat them well with the batter and deep fry till golden and set aside.
- Bring the gravy to a boil and add the fried chicken pieces and serve at once.

CHINESE HOT & SOUR SOUP

Preparation Time: 15-20 mins. • Cooking Time: 15-20 mins. • Serves: 8

1 chicken breast and carcass of 2 chickens
200 gms. cubed fresh paneer
2 spring onions sliced upto 4"
2 celery stalks cut diagonally
½" piece of ginger pounded
2 tbsps. soya bean sauce
2 tbsps. sugarcane vinegar
3 tbsps. brown sugar
1½ tbsps. cornflour
½ tsp. black pepper powder
2 eggs
salt to taste
1 pinch aji-no-moto

- Boil the chicken carcasses along with 1 breast in 8 cups of water. Add the ginger, celery, vinegar and salt to taste and cook over a medium flame till the chicken is soft. Strain the soup into a clean, heavy-bottomed vessel. Flake the flesh from the chicken bones and add to the soup.
- Add the brown sugar, soya bean sauce and pepper powder to the soup and replace on the stove. Place cornflour in half a cup of water and stir vigorously into the hot soup. Allow to boil. Taste for salt. When the soup thickens, add the whipped eggs from a height into the soup. Remove from the fire, add the cubed paneer and chopped spring onions and serve.

CHILLI HOT PRAWNS

Preparation Time: 20 mins. • Cooking Time: 15-20 mins. • Serves: 4-6

600 gms. prawns
1 tbsp. finely minced garlic
1 tbsp. finely minced ginger
1 pinch aji-no-moto
2 tbsps. tomato sauce
2 tbsps. soya bean sauce
2½ cups water
1 lettuce head
16 large cloves garlic ⎫
10 red chillies, preferably Kashmiri ⎬ *Grind together*
2 tbsps. sesame seeds ⎭
½ cup sugarcane vinegar
sesame oil
salt to taste

- Wash the prawns twice. Retain head and tail shell. Remove shell from the centre portion and devein. Wash twice and marinade in salt and soya bean sauce for 2 hours.
- Place 2½ cups of water in a flat vessel. Add the prawns, ginger, garlic, aji-no-moto and tomato sauce and bring to a boil. Once prawns are tender, remove from the fire.
- Grind the garlic, chillies, sesame seeds in the vinegar and cook it for 10 minutes over a low fire in ½ cup of sesame oil.
- Place finely chopped lettuce in a bowl and arrange the prawns with their heads up. Sprinkle the hot sauce on top of the prawns and serve.

SAUTÉED VEGETABLES

Preparation Time: 10 mins. • Cooking Time: 15-20 mins. • Serves: 4-6

100 gms. snow peas
100 gms. bamboo shoots
100 gms. broccoli
100 gms. chinese cabbage
2 tbsps. chopped celery
2 tbsps. soya sauce
1 tbsp. garlic strips
1 tbsp. green chillies cut into strips
1 large red pepper minced, fried
1 tsp. sesame seeds
2 tbsps. cornflour
sesame oil
salt to taste

- Wash the vegetables and set aside.
- Prepare the vegetables. Heat half cup oil till it smokes. Add garlic, green chillies, sesame seeds and fry well. Add salt and the vegetables and fry to and fro on high heat till the vegetable is tossed backwards and forwards and is almost cooked.
- Mix the cornflour in 1 cup of water. Place 1 cup water in a saucepan and boil. Add the soya bean sauce and cornflour water and mix well. Boil. Add fried sesame seeds and the fried minced pepper and taste for salt. Empty vegetables into a shallow dish and coat with the sauce.

PINEAPPLE CHICKEN

Preparation Time: 10 mins. • Cooking Time: 20 mins. • Serves: 4-6

1 chicken cut into 8 pieces
1 tin of pineapple slices
2 cups tomato sauce
1 cup celery stalks cut diagonally
1 cup spring onions cut diagonally
1 tsp. red chilli powder
½ cup cornflour
2 tbsps. soya bean sauce
2 tbsps. red Chinese chilli sauce
peanut oil.

- Wash the chicken pieces twice and marinade for 2 hours in salt, soya sauce, chilli powder and 1 tablespoon cornflour.
- Place half cup peanut oil in a chinese wok and add the chicken pieces to the hot oil. Lower the flame and allow the chicken to cook in 1 cup of water, stirring all the time. When the water almost dries up, add 1 cup of syrup from the pineapple tin. Cook till the chicken softens. Add 2 cups of tomato sauce, the celery and spring onions, as well as the chinese chilli sauce. Add water to the remaining cornflour in the cup, stir briskly and add to the chicken. Mix well in the wok for 7 minutes. Taste for salt.
- Serve decorated by pineapple rings.

PRAWNS WITH HONEY AND PEACHES

Preparation Time: 15 mins. • Cooking Time: 20 mins. • Serves: 5-8

400 gms. prawns
6 pieces of canned peaches
1 cup syrup from canned peach tin
½ cup honey
1 tbsp. pounded ginger
½ tsp. aji-no-moto
½ cup spring onions finely chopped
red pepper rings for decoration
1 tbsp. cornflour mixed with ½ cup water
1 tbsp. soya bean sauce
salt to taste
peanut oil

- Wash the prawns. Keep the heads and the tails. Remove centre shell, devein and wash twice. Marinade in the soya bean sauce for 2 hours.
- Place the prawns in 1 cup of salted water and boil till soft.
- Arrange the prawns in a bowl.
- Place the peach syrup and honey in a saucepan over a low flame. Add the pounded ginger, aji-no-moto, spring onions and corn flour mixed in half cup water and salt. Bring the mixture to a boil and pour it over the prawns. Top with the peach halves and red pepper rings.

. . . .

CHINESE STYLE BRAISED CHICKEN WINGS

Preparation Time: 20 mins. • Cooking Time: 20-25 mins. • Serves: 8-10

30 chicken wings with their tips cut off
8 spring onions white and green portion cut finely diagonally
½ cup soya bean sauce
½ cup tomato sauce
¼ cup honey
2 tbsps. minced fresh garlic
2 tbsps. minced fresh ginger
1 tbsp. finely chopped deseeded green chillies
1 tsp. aji-no-moto
½ tsp. black pepper powder
salt to taste
½ cup refined oil

- Wash the wings well and marinade in all the items except the oil, for 2 hours. Mix well and place in a cool spot.
- Heat the oil in a skillet and add the chicken wings and the marinade and turn up and down for 5 minutes. Cover and cook over a low flame for 20 minutes. Serve as a snack.

HONEY AND GINGER CHICKEN

Preparation Time: 15 mins. • Cooking Time: 10-12 mins. • Serves: 6

8 chicken breasts – boneless
¾ cups cornflour
1 cup extra cornflour
2 tbsps. sesame seeds – roasted
1 tbsp. finely sliced ginger
1 tbsp. finely sliced capsicum
1 bunch spring onions for garnishing
6 green chillies deseeded and chopped finely
6 eggs
1 cup honey ⎤ *Mix in a*
1 cup capsico or tobasco sauce ⎦ *glass bowl*
salt
sesame or til oil

- Cut each breast piece into 3 to 4 pieces depending upon the size of each chicken. Wash, salt and lightly boil along with ginger and chillies and set aside.
- Make spring onion curls and immerse them in ice water.
- Heat 2 cups of oil in a wok or kadhai. Mix the extra cornflour about ½ cup or more with the roasted sesame seeds and spread on a wooden board. Roll each piece of chicken in this dry mixture and keep aside.
- Beat ½ cup cornflour with 3 eggs. Make extra batter only if required. Coat the chicken pieces with this mixture and fry in batches in hot oil till golden. Sprinkle the honey and tabasco mixture on each batch and decorate with the finely cut capsicum and spring onion curls. Serve each batch immediately after it is ready.

AMERICAN CHOP SUEY

Preparation Time: 15 mins. • Cooking Time: 25 mins. • Serves: 4-6

200 gms. noodles
200 gms. cooked shredded chicken
6 spring onions cut julienne
1 capsicum cut julienne
1 orange carrot cut julienne
1/4 green cabbage cut julienne
2 thick celery stalks cut julienne
50 gms. french beans, washed, stringed and cut julienne
6 mushrooms, washed, finely sliced
2 tbsps. minced green chillies
2 tbsps. minced fresh ginger
2 tbsps. minced fresh garlic
1 tsp. aji-no-moto
1 cup tomato ketchup
1 cup chicken soup
1 tbsp. cornflour
2 fried eggs
salt
oil

- Boil the noodles in salted water, drain and twist into a circular coil in the form of a quarter plate and deep fry till golden and keep aside.
- Take a Chinese wok. Add 3 tablespoons of oil and stir fry the chilli, ginger, garlic, for 2 minutes. Then add the french beans, carrots, cabbage, celery, spring onion, capsicum, mushrooms and 1 more tablespoon oil. Stir fry for 7 more minutes.
- Add the tomato ketchup, the chicken soup and stir on a high heat. Add the chicken shreds and mix well for 2 minutes. Mix the cornflour with half a cup of water and add to the boiling mixture, and stirring vigorously, allow it to cook for 5 to 7 more minutes. Taste for salt and sweetness.
- Fry 2 eggs and set aside.
- Place the crisply fried noodles onto a flat dish. Top with the chicken, vegetable and tomato ketchup mixture. Place the hot fried eggs on top and serve.

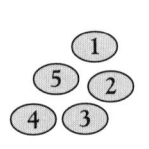

Chicken and Egg Fried Rice
Hot and Sour Soup (pg. 148)
Chilli Hot Prawns (pg. 148)
Pineapple Chicken (pg. 149)
Steamed Pomfret with Black Bean Sauce (pg. 146)

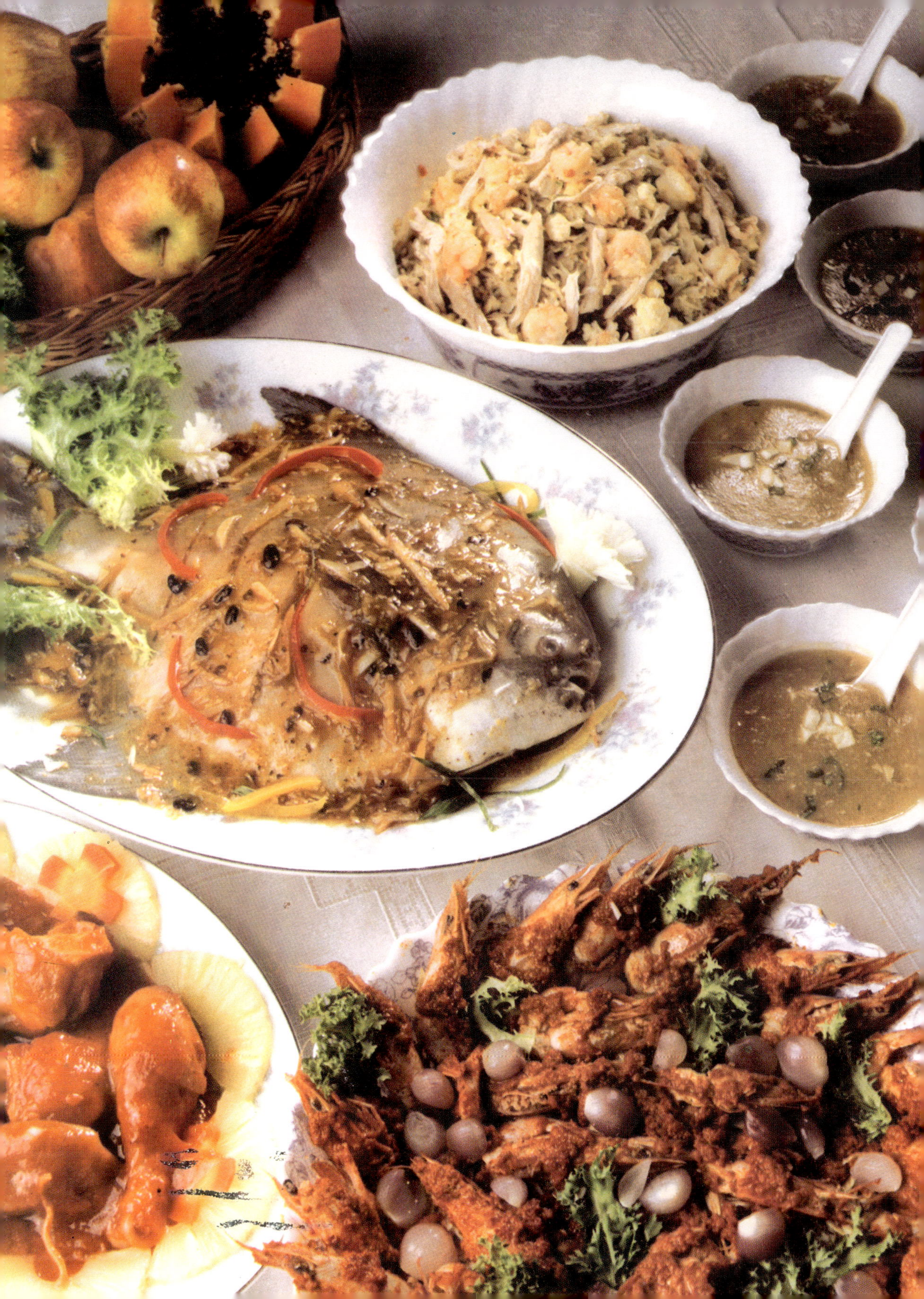

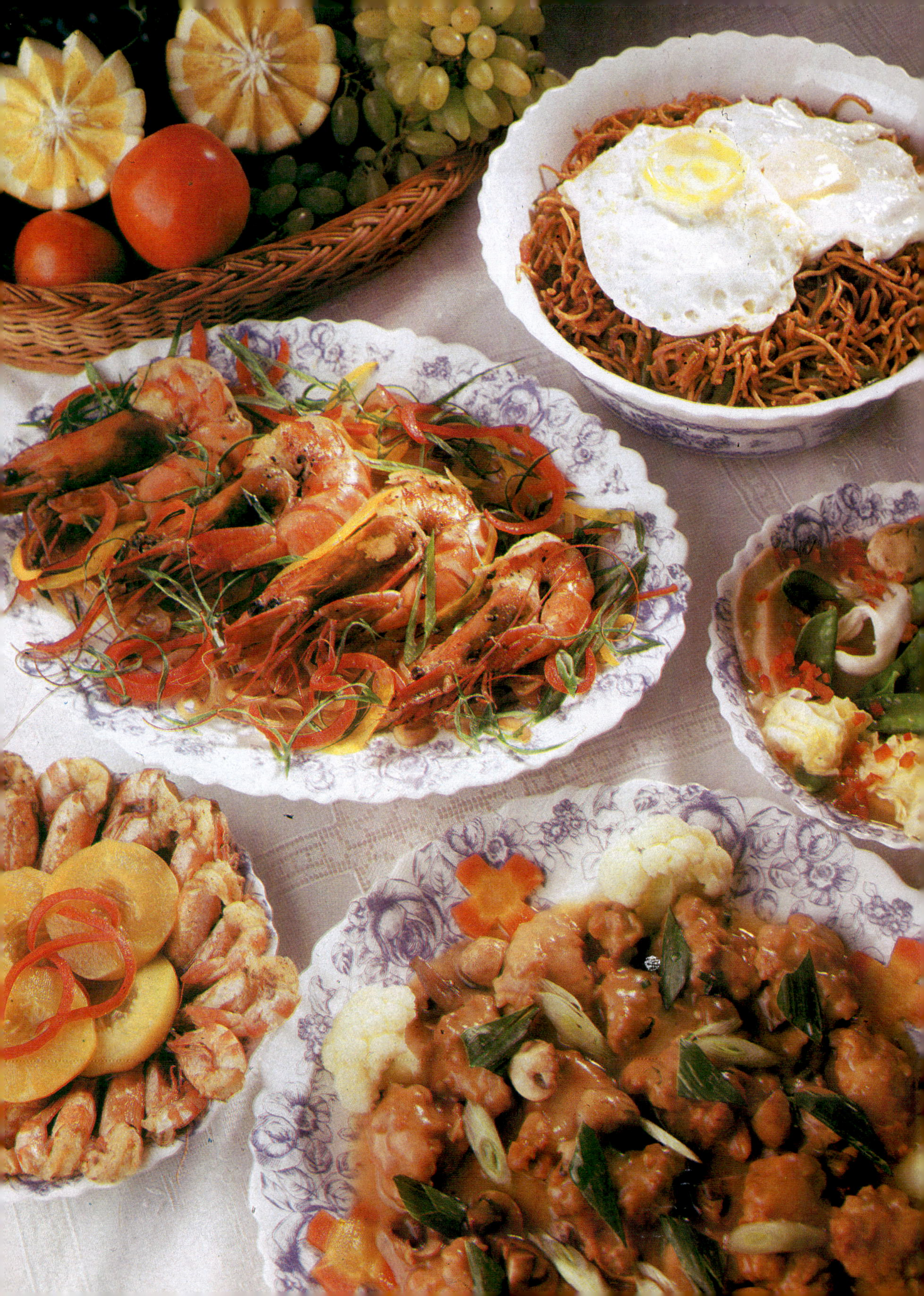

VEGETABLE HAKKA NOODLES

Preparation Time: 12 mins. • Cooking Time: 18 mins. • Serves: 4-6

These noodles are in great demand by my clients. They are very easy to make and are helpful if unexpected guests turn up.

200 gms. egg noodles or plain noodles
25 gms. yellow carrots cut julienne
25 gms. green french beans cut julienne
25 gms. green cabbage cut julienne
1 capsicum cut julienne
4 spring onions cut julienne
8 large cloves garlic cut julienne
2" ginger cut julienne
6 green chillies cut julienne
½ cup bean sprouts
½ tsp. black pepper powder
1 tsp. aji-no-moto
3 red chillies broken into 3 pieces each
2 tbsps. soya bean sauce (optional)
salt
oil or chilli oil

- Boil the noodles in salted water and when soft, drain and set aside.
- Take a Chinese wok and place 3 tablespoons of oil in it. Place on high heat and add the green chillies, ginger and garlic and stir for 2 minutes. Add the carrots, french beans, cabbage, capsicum and spring onions and lower heat and stir fry for 5 more minutes. Set aside.
- Place 3 tablespoons oil or chilli oil in the wok and place on a high heat. Add the broken red chillies to the oil, the bean sprouts, black pepper powder, soya sauce and aji-no-moto. Stir fry for 2 minutes and add the noodles. Stir fry for 5 minutes. When well blended, add all the stir fried vegetable mixture, cook for 3 more minutes mixing well with the noodles. Taste for salt and serve hot.

American Chop Suey (pg. 152)
Sautéed Vegetables (pg. 149)
Manchurian Chicken (pg. 147)
Prawns with Honey and Peaches (pg. 150)
Tandoori Bade Jhinge (pg. 180)

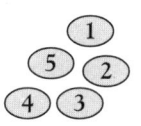

CHINESE PRAWN FRIED RICE

Preparation Time: 10 mins. • Cooking Time: 45 mins. • Serves: 10

500 gms. basmati rice
400 gms. deveined fresh prawns
4 tbsps. soya bean sauce
5 finely chopped green chillies
1" finely chopped fresh ginger
20 finely chopped garlic cloves
100 gms. finely chopped french beans
100 gms. finely chopped carrots
6 spring onions chopped diagonally
1 tbsp. of black pepper powder
4 eggs
2 tbsps. aji-no-moto
salt
sesame oil

- Wash the rice twice. Boil water in a large vessel and when it bubbles, add the rice and salt and cook till tender. Drain the rice in a colander.
- Wash the prawns 3 times and marinade in salt and 1 tablespoon of soya bean sauce. Set aside.
- Heat half a cup to one cup of sesame oil in a wok. When the oil heats put in green chillies, ginger, garlic, french beans, carrots, chopped spring onions and the prawns. Stir non-stop till the vegetables soften and the prawns are cooked. Remove the vegetables and prawns and wipe the wok.
- Place half a cup of sesame oil in the wok. Put in the boiled rice and sprinkle with 3 tablespoons of the soya bean sauce. Sprinkle the rice with the aji-no-moto and the pepper powder. Whisk the eggs, make a hole in the rice and pour the eggs and stir fry the rice and eggs.
- Add the vegetable mixture with the prawns and stir the rice well on a high heat. Taste for salt.
- Serve the rice with sweet and sour pineapple sauce.

PINEAPPLE SAUCE

Preparation Time: 15 mins. • Cooking Time: 45 mins. • Serves: 10

1 large tin pineapple slices
½ bottle tomato sauce or ketchup
½ cup cornflour
6 green chillies
2 tbsps. sugar
2 tbsps. grated ginger
2 tbsps. chopped garlic
1 tbsp. aji-no-moto
1 tsp. black pepper powder
2 cucumbers
1 small cauliflower
4 spring onions
salt
sesame oil

- Open the pineapple tin. Cut the slices into half inch pieces. Reserve the syrup.
- Chop all the vegetables into thin diagonal strips. Cut the cauliflower into florets.
- Take a vessel and place 3 tablespoons of sesame oil in it. Heat the oil and put in the chillies, garlic, ginger and diagonally cut spring onions. Reduce the flame and put in the tomato sauce. Add the pepper powder and aji-no-moto as well as the syrup from the pineapple tin. Take the cornflour and mix it in 1 cup of water. Stir and pour in a steady stream into the tomato sauce and keep stirring till the gravy is thick and the cornflour is cooked. Remove from the stove.
- Sauté the cucumber slices and the cauliflower florets in a little oil. Add a little salt and half cook the vegetables and add them to the sauce. Add the pineapple pieces and taste gravy. Add extra sugar only if you need it.
- Serve with fried rice or cutlets or patties.

DRUMS OF HEAVEN

Preparation Time: 10 mins. • Marinate Overnight • Cooking Time: 30 mins. • Serves: 7

24 large chicken wings
1 tbsp. mustard powder
4 tbsps. soya bean sauce
2 tbsps. brown sugar
½ cup good honey
1 tbsp. ginger-garlic paste
½ cup sesame seeds
½ cup poppy seeds
1 tsp. freshly ground black pepper
oil

- Cut the wing tip and reserve only the largest wing portion. Wash and with the help of a knife turn the meat from the bottom of the wing upwards so as to resemble a drumstick.
- Place ginger-garlic paste, pepper, salt to taste, soya bean sauce, brown sugar, mustard powder and honey in a bowl. Mix well and toss the wings into the mixture and marinate overnight.
- Splash a little oil on the drumsticks. Mix the poppy and sesame seeds together. Coat the drumsticks in the mixture, set them out in a baking pan and cook at 350°F for half an hour or till soft. Taste for salt. Serve with drinks.
- If you don't have an oven cook over a stove.

BROCCOLI WITH LEMON AND BUTTER BAKE

Preparation Time: 10 mins. • Cooking Time: 7 mins. • Serves 4-6

1 kg. broccoli florets
2 hard boiled eggs
1 cup fresh breadcrumbs
2-4 rashers back bacon (optional)
2 sour limes – juice removed
butter
pepper powder
salt

- Prepare the florets by cutting off the coarse lower stalks. Boil in salted water till stalks are tender.
- Fry the bacon and crumble when crisp. Set aside. Boil the eggs and grate the eggs and mix into the bacon.
- Place the broccoli in a baking dish.
- Heat 2 tablespoons butter and the lime juice and pour over the broccoli.
- Place 2 tablespoons butter and breadcrumbs in a frying pan and stir until golden brown.
- Cover the broccoli with the bacon and egg crumble and cover with the buttered breadcrumbs. Place for 7 minutes in a hot oven just before serving.

BIRD'S NESTS WITH CHICKEN MINCE OR STIR-FRIED VEGETABLES

Preparation Time: 20 mins. • Cooking Time: 40 mins. • Serves: 4

For the Bird's Nests you will need a metal tea strainer as large as an orange. The recipe below will make 4 nests. So if you want more bird's nests, double or triple the amounts.

4 large potatoes, peeled and grated
1 egg well beaten
1/3 cup flour
oil for deep frying

For the Sauce:
2 tsps. soya sauce
2 tsps. dry sherry
1/2 cup chicken slivers
1/2 cup chicken stock
2 tsps. cornflour

For the Chicken Mince Filling:
6 chicken breasts, minced raw
1 tsp. ginger-garlic paste
4 spring onions
1 tsp. minced fresh mint
1 tbsp. chopped celery
1 apple – skinned, cored, finely chopped
butter
pepper powder
salt

The Stir-Fried Vegetable Filling:
100 gms. baby corn
200 gms. red carrots cut julienne
100 gms. cucumbers – white cut julienne
100 gms. red bell peppers cut julienne
4 spring onions cut julienne
1 tsp. grated ginger
1 tsp. grated garlic
1 tsp. finely chopped green chillies
2 stalks celery cut diagonally
1/2 cup bean sprouts
oil

For the Bird's Nests:
- Heat oil in a kadhai or deep fryer. Combine the grated potatoes, flour, egg and salt to taste. Oil the metal tea strainer from inside and line the whole with one fourth of the mixture. Lower the strainer carefully into the hot oil till it is totally covered with the oil and allow to cook till golden brown. Remove from the oil and loosen the nest with the edge of a blunt knife. Set it on absorbent paper. Cook 3 more from the remaining mixture.

For the Sauce:
- Mix all the ingredients and keep ready in a bowl.

For the Chicken Mince:
- Place all the ingredients in a heavy based saucepan with 2 tablespoons butter and 1 cup water and cook over a low flame till soft.
- Pour the contents of the sauce bowl into a saucepan and add the minced chicken. Stir well till the sauce boils and thickens. Taste for salt.
- Stuff into the bird's nests and serve immediately. Decorate with red bell pepper if liked.

For the Vegetable Filling:
- Place 3 tablespoons oil in a wok, allow to heat and add the garlic, ginger, chillies, carrots, baby corn cut into bits, red bell pepper, cucumber and celery and stir fry for 7 to 10 minutes. Add salt to taste and a little more oil if you need it. When vegetables are cooked, add the bean sprouts and spring onions and cook for a further 5 minutes. Add a dash of black pepper powder and stir in all the sauce ingredients kept in a bowl.
- Stir well till the mixture comes to a boil and thickens. Taste for salt.
- Place the mixture in the bird's nests and serve immediately.

SECTION 13

CHRISTMAS SPECIALITIES

STUFFED ROAST CHICKEN

Preparation Time: 1½ hrs. • Cooking Time: 2½ hrs. • Serves: 30

30 small chickens, 600-800 gms. each
1 kg. soft, fresh breadcrumbs
600 gms. ginger-garlic paste (split into 400 gms. & 200 gms. portions)
5 kgs. mutton mince
3 kgs. brown onions, finely chopped
10 apples, cored and cubed
30 boiled eggs
2 bunches celery, thick stalks removed
1 packet fresh sage
2 tbsps. peppercorns, coarsely grated
2 cups white vinegar
2 cups sugar
salt
oil
1 bundle of white cotton cord (string) to tie and stitch the chickens

- Wash the chickens inside out thrice. Clean out the insides thoroughly. Salt the chickens inside-out and apply the 400 gms. ginger-garlic paste on the chickens and insides as well. Keep in a cool place.

- Heat 2 cups oil in a large dekchi and fry the chopped onions over a medium flame. When pink and soft add the mince, salt, pepper and 200 gms. of ginger-garlic paste and mix well.

- Cook the mince in its own juices for about 10 minutes. Add 1 litre water, cover and cook till soft. Add more water if required. Add the chopped apples, sage, vinegar and sugar and mix well. Cook the apples till soft. Adjust salt and pepper. The taste of sage should be strong. Mix in the breadcrumbs.

- Stuff each chicken with the mince and 1 boiled egg. Stitch the opening and tie up the legs.

- Heat a large kadhai full of oil. When the oil is hot and smoking, fry the chickens, a few at a time. Brown them well. Arrange the fried chickens in a large vessel and roast them in water with 2" pieces of celery. Cook the chickens till they are done. Serve with fluffy mashed potatoes, tender sautéed peas, boiled red carrots and french beans.

CHRISTMAS PUDDING WITH BRANDY SAUCE

I have been following this recipe for the last 20 years and it has never failed me. It makes 5 large (1 kg.) puddings. I use butter instead of suet.

Preparation Time: 2 hrs. • Cooking Time: 6 hrs. • Serves: 30-40

600 gms. black seedless currants
400 gms. golden raisins
400 gms. brown raisins
400 gms. sultanas
250 gms. orange peel, chopped finely
250 gms. glace cherries, chopped finely
200 gms. almonds, ground
3 apples, skinned, cored and grated
3 large carrots, skinned, cored and grated
400 gms. flour
600 gms. fresh soft breadcrumbs
400 gms. butter
500 gms. demerara sugar
4 tbsps. nutmeg-cardamom powder
1 cup liquid jaggery
6 eggs, whisked
1 bottle rum
1 bottle brandy
Oil for applying to the pudding basins.
Greaseproof paper for lining the basins

Brandy Sauce

500 gms. unsalted butter
300 gms. castor sugar
1 tbsp. vanilla essence
1 cup brandy

P.S.

Flaking the soft portion of the bread to get 600 gms. of breadcrumbs is a tedious process, so please see that 2 to 3 helpers are there to assist. Also the mixing of all the ingredients for the quantity given requires help.

- Put the breadcrumbs in a large dekchi. De-twig the raisins, currants and sultanas. Add the grated apples, carrots, peel, raisins, currants, sultanas, cherries and the almond powder to the breadcrumbs. Add the cardamom-nutmeg powder. Sprinkle the demerara sugar over the ingredients and mix well. Add the flour.

- Whisk the eggs and jaggery and add to the mixture. Add softened butter, rum and brandy and mix well so that all the items are homogenised.

- Heavily oil the pudding basins. Cut out greaseproof paper for the bottom and top of the puddings.

- Fill the pudding basins with the mixture leaving an inch at the top for the pudding to rise. Cover with oiled greaseproof paper. Seal tightly with the lid.

- Arrange the pudding basins in a tray at the base of a large flat dekchi. Fill enough water to come half way up the basins. Cover the dekchi and steam the puddings for 6 hours. Remove and cool.

- Before serving, steam the puddings again for 2 hours. Invert onto a dish and remove the greaseproof paper. Pour brandy over the pudding and light it. Serve with the lights dimmed so the flaming brandy is visible. Divide each pudding into 8 portions. Serve with Brandy Sauce.

- Place softened butter in a bowl and whisk in the sugar, vanilla and brandy. Chill and serve knobs of it with slices of Christmas pudding.

COQ AU VIN

Preparation Time: 1 hr. • Cooking Time: 45 mins. • Serves: 30

30 chicken breasts, each cut into 4 pieces
2 kgs. baby onions
2½ kgs. mushrooms
1½ bottles tomato sauce
1 kg. butter
20 gms. red pepper flakes
2 tbsps. freshly milled black pepper
¼ bottle brandy
½ bottle red wine
1 tsp. dried oregano

- Wash the mushrooms well. If large, cut into quarters. Skin the baby onions.
- Place half the butter in a large pan and gently sauté the mushrooms and the baby onions. Stir, cover and cook till soft.
- In a large dekchi place the rest of the butter and put in the washed, boneless chicken, salt, pepper, red pepper flakes and oregano. Stir gently and cover with a lid on which some water has been placed. Cook till the chicken is tender. Now add the tomato sauce and stir well and then add the wine. If the gravy is too watery, thicken it with 2 tablespoons of cornflour mixed in a cup of water.
- Add the brandy, the sautéed onions, mushrooms and simmer for 10 more minutes.
- Serve with sautéed baby carrots and finger chips.

CREPES SUZETTE

Our crepes suzette turned out exceptionally well. I did not add any liquor to the batter, but if you add 2 tablespoons of rum, or cherry or apricot brandy, it will enhance the flavour. An important point to remember is to let the batter rest for an hour or two before making the crepes. The quantity below is sufficient to make 28-30 crepes in a non-stick frying pan with a 7" diameter.

Preparation Time: 20 mins. • Resting Time: 2 hrs. • Cooking Time: 25-35 mins.
Serves: 10

For the Crepes:
250 gms. flour
700 ml. creamy milk
3 tbsps. castor sugar
6 eggs
50 gms. melted butter
2 tbsps. oil
1 tsp. vanilla essence
extra butter for frying
½ tsp. salt

For the Orange Sauce:
¾ litre onjus (orange juice)
400 gms. orange marmalade
extra orange rind, boiled and sweetened
250 gms. butter, soft till almost melted
275 gms. castor sugar
brandy for flambéing
vanilla ice-cream

- Place the flour in a bowl and mix in ½ teaspoon salt. Make a well in the centre and pour in the sugar, vanilla essence and the whisked eggs. Whisk well till it is free of granules.
- Add the milk slowly and mix till the batter is smooth and creamy. Allow this to stand for an hour or two.
- Meanwhile make the sauce. Beat the sugar and butter till light in a large saucepan. Add the Onjus, the orange marmalade and extra sweetened rind. Place on a low flame and allow to cook till slightly thickened.
- To make the crepes, heat the non-stick pan with a knob of butter. As soon as the butter is hot ladle some batter onto it and tilt the pan around to spread the batter evenly on the base of the pan. Let it set and then flip over to cook the other side. You should get a thin golden crepe. Finish the entire lot in this fashion. All together you should get 28-30.
- Place the crepe on a warm dessert plate. Place one scoop of vanilla ice-cream in the centre and fold the crepe over into a half-moon shape. Pour some warm orange sauce onto the crepe. Light brandy over a gas flame and pour the flaming liquid onto the crepe and serve immediately.

SECTION 14

SOME VERY UNUSUAL AND SIMPLE RECIPES

Sometimes you get fed up of your own cooking. The Club food does not appeal to you, nor your favourite restaurant's menu. You feel blue. Bored to death? Then turn these pages and make some of the most unusual meals you have ever tasted.

. . . .

GOLDEN PUMPKIN SURPRISE

(Mince, Apples and cashewnuts served in a Steamed Golden Pumpkin)

Preparation Time: 30-40 mins. • Cooking Time: 1 hr. • Serves: 8

1 round red pumpkin about 2 kgs., preferably with a stalk
1 kg. minced mutton
2 cups peeled, cored, cubed apples tossed lightly in lime juice
800 gms. large, skinned, deseeded and pureed fresh tomatoes
200 gms. finely chopped onions
1 cup tomato ketchup
1 tbsp. broiled, coarsely ground coriander seeds
1 tbsp. broiled, coarsely ground cumin seeds
1 tsp. coarsely ground black pepper
1 tsp. Kashmiri chilli powder
1 tbsp. freshly ground ginger-garlic paste
1 tbsp. freshly chopped mint
100 gms. whole large cashewnuts, fried
100 gms. very large red raisins
3 bay leaves
2 lettuce
2 green limes
salt to taste
pure ghee

- Marinate the mince with salt, ginger-garlic paste and black pepper powder and set aside.
- Prepare the pumpkin. Slice off the top generously so you have a wide mouth into which you can reach down with your hand to remove the seeds and soft strands. Take a small knife or tablespoon and scrape the insides of the pumpkin till smooth. Smoothen the inside of the sliced top also.
- Place a large vessel half filled with water on high heat. Add salt and immerse the pumpkin and sliced top, skin side up, into the water. Allow to cook till the inner flesh has softened, but the outer skin has retained its shape. Remove the pumpkin and drain the water from it by placing it with its mouth side on a wire rack. Cool.
- Place the chopped onions in a heavy based vessel with half a cup of pure ghee, and fry till the onions are pink and soft. Toss in the mince and keep stirring for 5 minutes, after which add some more ghee, half a cup or so, and brown the mince in its own juice over a low flame. Add all the ground spices, stir, add the pureed tomatoes, add 2 cups of

water and cook the mince till tender. Keep the flame low so the water and tomato pulp do not evaporate fast.

- Cook the mince till soft, adding water if necessary. Mix in the apples, fresh mint, bay leaves and tomato ketchup and cook for a further 10 minutes.
- Lightly fry the cashewnuts and raisins and set aside.
- Take a large flat dish and decorate it with washed lettuce leaves. Set the red pumpkin on the leaves in a diagonal way and put the steaming mince into it, so that half the mince is in the pumpkin and half of it is on the dish. Top the mince with the fried cashew nuts and raisins.
- This dish can be eaten with bread, parathas or a green peas pulao. The soft pumpkin flesh can also be served along with the mince.

A PASSION FOR PEPPERS

When I was young, we knew of only one kind of pepper, the green capsicum. Nowadays specialist farms in India grow imported types of peppers which are red, yellow, orange and even a purplish black. I have eaten the black coloured one a few times as they come rarely into the market. In my book JAMVA CHALOJI I had given the recipe of a green pepper pulao which I had learnt from my mother where the capsicum was stuffed with sweet and sour mutton mince. We stuff the other peppers with various mixtures and it makes welcome and novel eating for our guests. I would like to share these recipes with you.

DRY FRUIT STUFFED PEPPERS

Preparation Time: 15 mins. • Cooking Time: 75 mins. • Serves 5-7

3 green peppers
3 golden peppers
3 red peppers
2 large onions
4 tomatoes skinned and pulped
1 tsp. garam masala
1 tsp. chilli powder
1 tsp. grated fresh ginger
1 tsp. finely minced green chillies
2 tsps. finely minced fresh mint
2 tbsps. sweet raisins
3 tbsps. boiled, skinned, sliced almonds
10 dried apricots boiled in 1 cup water and 1 teaspoon sugar soaked overnight
1 pinch saffron
salt
ghee

- Wash and dry the peppers and carefully remove the stalks and set aside.
- Cook the onions in 3 tablespoons of ghee till soft and pink. Add the tomatoes, green chillies and cook for 5 minutes. Add the garam masala, chilli powder, ginger, mint and cook for a further 7 minutes. Add the raisins after washing them as well as the apricots after chopping them finely. Fry the almonds lightly, heat the saffron and sprinkle both into the tomato mixture. Dry the mixture over a low heat and stuff the peppers and place the stalks back in the peppers.
- Steam the peppers and cook them till soft or fry in oil and cook in 2 cups of water till soft.

MINCE STUFFED RED PEPPERS

Preparation Time: 10 mins. • Cooking Time: 50 mins. • Serves: 4-6

350 gms. minced mutton
8 red peppers
2 onions, finely chopped
3 large tomatoes, finely chopped
3 green chillies, deseeded and finely minced
2 stalks celery, finely chopped
1½ tsps. garam masala
1 tsp. Kashmiri chilli powder
1 tbsp. ginger-garlic paste
2 tbsps. white vinegar
1½ tbsps. brown demerara sugar
2 tbsps. seedless raisins
salt
refined groundnut oil

- Wash the red peppers and cut a small hole around the stalk. Deseed the peppers. Overturn and set aside.
- Fry the onions in a pan in 3 tablespoons of oil till soft and pink. Add the minced mutton, salt and the ginger-garlic paste and roast the meat till red. Add 2 cups of water and cook over a medium flame till the mince is soft and tender. If necessary add more water.
- Once the mince is soft, add the green chillies, tomatoes and celery and place on a low flame and stir well. Add the garam masala, chilli powder and seedless raisins. When the tomatoes have cooked to a pulp and are well assimilated in the mince, add the vinegar and the sugar. Remove the saucepan from the fire.
- Stuff the red peppers with the mince.
- Grease an aluminium or pyrex dish with oil. Arrange the peppers in the dish, add half a cup of water and allow to cook over a low fire or bake in an oven at 300°F till the peppers have softened.
- Serve immediately.

GOLDEN PEPPER PULAO

Preparation Time: 25 mins. • Cooking Time: 1¼ hrs. • Serves: 5-6

For the Rice:

500 gms. basmati rice
1 gm. saffron
2 onions cut long and deep fried
2 one inch pieces of cinnamon
10 peppercorns
6 cloves
4 large elaichis or brown cardamom
4 star anise
4 bay leaves
salt
ghee or oil for the fried onions

For the Peppers:

8 golden peppers
1 kg. shelled and deveined prawns
1 small bunch coriander washed and finely chopped
14-16 red Kashmiri chillies ⎫
2 whole large cloves garlic ⎬ Grind in sugarcane vinegar
2½ tbsps. cumin ⎬
½ tsp. black mustard seeds ⎬
6 black peppercorns ⎭
salt
oil

- Prepare a broad mouthed heavy bottomed vessel by scrubbing it well. Keep aside.
- Place a cup of oil in a dekchi over medium flame. When hot, add the ground masala and stir till it is red and almost cooked. Salt the prawns after washing them twice and add them to the masala. Reduce the heat to very low, cover the vessel and allow the prawns to cook in their own juices for 10 minutes. Cover and place some water on the dekchi cover. Keep adding a little water from time to time till the prawns are tender and soft. Mix in the chopped coriander and cool. Taste for salt.
- Wash all the peppers and with a sharp, pointed knife, cut a circle around the stalks and remove them intact. With your finger or a fine teaspoon remove the seeds in each pepper. Bang each lightly so any remaining seeds fall out. Take a small teaspoon and fill all the peppers well with the prawn mixture and then cover with their stalks.
- Wash the rice and place it in the prepared pan. Add salt, all the whole spices and the saffron after heating it lightly. Lastly add the fried onions along with 3 tablespoons of the ghee or oil it was fried in. Add water to cook the rice, then lower the peppers and arrange them close to each other so they stay upright. Place the dekchi on medium heat. Sprinkle more salt over the rice if necessary as the peppers will be absorbing it. Lower the flame to its lowest point and allow the rice to cook for 40 minutes till all the water is absorbed and the peppers are soft. If the rice remains hard add more water. It should be soft and not dry.
- Serve this pulao with cucumber or banana raita or a Parsi dhansakh dal.

RED PEPPER MUSHROOM PULAO

Preparation Time: 25 mins. • Cooking Time: 75 mins. • Serves: 5-6

For the Rice:

500 gms. basmati rice
4 nutmeg flowers or javantri (mace)
4 crushed green cardamoms
4 tomatoes skinned and pulped
3 large onions chopped and cooked in ghee
3 potatoes cubed and fried
1 tsp. sugar
salt
ghee

For the Pepper Stuffing:

8 red peppers
600 gms. mushrooms, washed and finely chopped
200 gms. golden raisins washed
200 gms. finely chopped onions
1 tbsp. grated fresh ginger
2 cups pulped tomatoes
1 tsp. garam masala
1 tsp. chilli powder
1 tsp. cumin powder
1 tsp. Parsi dhansakh masala
1 tsp. sugar
oil
salt

- Wash the peppers and cut a hole around the stalks and deseed them. Keep the stalks.
- Cook the onions for the stuffing till soft 3 tablespoons of oil. Add the mushrooms and the ginger, cook for 5 minutes and then add all the spices and sugar. Mix well and add the tomato pulp. Cook till the mixture dries up. Cool and mix the raisins. Stuff the peppers with the mixture. Place the peppers in a metal sieve, cover and steam them or cook in a dekchi in slightly salted water over a low flame or, cooking a rice cooker or, cook in the pulao rice. Taste the mixture for salt.
- Wash the rice and place it in a flat broad mouthed dekchi. Add the spices.
- Cook the onions till soft in 3 tablespoons of pure ghee and add the tomato pulp with salt and 1 teaspoon sugar. Give a quick boil and add the onion and tomatoes to the rice in the dekchi. Add sufficient water to cook the rice. If you are cooking the peppers in the pulao, then add the water and salt accordingly, as the peppers will absorb part of the salted water. Cook on a high heat till the rice comes to the boil, then lower the heat to very low. Cook till the rice is soft. If necessary, add more water if the rice is not soft and the water has dried up. Top with fried potatoes.
- Serve with a green salad and a thick Parsi Dhansakh Dal.

KHICHRI WITH VEGETABLE STUFFED GREEN PEPPERS

Preparation Time: 20 mins. • Cooking Time: 75 mins. • Serves: 5-6

For the Rice:

300 gms. basmati rice
175 gms. pink lentils
2 bunches spring onions, fried
4 cloves
10 peppercorns
4 crushed green cardamoms
100 gms. black currants, fried
100 gms. ladyfingers cut into ½" pieces and fried
1 tsp. turmeric powder
100 gms. green peas boiled
salt
ghee

For the Stuffing:

8 green peppers
100 gms. sweet potatoes peeled, cubed
100 gms. yam skinned, cubed
100 gms. carrots skinned, cubed
100 gms. french beans stringed, washed finely cut
4 large onions skinned and chopped
4 tomatoes skinned and chopped
1 cup dates stoned and chopped
½ cup tomato sauce
1½ tsps. garam masala
1 tsp. chilli powder
1 tbsp. sugar
½ cup fresh coriander
salt
oil

- Wash and dry the peppers and carefully remove the stalks and reserve them. Deseed the peppers and set aside.
- Heat a kadhai half full of oil and fry each of the vegetables separately, except the peas, till soft. Sprinkle salt.
- Cook the onions in a little ghee separately in a large dekchi. Add the tomatoes and cook till soft. Add the tomato sauce, garam masala, chilli powder, sugar, coriander and dates and cook for 5 minutes and set aside.
- Add all the fried vegetables one by one into the onion-tomato mixture and stir gently. Heat for a further 5 minutes. Cool and stuff into the peppers and replace the stalks.
- Wash the rice and pink lentils and place in a rice cooker or dekchi. Add the whole spices, turmeric powder, fried spring onions, salt, 1½ tablespoons pure ghee and sufficient water to cook the rice till tender.
- Steam or cook the peppers in oil and water till soft.
- Place the khichri on a flat dish. Place the cooked peppers on the rice and top with the fried lady fingers, boiled peas and fried black currants.

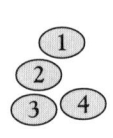

1. Fresh Fruit Salad with Brandy
2. Russian Salad in Watermelon (pg. 50)
3. Cheese Fish Fillets with Hot Tomato Sauce (pg. 142)
4. Fish Florentine (pg. 171)

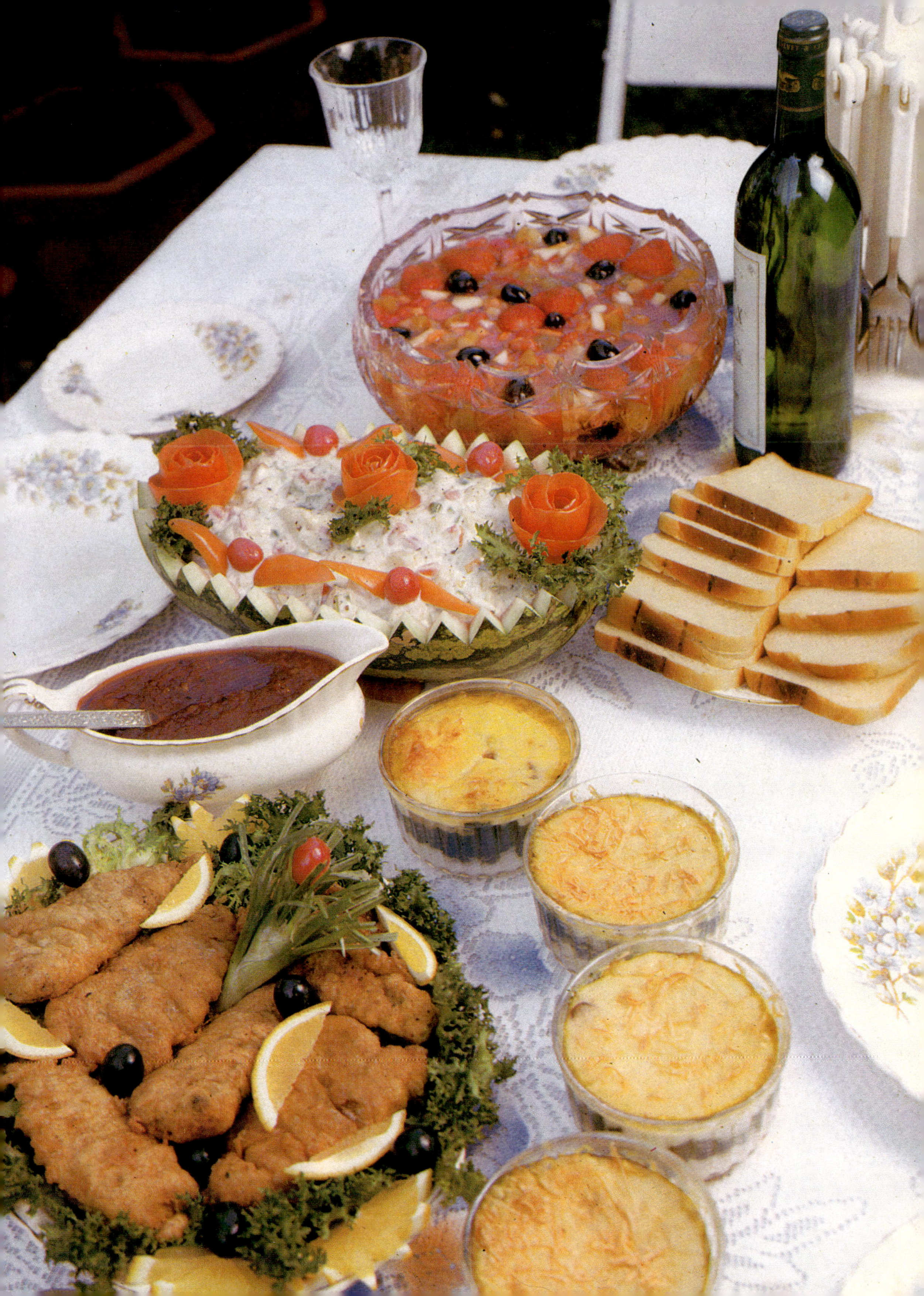

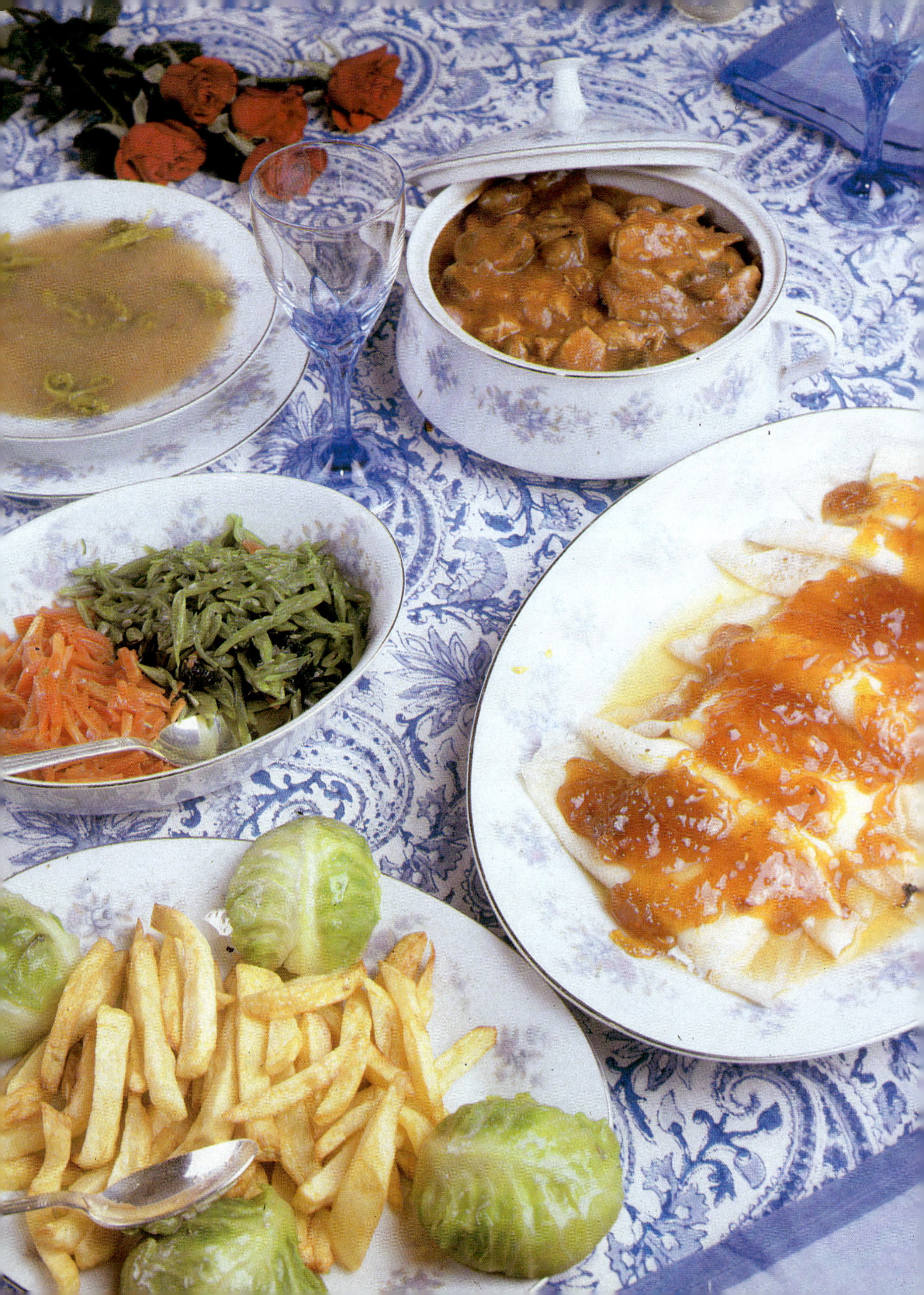

RED PEPPERS STUFFED WITH COTTAGE CHEESE AND PEACHES SERVED ON TOMATO RICE

Preparation Time: 20 mins. • Cooking Time: 75 mins. • Serves 5-6

For the Rice:
400 gms. basmati rice
1 kg. tomatoes skinned and liquidized with two cups water
1 tsp. black pepper powder
4 bay leaves
salt
ghee or butter

For the Stuffing:
8 red peppers
400 gms. cottage cheese
1 can peaches
2 tbsps. chopped celery stalks
1 tbsp. chopped parsley
salt
butter

- Wash the rice and cook in the tomato juice, pepper powder, bay leaves, salt and 2 tablespoons butter.
- Wash, dry and deseed the peppers and carefully cut away the stalks. Keep them aside. Braise the peppers after oiling them externally until they are soft. If the skin blackens, don't worry. Skin the peppers carefully.
- Make the stuffing by chopping the peaches into small cubes. Mash the cottage cheese in a bowl, add salt only if necessary and lightly mix in the peaches, celery and parsley.
- Stuff the red peppers carefully with the mixture. Place the cooked rice in a large pyrex dish and place the stuffed peppers after making 8 depressions in the rice.
- Place for 10 minutes in a hot oven and serve.

Coq Au Vin (pg. 160)
Crepes Suzette (pg. 161)
Asparagus Soup

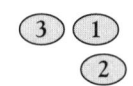

SECTION 15

A RICELESS LUNCH FOR MY FRIENDS

*(A Cool Starter, A Delicious Main Course
Ending In The Universal Favourite – Mango Ice-cream.)*

. . . .

CHICKEN WITH STRAWBERRY JELLY

Preparation Time: till jelly thickens • Serves: 6

1 packet strawberry jelly
2 cups flaked, boiled chicken
20 large fresh strawberries
2 cups mayonnaise
1 cup skinned, seedless, green grapes
1 cup chopped canned pineapple
2 egg whites
1 tbsp. finely chopped parsley
1 cup whipped cream

- Wash and hull the strawberries but retain the stalks of 8 large ones.
- Make the strawberry jelly according to the directions on the packet, but use less water. Place in the freezer till it thickens. Remove and place into a large bowl. Mix in the chicken, mayonnaise, sliced strawberries, sliced grapes, finely chopped pineapple and parsley.
- Beat the egg whites till stiff and peaks rise and then fold into the chicken mixture. Place in a fancy glass dish. Cover with foil and chill overnight in the refrigerator. The next day, slice the large 8 strawberries into fan shapes and place around the dish. Beat the cream and when stiff, pipe around the strawberries and decorate the top of the dish with lattice design or stars.

FISH FLORENTINE

Preparation Time: 30 mins. • Cooking Time: 1 hr. • Serves: 6

2½ cups of boiled, flaked, deboned pomfret or ramas fish
2 bunches of spinach (palak)
200 gms. sliced mushrooms
200 gms. grated cheese
1½ ltrs. milk
3 eggs
1 pinch soda-bi-carb
3 tsps. sugar
juice of 2 sour limes ⎤
pulp of 2 deseeded green chillies ⎦ mixed together
6 tbsps. flour (maida)
black pepper to taste
salt
butter

- Boil water in a saucepan. Add 1 teaspoon salt and soda-bi-carb. Cut off the spinach stalks, wash and add to the water and cook for 5 minutes. Strain in a colander, then grind fine in a mixer. Mix in the lime, sugar and chilli pulp and set aside.

- Place 3 tablespoons of butter in a large saucepan and add the flour. Fry for 3 to 4 minutes, add milk and whisk briskly till evenly mixed with the flour. Keep stirring till you get a smooth sauce. Add the mushrooms and cook for a further 5 minutes. Remove from the fire and cool for 10 minutes, stirring often. When cool, add 2 beaten eggs to the sauce and half the grated cheese.

- Take a large, baking dish and pour in half the sauce. Spread the spinach over it in a thin, smooth layer. Cover the spinach layer with the boiled, deboned fish then top with the rest of the white sauce. Whisk the remaining egg and spread on top. Thoroughly cover with grated cheese.

- Pre-heat the oven to 350°F for 10 minutes. Bake the Fish Florentine for 35-40 minutes till the top turns into a golden brown crust. Serve.

CREAMED MUTTON KASHMIRI STYLE

Preparation Time: 20 mins. • Cooking Time: 2 hrs. (40 mins. in pressure cooker)
Serves: 8

1 kg. choice mutton pieces from leg portion including nali or long bone
1 tbsp. ginger-garlic paste
4 bay leaves
12 kashmiri chillies ⎫
4 green cardamoms ⎪
15 black pepper corns ⎪ *grind*
6 cloves ⎬ *finely with*
10 garlic cloves ⎪ *a little*
1 tbsp. cumin seeds ⎪ *water*
1 tsp. fennel seeds ⎪
2 large finely chopped onions ⎭
4 large tomatoes, skinned and deseeded and made into pulp
200 gms. curd
fresh sprigs of mint for decoration
salt
pure ghee

- There are two ways of cooking this interesting dish. If you don't have time, you can use the pressure cooker, otherwise I would suggest that the meat be cooked on an open coal fire or gas stove.

- Marinade the meat in salt and ginger-garlic paste and allow to stand for 2 hours.

- Grind the masalas to a pulp and then place in a very heavy vessel along with half a cup of ghee. Keep on a medium flame and fry well till a delicate aroma arises and the masala is cooked. This should take 7 minutes. Add the tomato pulp and simmer for a further 10 minutes. Set aside.

- Place the marinated meat with bay leaves and half a cup of ghee on a stove and allow to fry till red. Add 4 cups of water and allow to cook till soft. Indian meat is very tough so this will take at least 2½ hours. If you wish, use a pressure cooker.

- When the meat becomes soft, put it in the cooked gravy. Strain the soup and add 1-2 cups to the masala gravy and let it simmer for 10 minutes. Whisk the curds and add little by little to the gravy stirring all the time. When the curd has been absorbed, allow to simmer for 3 minutes more before serving.

PAPETA MA GOSHT
(Mutton and Potato Stew for Bahadur Mody)

Preparation Time: 8 mins. • Cooking Time: 35-40 mins. • Serves: 6

This is the most popular dish of the Parsis next to Dhan-Dal. The child begins eating it from age 2 till he dies. Its blandness and the taste of the blending of the potato and the mutton essence makes it an all-time favourite

500 gms. mutton chunks
350 gms. large potatoes skinned and chopped, the size of the meat chunks
300 gms. large ripe tomatoes finely chopped
200 gms. brown onions, finely chopped
1½ teaspoons ginger-garlic paste
salt
100 gms. ghee

- Wash the mutton twice and marinade it in salt and ginger-garlic paste for at least half an hour.
- Place the chopped onions directly into the pressure cooker with 100 gms. pure ghee. Allow the onions to cook over medium heat till they are golden brown. Add the mutton and stir for 5 minutes non-stop.
- Add the finely chopped tomatoes and stir for 3 more minutes. Add the potatoes, stir and add 4½ cups of water and taste for salt. Cook in the pressure cooker till the meat is very soft and tender.
- If cooking for adults, add green chillies, chopped coriander, a pinch of turmeric, chilli and black pepper powder to this dish.
- When serving, decorate the dish with fresh curry sprigs and whole green chillies as shown in the photograph.

MANGO SHRIKHAND

Preparation Time: 2-4 hrs. • Serves: 15

10 gms. saffron
2 kg. yoghurt
1 kg. castor sugar
200 gms. sliced pistas or charoli
1 tsp. cardamom powder
2 tbsps. milk
6 alphonso mangoes when in season, skinned and cut into tiny pieces

- Heat the saffron and place in 2 tablespoons of hot milk in a cup.
- Take the yoghurt and hang it in a muslin cloth for 2 to 4 hours. Transfer to a stainless steel bowl and mix in the saffron and cardamom and gradually the castor sugar and whisk till smooth. Taste for sugar. Chill. Mix in mango pieces if available.
- Serve in little silver katoris topped with sliced pistas or charoli.

MANGO FREEZER ICE-CREAM

Preparation Time: Overnight • Serves: 10

13 large alphonso mangoes
2 litres creamy milk
1 kg. clotted cream or malai
2 condensed milk tins
2½ cups sugar

- Remove the mango pulp and discard the skin and stones. Keep in a cool place.
- Boil the milk in a large pan and add the sugar and the condensed milk. Cook over a medium flame for 12 to 15 minutes. Cool under a fan.
- Whip the mango pulp lightly for 2 minutes. Add it to the cooled milk. Lightly whip and mix the cream into the pulp mixture whilst it is coarse and has a granular texture. It will give a white and golden appearance to the ice cream. Freeze overnight.
- Pour the mixture into rectangular stainless steel or aluminium boxes so you can cut the ice cream into slices.

SECTION 16

AN EXTRA-ORDINARY LUNCH

CHEESE SOUFFLE

Preparation Time: 7 mins. • Cooking Time: 45 mins. • Serves: 6

3 tbsps. grated cheese
½ cup grated cheese
250 gms. butter
1 cup self raising flour
1½ cups milk
5 egg whites
6 egg yolks
1 tsp. freshly ground pepper
salt to taste

- You will need a round pyrex bowl with straight sides. A grease proof or a butter paper collar should be tied around its sides to hold the souffle as it rises.
- Pre-heat your oven to 400°F. Grease the pyrex dish with a little butter all over and sprinkle 3 tablespoons grated cheese on its base and sides.
- Melt the butter in a heavy based saucepan. Stir in the flour and cook over a low heat stirring all the while. Do not allow the roux to brown. Pour in the milk and whisk vigorously and cook over a slow fire till it is smooth and thick.
- Separate the yolks and the whites of the eggs and beat in the egg yolks one at a time into the milk and flour mixture. Add a pinch of salt and ¼ teaspoon pepper powder. Set aside. If you wish, add 1 teaspoon or more chopped parsley.
- Place the 5 egg whites in a bowl add a pinch of salt and whisk well till they stand out in stiff peaks. Gently stir the egg whites into the sauce and the rest of the grated cheese – reserving 1 tablespoon. Pour the mixture into the prepared greased pyrex dish till it is three-quarters full.
- For a decorative effect, cut a deep trench all around the centre of the souffle and sprinkle the remaining grated cheese on top of it.
- Place the souffle into the pre-heated oven. Turn the temperature down to 375°F and bake in the centre of the oven for 25 to 30 minutes until the top is golden brown and crusty.

HIMALAYAN MURGHI

Preparation Time: 40 mins. • Cooking Time: 60 mins. • Serves: 6

1 kg. chicken cut into 8 pieces
2 large finely chopped onions
4 large tomatoes – pureed
1 tbsp. paprika
1 tbsp. ginger-garlic paste
1 tsp. black pepper powder
1 tsp. mace powder
½ tsp. sage
½ cup tomato ketchup
200 gms. sliced mushrooms
½ ltr. milk
2 tbsps. flour (maida)
150 gms. grated cheese
4 large potatoes cut into finger chips
salt
butter
oil

- Cut the chicken into 2 leg pieces and 2 breast pieces. Then cut each into 2 so that you have 8 pieces. Wash well and marinate in salt, ginger-garlic paste, paprika, pepper powder, mace powder and sage for half an hour.

- Place 2 tablespoons of any refined oil along with 1 tablespoon of butter in a large saucepan and add the finely chopped onions and cook till soft. Add the chicken and cover and cook over a slow flame in its own juices for 7 minutes. Raise the flame and add the pureed tomatoes along with half a cup of water and cook over a medium flame till the chicken is soft and tender. Add half a cup of tomato ketchup to the chicken to give the gravy a strong red colour.

- Heat oil in a frying pan and when hot, fry the potato chips till golden brown in colour. Sprinkle salt and set aside.

- Take a saucepan and place the butter and flour in it and cook over a medium flame for 3 minutes. Add the milk and stir vigorously till you get a smooth sauce. Add the sliced mushrooms, salt to taste and bring to a boil. Remove from the fire when cooked.

- To serve, place the chicken on a flat dish, cover with the potato chips and pour the white sauce carefully over the chicken to give an appearance of snow on mountain-tops. Sprinkle grated cheese over the sauce and enjoy.

CURLED FISH FILLETS IN AN ALMOND SAUCE – FIT FOR A KING

Preparation Time: 30 mins. • Cooking Time: 45-50 mins. • Serves: 6-8

4 tbsps. self raising flour
3 whole pomfrets or 12 fish fillets
1 tin cheese
15 boiled almonds – flaked and golden fried in butter
200 gms. canned or fresh sliced mushrooms
1½ litres milk
2 tbsps. tabasco sauce
200 gms. butter
1 bunch parsley
3 sprigs thyme
1 sour lime
salt

- Cut each pomfret into four fillets. You will have 12 fillets. Wash and marinate in salt and the juice of 1 sour lime. Take each fillet by the tail end and slowly roll it up and insert tooth picks to allow the roll to retain its shape. After all the fillets have been rolled up, place them in a cool place.

- Make a nice thick roux with the butter, milk, parsley, thyme and self raising flour. Cook it well and add 2 cups of grated cheese to it. Keep aside. Try to get a nice lemony colour by cooking the flour well with the butter before adding the milk. Taste for salt. Never add salt before hand to any dish when you are using cheese as the cheese itself contains a lot of salt. Always taste the produce and add salt at the end, if required.

- Take a rectangular pyrex dish and butter bottom and sides generously. Place the fish rolls leaving gaps in between each.

- Whip the cheese sauce, add the canned mushrooms and tabasco and top each roll generously with the sauce. Allow the remaining sauce to cover the base of the dish. Spread the almond flakes onto the dish. Bake in a pre-heated oven at 375°F till golden brown.

- Serve with small gutli breads from your local bakery. If you like, cut the gutli into two horizontally and smear with garlic butter. Heat and serve warm with pickled onion rings and fresh green lettuce tossed in a lime and sugar dressing.

SAFFRON RICE
WITH MEATBALLS AND COTTAGE CHEESE

Preparation Time: 25 mins. • Cooking Time: 55 mins. • Serves: 8

2 gms. saffron
500 gms. basmati rice
250 gms. paneer (cottage cheese)
50 fried cocktail kababs
2 1" pieces cinnamon
4 mace flowers
2 star anise
3 green cardamoms coarsely crushed
10 black peppercorns
4 tomatoes skinned, deseeded, pulped
2 onions chopped finely
2 large onions skinned, sliced, deep fried
2 large potatoes, skinned, cubed, fried
1 cup sweet curds
½ cup raisins
½ cup dried apricots
½ cup broken cashew nuts
ghee
salt

For the Kababs

700 gms. minced mutton
350 gms. mashed potatoes
1½ tbsps. chilli powder
1 tbsp. turmeric powder
2 tbsps. dhansakh masala
1½ tbsps. ginger-garlic paste
1 tsp. garam masala + mace powder
3 finely chopped onions
1 cup finely chopped fresh coriander
¼ cup finely chopped mint
6 eggs
breadcrumbs
salt
oil

- Soak the apricots overnight in water. Rice can be cooked in a dekchi or in a rice cooker.
- Deep fry the onions till golden brown in 2 cups ghee. Remove the ghee, leaving 3 tablespoons in the vessel. To the fried onions, add all the whole spices, cinnamon, mace flowers, star anise, cardamoms and peppercorns. Fry for 2 minutes and add the washed rice. Add salt and water and cook till each grain is separate.
- Heat the saffron on a hot tava or griddle and mix it into the curds. Whisk.
- Fry the chopped onion in 2 tablespoons ghee and when soft, add the tomato pulp and salt. Mix well.
- Chop the paneer and add to the rice along with the cocktail kababs, cashewnuts and fried potatoes.
- Wash raisins, remove apricots from the water and add to the mixture along with curds and saffron.
- When the rice is ready, pour in the mixture and close the vessel with a lid or foil. Keep on a very low heat or dum, for half an hour before serving.
- Place the potatoes and mince in a thali or bowl. Add salt and the ginger-garlic paste and mix well. Add the chilli, turmeric, dhansakh and garam masala with mace powders.
- Mix in the onion, coriander and mint and form into a ball. Make a depression into the ball.
- Beat the eggs briskly and pour into the depression and mix well. Keep for half an hour. Taste for salt.
- Make small rounds and roll them in the breadcrumbs.
- Place a kadhai on the stove. Half fill with oil and allow to heat well. Drop in the meatballs a few at a time and fry till golden brown. You should get over 50 small balls.

TOPLI NU PANEER

(A Special recipe from Dhun Bana taught to me by Banoo Irani)

Preparation Time: 40 mins. • No Cooking • Serves: 4

2 tsps. essence of rennet
1 litre milk
coarse salt
small bamboo baskets 2½" high

- Wet the baskets and set aside.
- Rub each basket all over with some coarse salt.
- The milk should not be hot. Just lukewarm. Test the heat by dipping a finger in it. Add 2 teaspoons of the rennet essence, stir and set aside. Wait for 15 minutes. The paneer or junket will start setting.
- Take tablespoons of paneer and place into the toplis. Place the toplis side by side in a vessel so that the bottoms do not touch the base of the vessel. There will be a heavy drip of water from the paneers. After 10 minutes or so, transfer the paneer to your left hand. Then transfer to the right hand and then to the basket. Wait for a further 15 minutes.
- Allow the water to trickle down. Place the paneer water into a glass dish. Place the paneers in the water and chill in the refrigerator for 2 hours before eating them.

CARAMEL TOPPED VANILLA ICE-CREAM

Cooking Time: 10 mins. • Serves: 6-8

1 party pack vanilla ice-cream
300 gms. sugar
vanilla essence
warm water – 1 to 3 tbsps., as required

- Place the pack of vanilla ice-cream in the freezer compartment of your fridge.
- Place sugar and water in a heavy bottomed pan, over a low fire and stir evenly till the sugar gets caramelised and becomes a golden brown. Add vanilla and remove from the fire.
- Scoop vanilla ice-cream into champagne glasses and top with the boiling caramel mixture and serve immediately. To keep the sugar in liquid form, place in a vessel of hot water while serving.

SECTION 17

SOME FAVOURITE PARTY DISHES

TANDOORI BADE JHINGE

Preparation Time: 25 mins. • Cooking Time: 30 mins. • Serves: 5

20 jumbo prawns shelled and deveined – leave the shell on the tails
15 black peppercorns ⎫
1" fresh ginger ⎬ grind together
4 deseeded green chillies ⎭
1 cup yoghurt
½ tsp. asafoetida
1 tsp. aji-no-moto
butter

- Apply salt to the prawns and set aside. Whip the yoghurt in a bowl and add the ground masala, asafoetida and aji-no-moto. Mix vigorously, add the prawns and cover with the mixture and allow to marinate for at least 2 hours. Taste for salt.
- Skewer each prawn twice till it forms a U. Use very thin metal skewers and roast till tender over a coal fire, turning the prawns at least 3 times. Brush with a little butter before removing from the fire.

MANGO AND SLICED CHICKEN SALAD

Preparation Time: 20 mins. • Cooking Time: 25 mins. • Serves: 6

4 large chicken breasts deboned
6 large ripe alphonso mangoes
8 medium sized broccoli florets
2 cucumbers diagonally sliced and glazed
1 small endive salad or cos lettuce
butter
salt – pepper

Lime Sauce:

2 tbsps. cornflour
2 limes – juice removed
½ cup butter
chives – snipped 2" long
2 tbsps. sugar
salt and pepper

- Wash the chicken and cut into strips. Apply salt and pepper to taste and boil in 2 cups of water till tender.
- Cut the cucumbers diagonally, apply salt and cook in 1 cup water and a ¼ cup of butter till soft.
- Boil the broccoli florets in 2 cups of water and a pinch of salt and pepper and ¼ cup of butter, till soft.
- Drain the chicken, cucumber and broccoli and reserve all the juices in a small pan.
- Wash the endive salad or cos lettuce and layer the dish with the leaves.
- Place the cucumber strips in a circular pattern on the salad dish. Arrange the chicken strips on top of the cucumber strips.
- Peel the mangoes. Cut 3 strips from each cheek and 2 strips from the sides of the mango. Arrange the mango slices on top of the cucumber and chicken slices. Arrange the broccoli decoratively in between the slices.
- Place the cornflour, lime juice, sugar, butter, chives, salt-pepper in a small saucepan. Mix well. Add the reserved juices. Taste for salt. Add salt sparingly – the sauce must be sweet and sour.
- Place on a low flame and cook till the liquid becomes thick. Taste for sourness and sweetness. Add more lime juice or sugar only if needed. Remove from the fire and cool.
- Pour the sauce over the chicken and vegetables. Chill and serve.

PAHARI MURGHI

While catering to the P.V.M. Gymkhana in Mumbai, I concocted a number of dishes with fancy names. Amongst these, Pahari Murghi took the public's fancy, so that very often we are asked to cook this chicken at parties, navjotes and weddings for five hundred to fifteen hundred people at a time. The following quantities will suffice for a party of fifteen people.

Preparation Time: 45 mins. • Cooking Time: 1 hr. • Serves: 15

For the Chicken:

2 gms. saffron
4 whole chickens cut into 8 pieces each
5 large onions
8 large tomatoes
4 bay leaves
1 coconut grated ⎫
16 Kashmiri chillies ⎪
1 tbsp. badi sonf or fennel seeds ⎪ Grind
½ tbsp. black peppercorns ⎬ together with
½ tsp. cinnamon powder ⎪ half a cup
½ tsp. mace powder ⎪ of water
1 tsp. shahjeera powder ⎭
1 tbsp. ginger-garlic paste
8 boiled eggs
4 large capsicums
salt
oil

For the Kababs:

½ tbsp. ginger-garlic paste
500 gms. mince meat
1 tsp. garam masala
1 large finely chopped onion
1 tbsp. fresh coriander
1 tsp. chopped green chillies
2 eggs
2 cups bread crumbs
10 slices bread
salt
oil

- Heat the saffron and steep it in 1 cup hot water.
- Wash the chicken pieces apply salt, the ginger-garlic paste and set aside.
- Chop the onions and tomatoes finely and grind the masala till fine and soft.
- Take a very large, wide-mouthed vessel and fry the onions and bay leaves in 1 cup of oil. When the onion is golden brown add the ground masala and fry till red. Add the tomatoes and when soft, put in the chicken pieces and allow to cook, stirring all the time on a slow fire for 15 minutes. Add 3 cups of water and allow to cook till soft.
- Meanwhile, make the kababs. Mix mince, onions, coriander, green chillies, ginger-garlic paste and the garam masala with salt to taste. Make the mixture into a ball and make a hole in it. Beat the eggs well and pour them into the hole and mix the mixture vigorously. Soak the bread slices in water and drain the water out with both your hands. Add to the mixture and knead well into it. Then wet both your hands and make tiny little cocktail kababs. Roll in the breadcrumbs and deep fry in hot oil till brown.
- Once the chicken is cooked soft, add the saffron water to the gravy and simmer over a very low flame till the gravy is thick. Add the kababs, shake the vessel, cover and remove from the flame.
- Serve the chicken on a flat dish and decorate with the kababs, boiled eggs and capsicum rings lightly fried in oil.
- Serve with rotis or soft bread.

PEAR FLAN

Preparation Time: 30 mins. • Cooking Time: 40 mins. • Serves: 6

For the Pastry:
90 gms. butter
1¼ cups self-raising flour
4 tbsps. powdered sugar
3 egg yolks
1 tsp. vanilla essence
1 tsp. nutmeg-cardamom powder

Filling:
4 pears, peeled, cored and quartered
125 gms. butter
1 cup ground almonds
1 tbsp. flour
2 eggs – well whisked
4 tbsps. jam
⅓ cup powdered sugar

- Place the butter, sugar, egg yolks and vanilla into a bowl and whisk well. Gradually add the flour, nutmeg-cardamom powder and knead lightly, roll into a bowl, cover with cling film and chill in the refrigerator for half an hour.
- Roll the pastry and line a 23 cm. flan tin.
- Mix the butter and sugar in a bowl. Whisk well. Gradually add the ground almonds and flour along with the beaten eggs.
- Spread the butter, sugar, egg and flour filling into the pastry case. Place the pear quarters all around the case and in the centre of the filling. Bake at 350°F or 180°C for 30 to 40 minutes till the top becomes golden brown. Remove from the oven and brush the top with the jam.

COINTREAU ICE-CREAM

Preparation Time: 20 mins. • Chilling Time: Overnight • Serves: 6

300 gms. cream
3 egg yolks
3 egg whites
¼ cup cointreau
¼ cup water
½ cup to ¾ cup sugar, depending on taste

- Place the water, sugar, egg yolks and cointreau in a double boiler and whisk. Beat over the hot water until the mixture is thick. This will take 10 to 12 minutes. Remove from the heat and cool.
- Whip the cream till firm peaks form. Whip the egg whites with a pinch of salt till stiff. Mix the cream and egg whites gently into the cointreau mixture. Place into an ice-cream container with a tight lid and freeze overnight.
- Serve cut into cubes or slices.

A LUXURIOUS DIWALI MEAL WITH TWINKLING LAMPS, FLOWERS AND SPARKLERS

RAMAS FISH BAKED WITH SLICED POTATOES

Preparation Time: 20 mins. • Cooking Time: 1 hr. • Serves: 6-8

1 kg. ramas fish
450 gms. sliced boiled potatoes
100 gms. sliced boiled carrots
50 gms. sautéed onion slices
1 celery stalk cut finely, diagonally
1 small bunch parsley, washed and chopped
juice of two sour limes
15 black peppercorns ⎫
1 tbsp. chopped garlic ⎬ Grind together
1 tbsp. chopped ginger ⎭
¼ tsp. nutmeg powder
butter
salt

- Wash the fish after scaling it and remove 500 gms. of boneless pieces or fillets. Boil the rest of the fish to make stock and use the flesh to make cutlets or kababs.

- Wash and salt the fillets and marinade them in lime juice, parsley, celery and the ground pepper and ginger-garlic. Keep in a cool place for 1 hour.

- Select a rounded pyrex dish and grease the bottom lavishly with butter. Arrange the marinated fish fillets at the bottom. Top with the sliced, sautéed onions, carrots and overlapping potato slices. Top with all the remaining butter and sprinkle the nutmeg over the potatoes.

- Bake in a pre-heated oven at 375°F till the potatoes brown. Serve immediately.

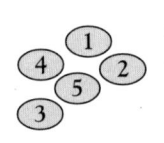

Pahari Murgh (pg. 182)
Curled Fish Fillets in Almond Sauce (pg. 177)
Golden Pepper Pulao (pg. 166)
Chicken Hawaiian Salad (pg. 57)
Boiled Mange Tout or Snow Peas

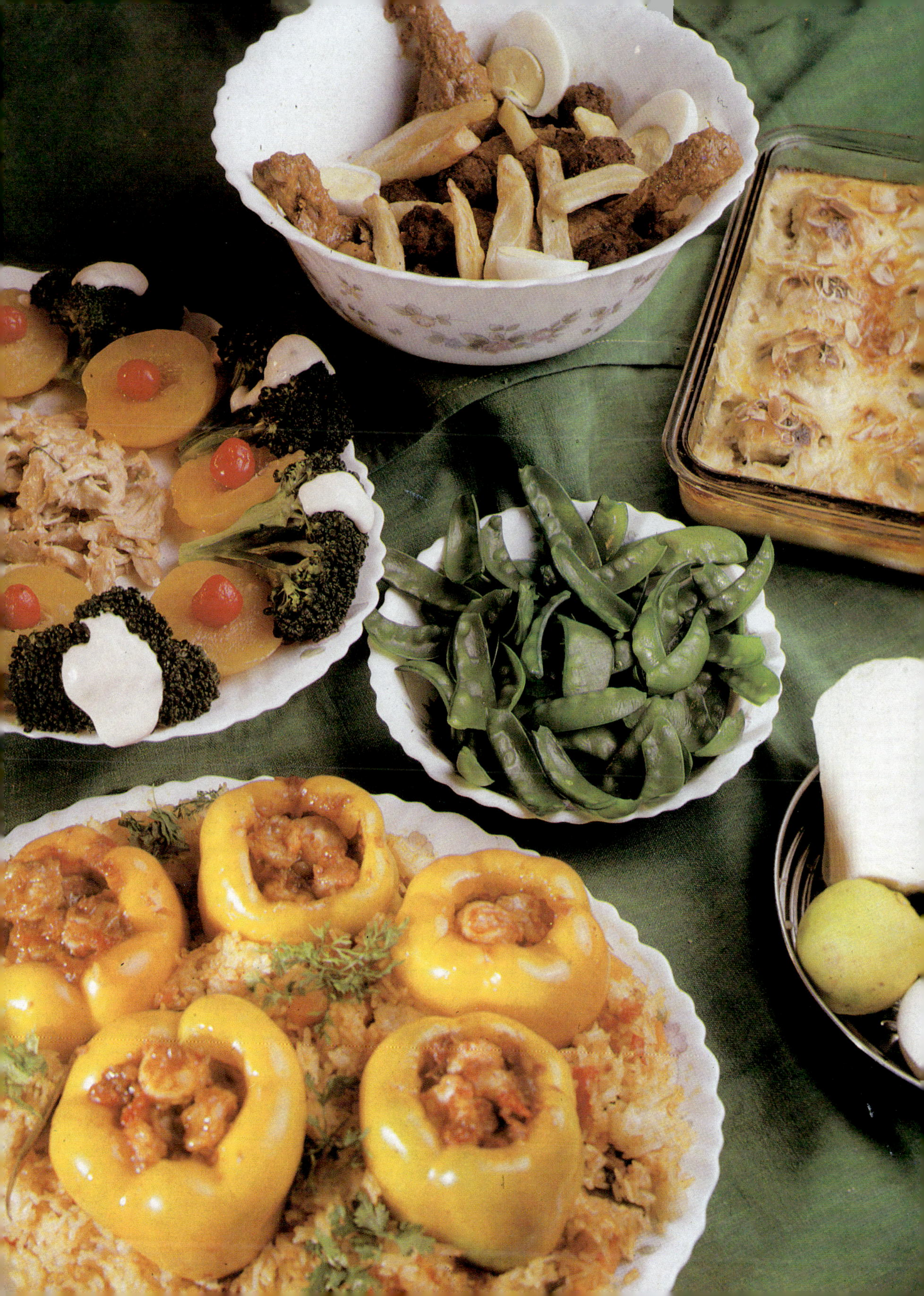

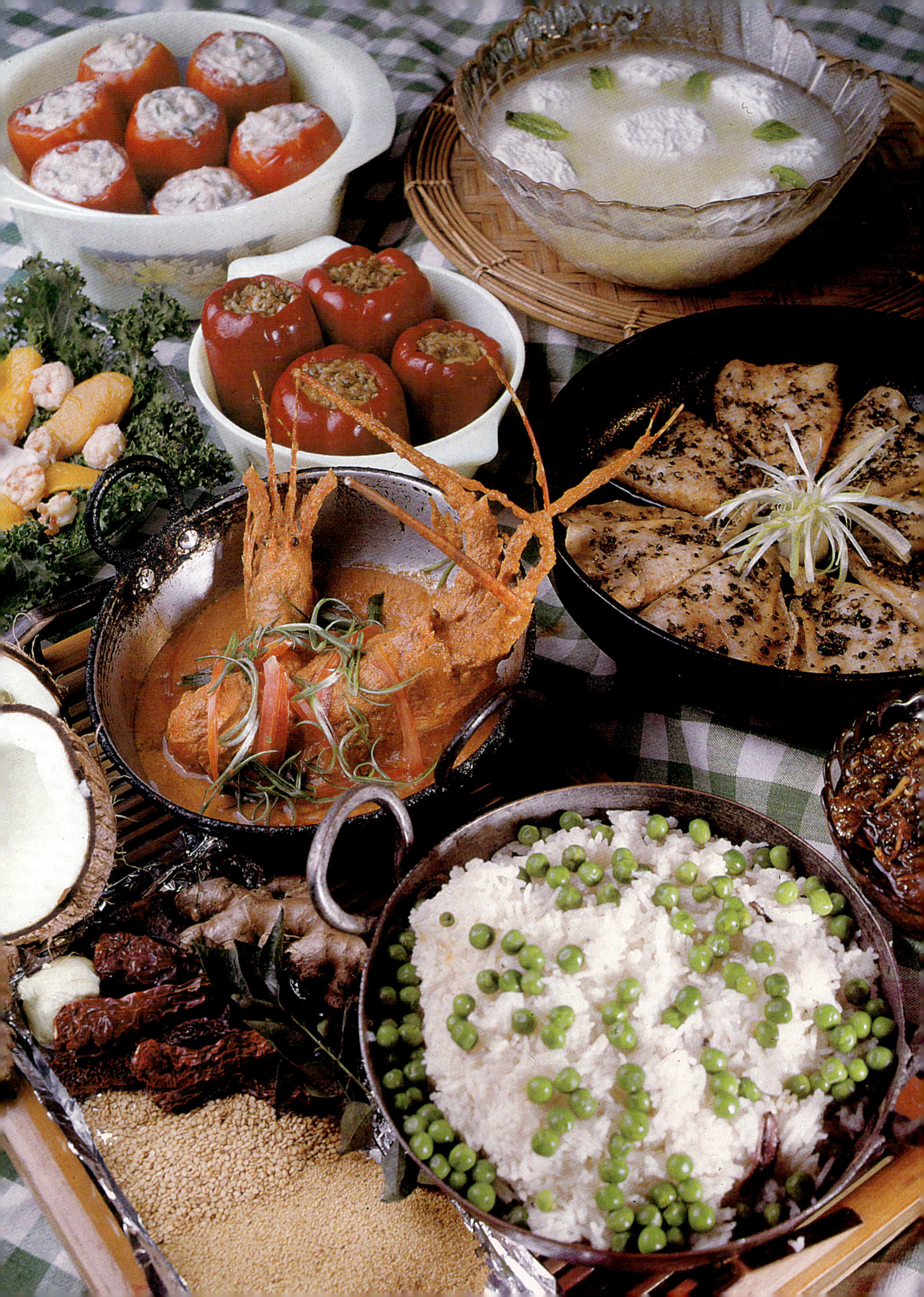

MOGHLAI GOSHT RASWALA

Preparation Time: 30 mins. • Cooking Time: 45 mins. • Serves: 6-8

2 gms. saffron
1 kg. mutton leg chunks with nali
2 large finely chopped onions
2 large tomatoes finely chopped
milk of half a coconut
100 gms. dried apple slices
100 gms. white seedless raisins ⎤
100 gms. dried apricots   ⎥ Soak overnight in 2 tbsps. sugar and water:
50 gms. dried figs   ⎥
25 gms. dried dates (kharak) ⎦
10 red Kashmiri chillies ⎤
10 black peppercorns   ⎥
1" piece cinnamon   ⎥
4 mace flowers   ⎥ Grind to a paste
1 tsp. carraway seeds   ⎥
1 tsp. poppy seeds   ⎥
1 tsp. sesame seeds   ⎥
1 tsp. coriander seeds   ⎦
3 green chillies slit and deseeded
salt
ghee

- Fry the onions and cook till soft and pink in ½ a cup of ghee. Fry over a low flame for 5 minutes and add 4 cups of water and bring to a boil. Add the coconut milk. Drop in meat chunks, cook in boiling water for 15 minutes and then simmer for 2 hours till tender. If you wish, you can cook the mutton in a pressure cooker in one fourth the time. Indian mutton is very tough and takes hours to cook.
- After the mutton has cooked, prepare the fruit gravy. Soak the apple slices for 5 minutes in warm water. Grind all the masala to a soft paste.
- Place the chopped tomatoes in a large pot with ½ cup of ghee and saffron. Allow the tomatoes to soften over a medium flame for 7 minutes and then add the ground masala. Fry well stirring for 5 minutes till red. Add the cooked mutton pieces, slit chillies and two cups of mutton soup and all the fruit and allow to simmer for 20 minutes before serving.

Topli-Nu-Paneer (pg. 179)
Crushed Black Peppercorns topped Fish Fillets
Mango and Prawn Salad (pg. 194)
Rice with Green Peas
Lobster Curry (pg. 27)
Mince Stuffed Red Peppers (pg. 165)
Chicken Stuffed Tomatoes (pg. 132)

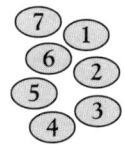

MUSHROOM AND TOMATO STUFFED OMELETTES

Preparation Time: 15 mins. • Cooking Time: 25 mins. • Serves: 6-8

For the Omelette:

8 eggs
¼ tsp. pepper powder
salt
butter

For the Stuffing:

150-200 gms. fresh mushrooms
1 large onion
2 tbsps. chopped parsley
2 tbsps. chopped garlic
1 tbsp. thyme
butter
salt

- Wash and slice the mushrooms and slice the onion finely. Cook them along with the garlic till soft in 2-3 tablespoons of butter. Taste for salt. Add a dash of tabasco. When the onion is soft, add the parsley and thyme and remove the vessel from the fire.
- Beat two eggs at a time in your mixie along with a pinch of pepper powder and salt.
- Cook and stuff the omelettes as described for prawn stuffed omelettes.

BEETROOT PICKLE

Cooking Time: 45 mins. • Serves 10-12

1½ kgs. small beetroots
750 gms. sugar
1 litre water
2 teacups sugarcane vinegar
125 gms. cornflour
1 dtsp. salt
1 tsp. cinnamon, clove, black pepper powder

- Wash the beetroots and cook in a pressure cooker for half an hour till soft. Skin and slice them.
- Place the sugar, vinegar and water in a heavy bottomed pan over a medium flame. When the sugar has melted after 10 minutes, mix the cornflour in 1 cup water and add it to the boiling sugar mixture and stir non-stop till you get a smooth sauce. Add the beetroot slices, sprinkle salt and spice powder and cook in the boiling syrup for 5 to 7 minutes. Cool, bottle and chill.

MUTTON KHURMA

Preparation Time: 30 mins. • Cooking Time: 1½-2 hrs. • Serves: 6-8

1 kg. mutton pieces with nali
1 tbsp. ginger-garlic paste
1 gm. saffron
½ cup cashewnuts ⎤ Grind together
½ cup raisins ⎦ with little water
1 tsp. black peppercorns
1 piece cinnamon
3 cardamoms
1 tsp. mace powder ⎬ Grind together with water
6 cloves
10 Kashmiri dried chillies
1 tsp. carraway seeds
4 large onions
5 large tomatoes, chopped
2 bay leaves
1 cup thick yoghurt (optional) or
1 cup thick cream
salt
oil

- Wash the mutton and marinate it in salt and ginger-garlic paste.
- Heat the saffron on a tava and allow to steep in a cup of hot water.
- Chop the onions and tomatoes finely, and place the onions in a large vessel with bay leaves and ½ a cup of oil. Place on a stove and allow the onions to turn golden brown. Add the meat pieces and fry till red, then add 4 to 5 cups of water. Put on a medium flame and allow to cook till tender. Indian mutton is very tough so. I would advise cooking it in a pressure cooker in 3 to 4 cups of water.
- Fry the spice masala in half a cup of oil. Add the tomatoes and stir well, then add the ground raisins and cashewnuts, saffron and whipped yoghurt. Stir well. Lower the flames and add the cooked meat and simmer till you have a nice thick gravy. Add the soup carefully, 1 to 2 cups only to the spicy gravy, or just as much as you need.
- Serve hot with a green salad and wheat chapatties or soft tiny loaves of bread.

SHAH-I-TUKHRA

Preparation Time: 35 mins. • Cooking Time: 45 mins. • Serves: 8-10

10 large ½" thick slices of bakery bread
2 litres milk
2 cups sugar
1½ cups water
50 gms. boiled, skinned, sliced almonds
50 gms. boiled, skinned, sliced pistachios
2 gms. heated saffron placed in half a cup of hot milk
½ tsp. crushed cardamom seeds
4-6 silver leaves
½ cup rose water
10 petals of pink roses
2 cups pure ghee

- Trim the four sides of each slice and cut into 2 or 4 neat triangular pieces.
- Make a thick syrup of the sugar and water, add the rose water and keep the syrup warm on a very low flame. Add the cardamom seeds.
- Heat the milk in a large, flat bottomed vessel, add the saffron and stir non-stop till it becomes two-thirds its original quantity.
- Place the pure ghee in a fry pan and fry all the bread pieces over a medium flame till golden. Immerse them into the syrup. Once they have swollen up, transfer them carefully into the milk. Allow the bread to soak up as much of the milk as possible. After half an hour, sprinkle the sliced nuts on top and then cover with the silver leaves and the pink rose petals. Serve chilled.

SHAH-I-TUKHRA (Method 2)

- This method is even better. Everything is the same except that you cool the milk and whisk in two well-beaten eggs. Place the milk in a rectangular pyrex dish or aluminium tray and carefully transfer the bread pieces onto it. Do not allow the pieces to disintegrate. Sprinkle with the sliced nuts and bake in a pre-heated oven at 350°F till golden. Cover with the silver leaves and serve warm. Omit the pink rose petals.

SECTION 18

A LUNCH FOR FRIENDS

. . . .

PRAWN STUFFED AVOCADOS

Avocados are an acquired taste. They are eaten a great deal in America. In India, we normally eat this fruit or vegetable in Five Star Hotels or in the houses of the rich. My friend Amy Jehangir who lives in Khandala has a tree in her garden and from the time I met her, I have been interested in eating this fruit-vegetable in salads. It is far tastier to eat with a mixture of prawns, mayonnaise, gherkins and cheese, than merely chopped up.

Select fine shining fruit – not raw, not soft. Cut each into two horizontal pieces. Remove the large seed in the centre and rub the white flesh with sour lime juice so that the flesh does not darken. The two centres in each half should be stuffed with whatever fillings you personally desire.

Preparation Time: 20 mins. • Serves: 8

4 avocados
1 cup prawns deveined, boiled, cooked
3 hard boiled eggs – chopped
4 gherkins – chopped
1 stalk celery chopped finely
1 tbsp. tabasco
4 sliced tomatoes
1 cup mayonnaise
1 tbsp. fresh chopped dill
salt to taste

- Cut each avocado into two pieces. Rub each cut piece with lime juice.
- Mix all the items except the tomatoes, together in a bowl and chill the mixture for 2 hours.
- Just before sitting down to your meal, place each avocado half on a plate decorated with tomato slices. Fill the centre with the cold mixture and serve as a starter.
- You can substitute boiled, flaked chicken for the prawns or bits of cheese and pineapple.

DARAIUS'S CHICKEN DELIGHT

Preparation Time: 40 mins. • Serves: 8

1 can pineapple rings
4 chicken breasts boiled and slivered
2 cups cheese sauce
½ cup white wine
1 cup mayonnaise
1 tbsp. pickled green peppercorns
6 boiled eggs – halved
stuffed olives – sliced
little bunches of black and green grapes
iceberg lettuce

- Assemble pineapple rings on a small silver salver or flat dish. Place the slivered chicken on top and pour some mayonnaise sauce over the chicken. Arrange the boiled eggs neatly around the pineapple slices.
- Beat the wine into the cheese sauce. Add the pickled peppercorns and gently pour over the mayonnaise sauce. Arrange the iceberg lettuce, olives and bunches of grapes in an attractive way around the pineapple and egg. Chill and serve.

CHICKEN PATTIES WITH HOT MUSHROOM SAUCE

Preparation Time: 20 mins. • Cooking Time: 30 mins. • Serves: 8-10

For the Patties:

6 chicken breasts boiled and shredded
¼ cup heavy cream
¼ cup chopped parsley
1 tsp. black pepper powder
¼ tsp. nutmeg powder
4 cups mashed potato
1 tsp. aji-no-moto
2 cups bread crumbs
4 eggs
salt
oil

For the Sauce:

2 cups tomato sauce
200 gms. fresh mushrooms
2 tbsps. tabasco sauce
1½ tbsps. fresh thyme
1 tbsp. fresh basil
2 green chillies
1 tsp. cornflour
salt
butter

- Place the chicken, mashed potatoes, cream, parsley, pepper and nutmeg powders and the aji-no-moto on a large thali or tray. Mix well and add salt. Allow to stand for half an hour and then shape into small patties.
- Whisk the eggs. Dip the patties in the whisked eggs and cover with bread crumbs and deep fry in a kadhai till golden brown. Keep warm.
- Keep the sauce ready before you fry the patties. Chop the mushrooms into slices after thoroughly washing them. Heat a frying pan with 2 tablespoons butter. Fry the mushrooms lightly and add the tomato and tabasco sauces, thyme, basil and 2 chopped green chillies. Mix 1 teaspoon cornflour in 3 tablespoons of water and add it to the sauce and keep stirring till you get a smooth finish. Taste for salt.
- Serve two patties in each plate along with the mushroom sauce. If you like, you may decorate the patties with parsley and the sauce with thin strips of spring onions.
- You will be able to make 15-20 small patties out of the above quantity of chicken and mashed potatoes.

LIVER WITH ORANGES

Preparation Time: 20 mins. • Cooking Time: 30 mins. • Serves: 6

1 goat's liver
1 large onion cut into rings
2 malta oranges – skinned and sliced
1 tsp. ginger-garlic paste
½ tsp. freshly ground black pepper
2 tbsps. soya sauce
½ cup tomato sauce or ketchup
1 tbsp. sugar
1 tbsp. green Chinese chilli sauce
ghee
salt

- Skin the liver. Wash and cut into diagonal 2½" slices as thick as our fingers. Salt and marinate in the ginger-garlic paste and set aside.
- Take a fry pan and place 2 tablespoons of ghee in it. When the ghee heats, add the onion rings and 1 tablespoon of soya sauce and shake the pan and cook the onions till slightly soft. Do not allow the rings to burn or become brown. Place the rings in a pyrex dish.
- Wipe the same pan and add 1 tablespoon ghee and 1 tablespoon sugar. When the sugar is lightly caramelized, place the orange slices in circles in the pan and shake it till both sides have become caramelized.
- Take a large heavy bottomed skillet. Place 3 tablespoons of ghee in it and when hot, place the liver in it. Lower the flame and sprinkle the liver with the black pepper, 1 tablespoon of soya sauce, the tomato sauce and green chilli sauce. Stir and cover the skillet and cook for 15 minutes over a very slow fire. Cook the liver, onion rings and orange slices only just before the dish is to be served.
- Take a rectangular or round pyrex dish. Arrange the liver in the centre and cover with the onion rings. Arrange the orange slices around the edges of the dish.

APPLE SURPRISE

Preparation Time: 10 mins. • Cooking Time: 40-45 mins. • Serves: 8

8 golden apples, peeled, cored, quartered and sliced
2 cups quaker oats
125 gms. butter
1 cup sugar
½ cup self-raising flour
½ cup honey
½ cup orange juice
½ cup coarsely chopped walnuts
½ tsp. cinnamon powder
½ tsp. nutmeg powder

- Grease a large baking dish and arrange the apple slices so that they overlap each other. Mix the sugar and orange juice and sprinkle over the apple slices.
- Combine the oats, flour, cinnamon and nutmeg powders and the walnuts in a bowl. Mix well.
- Heat the butter and honey gently and add to the oat mixture. Sprinkle the mixture evenly over the apple slices.
- Bake in an oven at 350°F for 35-40 minutes till golden brown and the topping is crisp.
- Serve hot or cold. If you wish, serve with whipped, sweetened cream.

CHOCOLATE ICE-CREAM

Preparation Time: Nil • Cooking Time: 30 mins. • Serves: 4-6

½ litre milk
½ tin condensed milk
¼ kilo clotted cream or malai
1 cup sugar
2 full tsps. cocoa powder

- Heat the milk and add the sugar. When it comes to the boil, add the condensed milk and stir over a low fire for 10 minutes.
- Mix the cocoa powder in half a teacup of water. Stir well and add it to the milk on the fire. Cook for 5 more minutes and then cool the milk.
- Beat the cream lightly and add it to the milk mixture. Chill in a flat pan or tin and then freeze overnight.

SECTION 19

A LUNCH WITH MY FAVOURITE COUSINS

TIGER PRAWN AND RIPE MANGO SALAD

Preparation Time: 25 mins. • Cooking Time: 30 mins. • Serves: 8-10

6 ripe, skinned alphonso mangoes, flesh sliced
20 large deveined tiger prawns
2 sliced avocados
1 cup mayonnaise
¼ cup parsley finely chopped
2 tbsps. tabasco sauce
½ tbsp. coarsely pounded peppercorns
6 sliced tomatoes
2 sliced red radish
2 sliced cucumbers
butter

- Wash and slice all the vegetables, avocado and mangoes and arrange in little clusters on a salver. Refrigerate.
- Heat butter in a skillet and add the washed, salted, deveined prawns. Grate some pepper on top of them and turn them upside down once. Add 2 tablespoons of water, cover and cook till all the prawns have become soft. Place them on the salver of vegetables.
- Dribble the mayonnaise after adding the parsley and tabasco on the vegetables. Serve chilled.

ROAST MUTTON CHOPS
WITH A SPICY MUSHROOM SAUCE AND BROCCOLI

Broccoli is a green vegetable very much like cauliflower. In fact, they are identical except for colour and flavour. It is available at specialists shops in Crawford Market in Bombay. I clean the stalks of their skin like covering as they are delicious to eat. The best way to eat this delicious vegetable is to plunge the stalks and curly heads in salted boiling water. After the vegetable is cooked, butter and eat it.

Preparation Time: 2 hrs. • Cooking Time: 45 mins. • Serves: 4-6

2 brocoli heads
8 double chops
200 gms. fresh mushrooms, sliced
2 carrots – cut into sticks or slices
4 mashed potatoes
4 tbsps. milk
1 tomato – peeled and deseeded
1 tiny onion sliced
1½ tsps. ginger-garlic paste
1½ tsps. cornflour
1 tsp. ground black pepper
oil
butter

- Indian chops can be tough, so wash and place them on a wooden board and beat them a little with a meat tenderizer. Then marinate them with salt, pepper and the ginger-garlic paste.
- Scrape the carrots and cut them into slices. Boil in salted water, drain when tender and set aside.
- Take 3 tablespoons oil and place in a skillet. When hot, put in the chops and turn them to seal their juices. Lower flame and add ½ cup of water, cover and cook till tender. If you prefer, cook them in a pressure cooker.
- Remove the chops onto a flat pyrex dish. Scrape the pan juices, add 1 tablespoon of butter and the sliced mushrooms and stir till they brown. Mix in the tomato and onion and allow to simmer.
- Place the cornflour in a teacup with ½ cup of water. Stir well and mix into the cooking mushrooms. Stir non-stop till you get a smooth gravy. Set aside. Taste for salt.
- Boil the broccoli after cutting it into florets. Taste for salt and drain when cooked.
- Heat the mashed potatoes in the milk, add 2 tablespoons of butter. Taste for salt.
- Decorate the chops in a pyrex dish by pouring hot mushroom sauce on the meat and surround with carrots, mashed potato mounds and broccoli.

BOUILLABAISSE – OUR FAMILY STYLE

My husband is very fond of a fish dish we eat at home. He often says it tastes better than the bouillabaisse he ate in Marseilles. We eat this soupy dish with fluffy, white basmati rice dotted with green peas. For each person you will need 1 baby lobster (optional), 2 large prawns and 3 pieces of filleted fish. I use Ramas fillets because next to Hilsa, this is the tastiest fish to be found in India.

Preparation Time: 35 mins. • Cooking Time: 1 hr. • Serves 6

6 baby lobster tails, deveined
12 large, shelled, deveined prawns
18 pieces of filleted ramas 2" x 2" thick
6 skinned, deseeded, tomatoes
½ cup sliced garlic
½ cup finely chopped parsley
1 tbsp. finely chopped mint
2 tbsps. finely chopped coriander
1 tbsp. finely chopped deseeded green chillies
1 tsp. red chilli powder
1 tsp. coarsely ground roasted cumin seeds
2 sour limes
2 tbsps. cornflour
3 large, finely chopped onions
1 tsp. aji-no-moto
salt
oil

- Wash all the fish well, devein the lobsters and prawns, salt and set aside.
- Fry the chopped onions in a large vessel till soft and pink in half a cup of oil. Toss in the fish, lobsters and prawns and cook with the onions for 5 minutes. Add the sliced garlic, parsley green chillies, mint and coriander, chilli powder and ground cumin.
- Chop the tomatoes finely and add to the fish. Add 7 cups water and allow the fish to cook over a high flame.
- Taste the soup for salt when the fish is ready. You can put in 1 teaspoon of aji-no-moto if you like.
- Take 2 tablespoons of cornflour and make a paste with some of the soup. Add it to the boiling soup and shake the pot from side to side.
- If eating the soup with bread, add 1 tablespoon prepared mustard (optional).
- If you are serving this soup with rice, eat it in large soup plates and serve with quartered lime pieces and fried papadums.

APRICOT ICE-CREAM

Preparation Time: 45 mins. • Chilling Time: Overnight • Serves: 6

1 large can Australian apricots
250 gms. dried apricots
4 egg yolks
caster sugar as required
300 gms. cream
4-6 tbsps. sugar
1-2 tbsps. brandy
2-4 tbsps. Grand Marnier Liqueur

- Place the dried apricots in 2 cups of water and cook till soft. Process in a liquidiser till pulpy.
- Whisk egg yolks, add 1-2 tablespoons sugar and whisk well. Warm the cream gently and add the egg yolks to it. Mix well and place on gentle heat till slightly thick. Remove from the fire. Cool.
- Add the apricot pulp and the Grand Marnier to the yolk and cream mixture and place in a covered ice-cream container. Freeze overnight.
- Combine the canned, drained apricots, with 1-2 tablespoons sugar and 1-2 tablespoons brandy. Chill in the refrigerator overnight.
- Serve the ice-cream with the canned apricots. Many of our Indian friends however prefer to make the ice-cream without the brandy and the liqueur. It tastes good.

RICE AND ALMOND KHEER

Cooking Time: 1 hr. • Serves 6

2½ teacups sugar
200 gms. basmati broken rice
2 litres rich creamy milk
50 gms. almonds boiled, skinned, sliced
50 gms. almonds boiled, skinned, coarsely ground
5 crushed green skinned cardamom seeds
1 tsp. vanilla essence
silver paper or varkh

- Wash and cook the basmati rice in a pressure cooker along with 3 teacups of water. Cook till soft. Mash up the rice.
- Heat the sugar and milk till both are well mixed. Allow to boil and put in the cardamom seeds and ground almonds. Then lower the flame and add the cooked rice and simmer for half an hour. Keep stirring non-stop till the mixture becomes sticky and thick. Remove from the fire, add the vanilla, mix, and pour into 6-8 small bowls or katoris.
- When cold, sprinkle the sliced almonds and cover with the silver paper.

SECTION 20

A SPECIAL LUNCH FOR EASTER

MUSHROOM AND CHICKEN SOUP GARNISHED WITH GHERKINS

Preparation Time: 15 mins. • Cooking Time: 45 mins. • Serves: 8

1 small chicken
2 tbsps. butter
1 stick celery
2 packets fresh mushrooms
cornflour
4 gherkins
2 spring onions
1 fresh lettuce
pepper
salt

- Cut the chicken and place in a pan with 10 cups of water, salt, celery and 2 spring onions, finely chopped. Cook the soup till the chicken is tender. Strain the soup into a heavy based saucepan and reserve. Flake the chicken after deboning and skinning the pieces.
- Take 2-3 tablespoons cornflour mix with ½ cup water and add it to the soup.
- Wash the mushrooms and slice finely.
- Add butter and the mushrooms to the soup and keep on a high flame stirring all the time till the liquid is brought to a boil. Lower flame and cook for a further 12-15 minutes. Add the chicken.
- When ready to serve, line each soup bowl with lettuce leaves. Pour the soup into 6-8 equal portions. Garnish with coarse, freshly grated black pepper and gherkin fans – one for each plate.
- To make the gherkin fans, halve the gherkins and slice them but keep all slices attached to one end and then spread them out – splay them and place one on the centre of each soup plate.

COLD RAMAS MOUSSE

Preparation Time: 40 mins. • Cooking Time: 30 mins. • Serves 8-10

500 gms. boiled, boned, flaked fish
100 gms. cream – whipped
3 tbsps. gelatine
2 tbsps. red wine (optional)
1 tbsp. freshly ground black pepper
2 cup boiled fish stock or chicken clear soup
2½ cups milk
2 bay leaves
¾ cup self-raising flour
1 stalk celery
1 small carrot
2 single spring onions
¼ tsp. nutmeg
1 small piece of fresh ginger
2 small packets of butter
2 green chillies – deseeded
1 tbsp. tabasco or capsico sauce
canned pineapple slices and canned cherries for decoration
juice of 2 sour limes
1 star anise or badian

- Cut the ramas in slices after removing the scales. Cut up the head and tail. Remove the gills and intestines from the fish and wash the head, tail, and all the sliced pieces twice under running water. Salt the fish, and marinate in sour limes juice.

- Place the fish in a large vessel, along with 6 cups of water, a few whole black peppercorns, star anise, sliced spring onions, 1 sliced carrot, coarsely chopped stalk of celery and a small piece of ginger cut into strips.

- Cook the fish in an open vessel till it is tender and soft. Then drain the soup and set aside and if you wish, use it instead of the chicken soup. Flake the fish and throw away all the skin and bones. We will need 500 gms. of the white boiled fish.

- Take 2½ cups of creamy milk and heat it in a saucepan. In another saucepan, heat 1 small packet butter and fry the flour in it over a very low flame. Stir for 2 minutes and pour in the hot milk and stir non-stop till you get a smooth white sauce. Add salt.

- Blend the fish and green chopped chillies in a mixer grinder along with a half cup of the reserved fish soup. Taste the mixture for salt. Add to the white sauce.

- Slowly mix in the black pepper, wine, tabasco sauce and cream with the fish. The cream should be very lightly beaten.

- Take 1 tablespoon of gelatine and melt it in half a cup of fish soup till it dissolves. Cool. Chill for half an hour. When it starts to thicken pour it into the fish mixture. Pour the fish in a glass bowl and even out the surface with a spatula. Chill.

- Boil the rest of the gelatine in a saucepan with 1 cup of fish soup. Set aside.

- Decorate the top of the mousse with a nice arrangement of the pineapple slices and cherries, and pour the gelatine evenly over the surface of the bowl. Cover with foil and chill overnight.
- You can use any other type of decoration if you wish. I like to use finely sliced carrots made into flowers over a base of mashed potato with tomato roses and green leaves made from the tops of spring onions.
- Serve accompanied by thick slices of chilled, ripe, skinned Alphonso mangoes and lettuce leaves.

CHICKEN WITH VEGETABLES, CHIPS AND FRUIT

This is a wonderful dish for a party or for someone who is not well or recovering from an illness. Without spices and chillies, it's a tasty treat especially when it is laid out in individual plates.

Preparation Time: 20 mins. • Cooking Time: 45 mins. • Serves 4-6

8 large pieces of chicken
4 tbsps. cornflour
salt and pepper
¼ tsp. caraway seeds
2 tsps. sliced garlic
1 tsp. sliced ginger
2 tsps. chopped parsley or fresh coriander
8 peach halves, preferably canned
4 potatoes
8 broccoli florets
4 carrots – cut into sticks
2 spring onions for decoration
butter
juice of 1 lemon (optional)

- Wash the chicken and coat with cornflour, salt and pepper powder.

- Place 3 tablespoons of butter in a wide mouthed pan and allow to heat. Drop in the chicken pieces skin side down and allow to turn brown-red. Turn and cook for 5 minutes. Then lower the flame, add 2 cups of water, cover and allow to cook till tender.

- Remove the pieces of chicken onto a tray and retain any pan liquid leftover in a bowl. Then add 1 tablespoon of butter to the pan and fry the caraway seeds, ginger and garlic. Add 1 tablespoon cornflour and stir vigorously. Then add the retained pan juices, a little water if necessary, the lime juice and a pinch of lemon colouring. When it comes to a boil add the chicken pieces and cover and allow to simmer for 5 minutes.

- While the chicken is cooking, cut the potatoes into chips and fry them. Cut the carrots into sticks and boil them in salted water and drain. Do the same with the broccoli. Cut the spring onions into thin strips and place in a bowl of cold water.

- When it's time to eat, lay out the plates and decorate each plate with one chicken piece coated with gravy, some chips, a floret of broccoli, a couple of sticks of carrot, spring onion strips and half a peach. Sprinkle the parsley or coriander on top of the chicken.

HERB, PRAWN AND FISH PULAO

Preparation Time: 25 mins. • Cooking Time: 45 mins. • Serves 8-10

300 gms. basmati rice
200 gms. large deveined prawns
200 gms. pomfret, ramas or surmai fillets three inches in size
1 kg. tomatoes, skinned and deseeded
4 spring onions
2 large capsicums - chopped finely
1 stalk celery – chopped into 1" pieces
2 tbsps. oregano ⎤ optional only
2 tbsps. thyme ⎦ if available
1 whole pod garlic sliced
2 tsps. chilli powder
1 tbsp. roasted cumin powder
½ tsp. cardamom-nutmeg powder
1 star anise
4 bay leaves
½ cup chopped coriander
2 gms. saffron
2 tsps. sugar
salt
ghee

- Boil the rice, along with 2 bay leaves, 1 star anise and 2 tablespoons ghee and salt. Drain the rice when soft and strain in a colander and set aside.
- Take the skinned, seedless tomatoes and cut them up into small pieces. Place in a large dekchi, add 2 teaspoons sugar and salt to taste and 2 bay leaves. Gently poach till tender on a very low flame. When soft, add the cardamom-nutmeg powder and remove from the fire.
- Chop the spring onions diagonally and place them along with the sliced garlic in a large pan with ½ cup of ghee. Add the chilli, roasted cumin powders and saffron heated on a skillet and crumbled. Add 1 cup water and the prawns and cook till prawns are tender. Add chopped capsicums, the herbs – celery, chopped oregano and thyme and toss in the tomato mixture. Place again on a low flame and add the salted fish fillets. Shake the pan from side to side so as not to break up the fillets. Taste for salt. Add 1 cup of water and allow to simmer for 7 minutes till the fish is cooked.
- Once the fillets are cooked, spread some rice on the bottom of a clear pyrex dish. Cover with a layer of fish and prawns. Then make another layer of rice and top it with the prawn and fish mixture.
- If you like, you can bake the dish for 15 minutes or serve it straightaway, topped with the chopped coriander.

AN INDIAN CHEESECAKE

Preparation Time: 7 mins. • Cooking Time: 1 hr. • Serves: 6

750 gms. best quality saltless paneer
1 cup buttermilk
4 eggs
½ cup honey
½ cup powdered sugar
2 tsps. grated lime rind
1½ tsps. lime juice
cream for decoration
fruit for decoration
strawberry or raspberry sauce or crush

- Mash the paneer until soft and place in a mixie or bowl. Beat in the eggs one at a time. Add the sugar, buttermilk, honey, lime rind and lime juice. Mix well.
- Place the mixture in a baking tin, preferably a springform tin or you will have difficulty extricating the cake. Place a pan or tray of water in the oven. Place the cake pan into it and bake for 1 hour at 350°F. Cook till the top feels firm. Allow to cool before you remove the cake from the pan.
- Decorate with piped cream and fruits.
- Serve with a strawberry or raspberry sauce or crush.

SECTION 21

A SHIKAR BIRD REARED FOR LOCAL CONSUMPTION

Until 1947 or so, Shikar played a very important part in the life of an aristocratic Indian, especially the royal houses of India who would try to entertain their British masters lavishly at Shikar camps.

Bharatpur, in Rajasthan, has a huge bird sanctuary and I remember reading years ago of how the then Maharaja invited the British Governor General of India and his court to a shoot. The jheel or lake where the birds rested, was said to have been covered by dark clouds of dying birds falling prey to the firing of the hunters' bullets. By 4 p.m. they had counted 20,000 birds slain. An ego trip never to be copied by any other state in the British Raj.

Most of these shikar birds were made up of large swarms of geese, mallards or wild ducks which came to rest on the jheel on their way south. Giant swans and Sarus cranes came all the way from Russia and settled down here for several months in the year. Now they are coming less and less in numbers every year.

So to come back to our shikar birds, even today, we get quails, the prince of birds, in our market in Mumbai. You have to give advance notice to the suppliers who, instead of hunting the birds, now grow them for the market. In India, the quails are popularly known as Bater and because they are small in size they are cooked whole so you need atleast one whole if not two birds per person.

The other birds closely akin to each other are the grouse and the pheasant and the famous partridge. I have been fortunate in seeing them wild, whilst on my archaeological digs in Gujarat and Rajasthan. Teetars are very common in isolated fields.

Venison was highly prized and deer are still hunted in the jungles. I was fortunate in seeing Rajput men prepare for a boar hunt on camelbacks with long spears at Binjor, near the Indo-Pak Border. Wild Boar meat is highly prized as being very sweet and succulent because it eats tubers. It is a bane to the farmer.

BATER SHAHZADA OR BAKED STUFFED QUAILS

There are specialised shops which sell quails. You have to telephone them 2 to 4 weeks in advance and specify the size and number of birds you require. Cook them on the day after they arrive, after marinating them in my aromatic tandoori masala. This recipe is of my own making and turns out wonderfully well. You will need at least one whole quail 250 gms. to 300 gms. in weight for each person. I cook eight quails at a time. I find it's easier and more tasty than looking after 12 or 24 of them. If you have 8 quails to bake, they can all be placed simultaneously in the oven instead of placing them turn by turn. When the last batch is ready, the first has grown cold. So the smaller the number, the better.

Preparation Time: 30 mins. • Cooking Time: 35-50 mins. • Serves: 4

8 quails – each roughly 250 to 300 gms.
500 gms. mashed potatoes
150 gms. boiled, skinned almonds
150 gms. boiled, skinned pistachios
juice of 3 sour limes
1 bunch of spring onions, cut julienne
3 carrots cut julienne
1 tsp. black pepper powder
½ tsp. mace powder
1 tbsp. coarsely ground pepper
1-1½ tbsps. rock salt
2 cups thick cream
½ cup brown demarara sugar
pure ghee

- Wash the quails inside and outside and then marinade in the rock salt, coarsely ground pepper and sour lime juice. Refrigerate overnight.
- The next day make mashed potato upto 500 gms. Mash finely. Add salt to taste.
- Place a little ghee in a small fry pan and cook the carrots and spring onions very lightly in it. Add the pepper powder, mace and the mashed potatoes. Stir well. Stuff the quails with this mixture.
- Place one cup ghee in a large baking pan and warm it and lay out the quails neatly in rows upon it. Allow the ghee to heat and brown the quails on both sides. Add a few drops of water and bake for 1 hour at 350°F. Keep turning the birds.
- Heat half a cup of ghee in a small sauce pan. Chop the pistachios and almonds finely and cook in the ghee till golden. Add the cream and the brown sugar and stir over a very low flame.
- Pour this mixture over the quails in the oven and keep basting them repeatedly for 20 minutes. Test the birds for tenderness. Serve straight from the oven in individual plates, spooning the cream gravy over each bird.

BATER ZAFRANI – QUAILS IN SAFFRON SAUCE

Preparation Time: 20 mins. • Cooking Time: 1-1¼ hrs. • Serves: 4-6

8 quails – each 250 gms. to 300 gms.
2 gms. saffron
300 gms. thick cream
200 gms. thick sweet curds
200 gms. skinned, deseeded tomatoes
200 gms. finely chopped brown onions
4 whole red Kashmiri chillies
1 tbsp. black pepper powder
1 tbsp. coarsely ground, broiled cumin seed
1 tbsp. ginger-garlic paste
pure ghee
salt

- Wash the quails inside and outside and marinade them in salt, ½ tbsp. pepper, ginger-garlic paste and whisked curds. Place overnight in the refrigerator.
- The next day place the finely chopped onions in a frying pan and cook in ½ cup pure ghee till soft and translucent. Add the whole kashmiri chillies, do not break the stem but keep it intact on the chilli, the black pepper powder and the coarsely ground cumin seed. Cook over the fire for 5 minutes and then add as many quails as fit into the pan and turn them up and down for 10 minutes. Remove them onto a baking pan and add the rest of the quails and cook them in the leftover gravy for 10 minutes.
- Arrange all the quails in a baking pan and pour the gravy in the pan on top of the birds. Place tomatoes in the same frying pan and cook for 5 minutes on a high heat. Sprinkle a pinch of fine salt over the tomatoes and mix vigorously to a pulp. Pour this over the birds along with 2 cups of water and cook in an oven at 350°F for 1 hour. Add more water if all the juice dries up.
- Heat the saffron on a tava or skillet for 2 minutes. Place between butter paper and crush with a pestle and sprinkle on top of the cream. Sprinkle fine salt on the cream and whisk lightly and pour over the quails and cook for 15 more minutes.
- Serve each bird on individual plates along with the pan juice or gravy.

Dr. Katy Dalal had a distinguished academic career having won the Wordsworth Scholarship and a gold medal for obtaining the highest marks at the Inter Arts Examination at the Mumbai University. She completed her Ph.D. on Archaeology from Pune University. She has numerous articles published on this subject to her credit and has taught Ancient Indian Culture in different Mumbai Colleges.

Having special skills in cooking and a wealth of family recipes handed down to her from generation to generation, she decided to go into the catering business in a small way. Encouraged by the response and a growing demand for party fare, she expanded her business and catered at Gymkhanas, Clubs, Parsi Navjotes and Weddings, creating many new varieties. She also offers a large variety of Continental, Gujarati, Jain, Udipi and Chinese fare.

Her first book "JAMVA CHALOJI — Parsi Delicacies for All Occasions", published in 1998 was a great success and a complete sellout within a span of 6 months. It has run into three editions.

Another book "PULAOS & BIRYANIS — A Tribute to Indian Cuisine", is also a fastseller both in India and abroad. It contains Pulao recipes with chicken, mutton, mince, eggs, fish, prawns and various vegetables. The author has included authentic Moghlai recipes after careful research in the culinary practices of those times as well as modern recipes created by herself which have found favour with people of all communities. She has researched in regional cuisines of Hyderabad, Bengal, South India and produced rich fare to suit all tastes. This book is also in its second edition.

Other Cookbooks available from Vakils, Feffer & Simons Pvt. Ltd.:

Jamva Chaloji – Parsi Delicacies for all Occasions
– *Katy Dalal*

Pulaos & Biryanis – A Tribute to Indian Cuisine
– *Katy Dalal*

Jamva Chaloji – 2 – More Parsi Delicacies to tickle your Palate
– *Katy Dalal*

Cooking Delights of the Maharajas
– *Digvijaya Singh*

Food Heritage of India
– *Vimala Patil*

Rotis and Naans of India with Accompaniments
– *Purobi Babbar*

Eat and Stay Slim with Soups and Salads
– *Purobi Babbar*

Prasadam – Food of the Hindu Gods
– *Nalini Rajan*